Emerald Cities

Emerald Cities

Urban Sustainability and Economic Development

JOAN FITZGERALD

OXFORD
UNIVERSITY PRESS

2010

OXFORD
UNIVERSITY PRESS

Oxford University Press, Inc., publishes works that further
Oxford University's objective of excellence
in research, scholarship, and education.

Oxford   New York
Auckland   Cape Town   Dar es Salaam   Hong Kong   Karachi
Kuala Lumpur   Madrid   Melbourne   Mexico City   Nairobi
New Delhi   Shanghai   Taipei   Toronto

With offices in
Argentina   Austria   Brazil   Chile   Czech Republic   France   Greece
Guatemala   Hungary   Italy   Japan   Poland   Portugal   Singapore
South Korea   Switzerland   Thailand   Turkey   Ukraine   Vietnam

Copyright © 2010 by Oxford University Press, Inc.

Published by Oxford University Press, Inc.
198 Madison Avenue, New York, New York 10016

www.oup.com

Oxford is a registered trademark of Oxford University Press.

Library of Congress Cataloging-in-Publication Data
Fitzgerald, Joan, Ph.D.
Emerald cities : urban sustainability
and economic development / Joan Fitzgerald.
p. cm.
Includes bibliographical references and index.
ISBN 978-0-19-538276-1
1. Urban policy—Environmental aspects—United States.
2. City planning—Environmental aspects—United States.
3. Urban economics—Environmental aspects.
4. Sustainable development—United States.
I. Title.
HT123.F58 2010
307.1'160973—dc22   2009023534

3 5 7 9 8 6 4 2
Printed in the United States of America
on acid-free paper

For Robert Kuttner, always.

Contents

Acknowledgments, ix

1 Sustainability as Economic Development, 1

2 Cities and the Green Economy, 11

3 Renewable Cities, 31

4 Building the Energy-Efficient City, 78

5 Is There Treasure in Our Trash?, 116

6 Creating a Green Transportation Economy, 145

7 Only Connect, 176

Notes, 185

References, 213

Index, 239

Acknowledgments

A SINGLE-AUTHORED BOOK IS SELDOM WRITTEN SINGLEHAND-EDLY and I have had much support along the way. I thank Daphne Hunt for her capable research assistance on several chapters. I am grateful to many students who provided research assistance: Natalie Brodski, Neenah Estrella-Luna, Erin Hoffer, Krista McCarthy, Alison Napoli, Jennifer Perrone, Noam Perry, and Prema Popat. Even my mother and brother, LaVerne and Gary Hufnagel, have been involved, providing quite a newspaper clipping service and asking very good questions about the book.

Thanks to Susan Christopherson, Ken Geiser, David Hochman, David Pellow, and George Sterzinger, who commented on specific chapters. Ross Gelbspan and Michael Renner reviewed segments as well. Many practitioners doing the work described in this book have taken time out to do several extensive interviews, including Sadhu Johnston, Chicago; Erin Flynn, Portland; Richard Steubi, Cleveland, and Greig Smith, Los Angeles. Of course, any errors remain mine.

Kathleen Simmons, our executive assistant at the Law, Policy, and Society program, has been essential in many ways—she prepared the manuscript, the bibliography, the tables and charts, and tracked down many a detailed statistic. Her assistance has been invaluable throughout.

Much of the research for the book was done while I was on sabbatical from Northeastern University. I thank Elliott Sclar, Director of the Center for Sustainable Urban Development at Columbia

University's Earth Institute and Rogan Kirsch, Associate Dean of the Robert F. Wagner Graduate School of Public Service at New York University, who were my academic hosts at the beginning and end of my sabbatical year.

Financial support for the writing of this book was provided by the Rockefeller Brothers Foundation and the Annie E. Casey Foundation. I thank program officers Michael Northrop and Patrice Cromwell, respectively. I thank my editor at Oxford University Press, Terry Vaughn, for understanding and supporting the message of this book.

It is family that makes it all worthwhile. My expanding extended family has been a source of joy and support, and I thank them simply for being there: Shelly Fitzgerald and Vincent, James, and Amaryah Lorenzo; Jessica Kuttner and Jack, Owen, and Eli Stewart; Gabriel Kuttner, Danielle Perry, and Alexander Kuttner. And to my husband, best friend, biggest fan, and tough-tender editor, Bob Kuttner, to whom this book is dedicated.

Emerald Cities

1

Sustainability as Economic Development

A S AN URBAN PLANNER INTERESTED IN SUSTAINABLE DEVELOPMENT, I found myself making a pilgrimage to several European cities known for incorporating practices associated with sustainability and for reducing their carbon emissions. My goal was to identify practices that could be replicated in the United States. It was in Freiburg that I experienced an "aha moment." What I learned is that a city's sustainability and climate change strategies could also be engines of economic development.

Freiburg, a university town of 216,000 in the Ruhr Valley of southwest Germany, epitomizes how a city can work creatively to integrate environmental and economic-development goals. Freiburg is home to Vauban, a large green neighborhood of about 20,000 residents that illustrates the city's commitment to renewable energy and sustainable development. On this visit, my guide is Wulf Daseking, the city's director of planning. As we walk through blocks of colorful apartment buildings nestled along narrow streets designed more for children playing than car traffic, he points out solar arrays on the building tops and explains passive solar elements such as louvered shades on the balconies of some buildings that move to let in or block out sun depending on the time of day and season.

We don't have to watch for cars, as there are hardly any. Residents cannot park on the streets; if they have a car, it must be parked in a garage just outside the neighborhood. Most residents bike to work or take advantage of the free tram passes the city provides to discourage car use. He points to a combined heat and electricity plant (80 percent wood chips and 20 percent natural gas), which, along with solar energy, provides 65 percent of Vauban's power.[1] The power for this neighborhood is 95 percent from renewable sources. Vauban goes beyond anything we are thinking of in the United States under the banners of smart growth, transit-oriented development, or the new urbanism. It is what urban planning should be in what commentator Thomas Friedman calls the energy-climate era.

On our way back to the center city (where cars are prohibited), Mr. Daseking detours to show me several of the city's solar buildings. "And here's the Fraunhofer Institute for Solar Energy Systems—Europe's largest solar energy research organization," he announces. He then tells me about at least five solar companies in the area that got their start at the Institute. My ears perk up. "So," I ask, "Freiburg's commitment to sustainable development is also creating economic development?" "Well, of course," he responds, as though the connection was obvious.

I had been visiting many of Europe's sustainable cities, but this was the first time any of my guides talked explicitly about linking their sustainability or climate change agenda to economic development. How and why did it happen in Freiburg?

FREIBURG'S GREEN ECONOMY

Freiburg's transition began when a nuclear power plant was proposed for the region in 1975. Citizen activists were successful in stopping the plant, and soon began a movement to promote solar and other renewable energy alternatives. It took until 1986 to develop a citywide strategy in which the city adopted guidelines for an energy and development policy, SolarRegion. By then, the city's intense environmental movement had already attracted the Fraunhofer Institute. At this point several environmental organizations, businesses, and research institutes began to promote renewable energy, particularly solar energy.

The three pillars of the SolarRegion strategy are energy conservation, use and development of new technologies, and use of renewable energy.[2] Each leg, in turn, contributes to an economic development strategy. The crucial development was moving beyond just using solar energy to producing solar panels locally. To promote renewable energy and economic development goals, Freiburg created local demand for solar technology by installing solar photovoltaic (PV) systems on public buildings—city hall, schools, the train station, a stadium, and others, now totaling over 900 installations. A city ordinance requires new buildings to use some solar energy in addition to satisfying strict building energy efficiency requirements. The emphasis isn't all on solar; the landfill has a ground-mounted solar PV system, two wind turbines, and a landfill gas plant that all produce energy.

In addition to leading by example, the city passed an ordinance in 2004 that requires the city to obtain 10 percent of its electricity from renewable sources by 2010, a goal that has not quite been met as of this writing.[3] Perhaps most important, in 1989 Freiburg became one of 40 German cities that implemented a feed-in tariff through which residents and businesses that install renewable systems can sell power back to the grid at a fixed price.[4]

Fraunhofer is now the largest solar research institute in Europe, employing 500 scientists who conduct basic and applied research on solar cells, off-grid power supplies, hydrogen technology, and related technologies. It is one of 80 research centers in the Fraunhofer-Gesellschaft, Germany's primary applied research organization. Germany's first self-sufficient solar building opened in Freiburg in 1992 for Fraunhofer researchers to test fuel cell and other systems. This research facility, which had a €32.3 million budget in 2007, has led to numerous solar technology and building efficiency product inventions and innovations.[5] Much of the research is in collaboration with industry, and to date the institute has spun off 14 companies, almost all of which are located in the Freiburg region. The city also developed a technology park that is home to many of the area's 80 solar businesses and research centers.[6]

Despite increased foreign competition in solar production, Freiburg's solar companies are thriving. Solar-Fabrik, the first solar panel producer to locate in Freiburg, illustrates how companies evolve into global companies to stay competitive. One year after opening its zero-emissions production facility in 1997, Solar-Fabrik was producing 25 percent of Germany's solar modules. The company added a new production facility in 2002 and expanded the original one in 2005, taking employment up to 199. In the early 2000s, branch offices opened in South Africa and Kenya. When growth was limited by unreliable cell supply, Solar-Fabrik began buying suppliers to ensure reliability of major inputs.[7] And Solar-Fabrik has entered into long-term supply agreements with companies (though not local ones) to ensure a steady supply of inputs.

As long as these solar companies also keep research and production in place and the Fraunhofer Institute continues to spin off new companies, Freiburg will remain a center of renewable energy research and production. The city employs about 2,000 directly in the solar industry (including research and development, production, design, and installation), but claims a total of 10,000 employed in a loosely defined environmental sector that even includes tourism associated with solar and other sustainable development aspects of the city.[8] While renewable technology and related industries comprise only 3 percent of Freiburg's labor market, the city has transformed itself into a leading center in renewable energy technology development.

TAKING THE LOCAL MODEL NATIONAL

Interestingly, these pioneering urban policies of Freiburg and other German cities—led by the city of Aachen—influenced the German federal government to spur the development of both the solar and wind technology industries.[9] As noted by Sigmar Gabriel, German Minister for Environment, "The systemic expansion of renewable energy is not only good from the environmental and climate policy point of view but also for innovation, growth, and employment in Germany."[10]

It's not that Germany hadn't been promoting renewable technology until Aachen got the idea. Federal research and development funding, direct subsidies, tax allowances, and loans for renewable energy have been in place since the 1970s. These policies were mostly motivated by environmental concerns brought to the forefront by the emergence in 1979 of the Green Party, which focused on environmentally sustainable development and social justice issues. Legislation in 2002 to phase out nuclear power by 2021 motivated even more investment in renewable energy.

As we'll see in chapter 3, while the United States dramatically reduced investment in research and technology development in renewable energy, Germany was forging ahead. Germany's first feed-in tariff was implemented in 1991 (see text box on pp. 6–7).[11] The 1999 100,000 Roofs program subsidized installation of solar systems as part of an industrial policy goal to expand the solar market. This €510 million program expanded solar capacity from 50 MW to 350 MW by 2003, with more than 2,250 installations connected to the grid.

The five-year program spent €460 million to provide guaranteed low-interest loans with no repayment for the first ten years to those who installed rooftop systems.[12] A new feed-in tariff established in 2000 added specific payments for solar power based on the model pioneered by German municipalities. The new feed-in tariff drove unprecedented solar energy market growth, and the policy diffused internationally to Spain, the Czech Republic, and even as far as South Korea.[13] At the same time, the Market Incentive Program offered €203 million in grants for commercialization and deployment of renewable energy systems and for export promotion.[14]

By 2002, 30 percent of the world's new solar installations were in Germany. The policies spurred a tenfold increase in the PV market between 1999 and 2003, while the cost dropped 20 percent.[15] Germany remains a leading world installer of solar capacity, but has dropped behind Japan and China in production. Of the 3,733 megawatts of solar cells manufactured worldwide in 2007, 920 were produced in Japan, 820 in China, and 266 in the United States.[16]

The feed-in tariff and related policies have led to Germany's becoming the world's largest producer of wind energy since 1997 while only increasing the retail price of electricity by about 1.2 percent (U.S. installed capacity moved ahead of Germany at the end of 2008).[17] The German Wind Energy Association reports that in 2007, German turbine and component manufacturers held 37 percent of world market share, with €6.1 billion in revenue, a 21 percent gain from 2006. The association estimates that Germany will have developed at least 45,000 MW of wind energy by 2020 and an additional 10,000 MW in offshore wind, totaling 25 percent of the country's electricity consumption.[18]

Employment in renewable energy has been increasing along with exports. Employment was only about 3,000 when the 1991 feed-in law was enacted; it grew to 50,000 by 1998, then to 120,000 by 2002. Renewable energy employment increased to almost 250,000 in 2007. Of these, 84,300 are employed in wind and 63,000 in solar power. The German government projects that 400,000 people will be employed in the renewable energy sector by 2020.[19]

One note of caution in this success story is that the cities that began the policy innovation are not necessarily the ones that gain the most from the federal government's renewable energy policy. The German government is directing many of the new production facilities to cities in the East, where significant infrastructure investments were made following unification. Unemployment in the East has been high,

Germany's Feed-In Tariff

Germany, like several European and other countries, has used feed-in tariffs to stimulate demand for renewable energy and to create jobs and an export industry in renewable technology. The feed-in tariff is the dominant policy tool for promoting renewables in Europe, with 18 EU countries employing them. Feed-in tariffs require grid operators to purchase all renewable power available to them from renewable energy generators at prices set by the government. The prices are set for a specified time period (varying, but usually around 20 years), with the amount of subsidy usually dropping over time (although fixed tariffs exist, they do not have the benefit of lowering costs). The idea is to guarantee suppliers of renewables a price above production cost so as to create a stable market that encourages investment in technologies and reduces the unit cost of production. For most, tariffs vary for different technologies. The costs of feed-in tariffs are paid by suppliers and passed on to consumers.[a]

Germany's 1991 electricity feed law (EFL) set the price for wind and solar at 90 percent of the retail electricity rate and hydropower, landfill gas, sewage gas, and biomass at 80 percent.[b] A new law, the Renewable Energy Sources Act (EEG), was enacted in 2000 to make some policy corrections and strengthen the EFL.[c] Its goal is to double the amount of renewable power from 1997 levels by 2010 and obtain 20 percent of electricity from renewable sources by 2020.[d] The 2000 Renewable Energy Law continues the commitment to doubling the percentage of renewable energy by 2010. And German national banks offer loans at 1–2 percent below market for the first 75 percent of project costs for renewable production initiatives.[e]

Key elements of Germany's feed-in tariff are long-term contracts, guaranteed purchasers, and pricing that provides an adequate rate of return for renewable suppliers. Further, the feed-in tariff is integrated into other long-term efforts to promote the development of an appropriate mix of renewable energy sources.[f] The law promotes a diverse ownership structure for renewable energy that includes power companies, municipalities, farmers (particularly with wind), and residential solar PV producers.[g] While critics point out that Germany's relatively low solar resource means that it can take several years for a photovoltaic cell to generate as much power as it took to manufacture it,[h] German companies have developed expertise in building a product with enormous export potential.

(continued)

aSawin, 2004; Rickerson, 2002. For a more detailed explanation of how feed-in tariffs work in different counties, see Sijm, 2002.

bSee http://www.wind-works.org/FeedLaws/Germany/ARTsDE.html (accessed June 15, 2007).

cA key difference in the new law is that it differentiates among energy producers, with low-cost producers compensated at lower rates than higher-cost producers to provide more incentive for developing installations on lower-quality sites. This change was needed because concentration of wind energy in the northern part of the country (with higher winds) overburdened utilities there. Another difference is that grid operators are required to purchase power from local producers (an equalization program was added to reduce the cost differentials paid by grid operators in different parts of the country for renewable power). Network utilities are also compensated for supplying the grid with electricity from renewable sources.

dRenewable Energy Sources Act. Available at www.bmu.de/files/pdfs/allgemein/application/pdf/res-act.pdf (accessed June 15, 2007).

eOther policies include the 100,000 Roofs Program, which subsidizes installation of new solar panels. This program has stimulated growth in installed PV capacity from 50 MW in 1998 to 350 MW. The Market Stimulation Program provides grants and loans to individuals, schools, and businesses for installing renewable heating systems. Other grants totaling $270 million in 2003 were earmarked for commercialization of renewable energy systems and another $40 million for export promotion (Runci, 2005).

fKlein et al., 2007.

gThe tariff can be paid to commercial and residential providers. Residential users who purchase solar PV systems for their homes, for example, can feed in electricity they do not use to the grid at the subsidized rate, ensuring a quite attractive payoff from their initial investment in the system.

hKrupp and Horn, 2008: 39. Germany's solar energy potential is approximately 1,000 kilowatt hours per square meter.

and companies are taking advantage of skilled workers at lower wages than in the West.[20] Despite this targeting by the national government, Freiburg still benefits from its early leader status and its strength in research.

CAN CITIES LEAD THE WAY IN THE UNITED STATES?

I had come to Europe to see how urban planners were incorporating sustainability into their practice and to see how city climate change action plans were working, and what, if any, were their links to economic development. Before this tour I had written an article on green jobs in a January 2007 special-focus section of *American Prospect* magazine, titled "Emerald Cities," in which I argued that the transition to a low-carbon economy could be an engine of economic development for many U.S. cities and states. But I didn't have a lot of evidence. Seeing the local-to-national diffusion of policy in Germany gave me hope that it could occur in the United States. In the absence of national leadership during the Bush years, cities and states have been leading on climate change and renewable energy and other "green" or "clean" technologies. My goal is to tell the story of what these cities are doing. Those making the link, the "emerald cities," are the subject of this book.

To find emerald cities, I started looking at various rankings of green or sustainable cities in the United States. Although methodologically flawed, these rankings provided a rough starting point. For the most part, the lists did not include meaningful measures of green economic development. Conspicuously absent from the lists were any rust belt cities. Yet green strategies crop up in improbable places. One day I picked up *U.S. Airways Magazine* on a shuttle flight to find on the cover "Syracuse, New York—the Emerald City!" Intrigued that a city that hadn't made any lists had used my book title, I soon made a trip there to find out what was going on. That led me to investigate other rust belt cities that might be seeking to transform themselves into green cities.

My interviews took me to many places. I attended several national and international conferences on various aspects of urban sustainability and climate change and on the green economy and used these opportunities to interview key actors in the field on the question of linking city climate change and economic development strategies. I visited renewable energy companies and interviewed elected officials and city planners as well as representatives of key networking organizations of cities committed to sustainable development.[21]

The opportunity for linking sustainability and economic development is real. But there are also many challenges. Cities cannot solve the climate crisis without international treaties and national policies to support them. But national policy gets played out in particular places, and cities can employ economic development strategies to support the development of renewable energy and clean carbon-reducing technologies. There are many outstanding questions on what cities can and should be doing to become players in an energy-climate era. Can cities create enough demand for renewable energy or green building products to stimulate new manufacturing jobs? Or is this the job of national policy, with little role for city or regional planning organizations? What can national governments learn from city and regional efforts? Which green technologies can take hold in which cities? Can green economic development help revitalize the economies of rust belt cities? These are the questions this book seeks to answer.

As an urban planner whose career has followed a long-standing tradition in the field of seeking social justice through planning, I have another question, which dominates this book: How can policies to promote sustainability and decrease greenhouse gas emissions be implemented in such a way that they not only contribute to urban economic development but also push forward the equity agenda that is at the root of progressive economic development? As we will see, few cities are linking all three agendas.

THE GLOBAL RECESSION AND THE GREEN ECONOMY

Since I began researching this book, the United States has entered the worst economic downturn since the Great Depression and Barack Obama has been elected president. Already, President Obama has shifted the country's position on climate change dramatically. He has also elevated the importance of urban policy by creating a new White House Office of Urban Affairs. And in his campaign speech to the NAACP, candidate Obama talked about working throughout his life to "help build an America where economic justice is being served," and how his presidency would do the same. These combined factors could help spur intensification of progress toward linking sustainability, economic development, and social justice.

During the campaign, Obama supported the United States becoming one of the signatories of the Kyoto Protocol in the next round of negotiation (in Copenhagen in December 2009) and made a commitment to cutting U.S. greenhouse emissions by 80 percent by 2050. Much of the president's ability to make the United States a climate change leader will hinge on passing the global warming bill released in April 2009 by Representatives Henry Waxman of California and Ed Markey of Massachusetts. The bill establishes a controversial carbon cap-and-trade program that would set national limits on greenhouse gas emissions and establish a credit and permit trading system for polluters.

While campaigning, Obama also supported a 10-year, $150 billion clean energy plan, a "green new deal" that would create five million jobs. Organizations supporting a green recovery lost little time in getting out reports on how the funds should be allocated. The Center for American Progress and a coalition of labor and environmental groups commissioned researchers at the Political Economy Research Institute at the University of Massachusetts Amherst to produce a guide, *Green Recovery: A Program to Create Good Jobs and Start Building a Low-Carbon Economy*, which outlines a $100 billion short-term clean energy and jobs stimulus that would create two million jobs in two years through renewable energy, energy efficiency, public transportation, and related sectors. The Apollo Alliance put out *The New Apollo Program: An Economic Strategy for American Prosperity*, which advocates for a 10-year, $500 billion investment in renewable energy, energy efficiency, and related sectors to create five million jobs. The Center for Transit-Oriented Development's *Jumpstarting the Transit Space Race: How the New Administration Could Make America Energy-Independent, Create Jobs and Keep the Economy Strong* argues for a massive investment in public transportation as economic stimulus and as urban and environmental policy.

Although perhaps less than these organizations called for, President Obama's $780 billion stimulus package, the American Recovery and Reinvestment Act, commits sizable amounts to green projects, much of which will be channeled to cities. It is a unique opportunity to link urban sustainability and economic development. And with $500 million of stimulus money earmarked for job training in green occupations, there is also an opportunity to advance a social justice agenda that moves disadvantaged individuals into the green economy.

The twin challenge of engineering a recovery from the worst economic crisis since the 1930s and saving the planet from devastating climate change has a common element. Both goals require substantial public investment in 21st-century industries and technologies and in public goods. While much of the financing and overarching regulatory policies are national and even international, cities remain on the front lines of the innovations.

2

Cities and the Green Economy

The battle against climate change will be won or lost in cities.
—Nicky Gavron, Deputy Mayor of London
(2000–2003, 2004–2008)[1]

Cities consume 75 percent of the world's energy and produce 80 percent of its greenhouse gas emissions. Paradoxically, they are also the greenest places on earth when it comes to efficiency, because of their density. Urbanist Jane Jacobs underscored the value of density for creating civically engaged, vibrant neighborhoods, but only recently have we focused on how density results in greater energy efficiency and reduces auto use. Still, cities can and must do much more than rely on their spatial patterns. Absent a comprehensive national policy in the United States prior to 2009, many American cities have been implementing strategies that contribute to reducing greenhouse gas emissions, air and water pollution, and reliance on fossil fuels.

Cities such as Austin, Boston, Chicago, New York, Los Angeles, Portland, San Francisco, Seattle, and others have adopted policies requiring renewable energy and green buildings; they have added trees, green roofs, and parks to improve air quality and reduce storm water runoff; and invested in public transportation, bike paths, and walkways to reduce car use. Many of these same cities are leaders in "smart growth" practices such as providing incentives for development that is close to public transportation, building around existing commercial centers, preserving open space, reusing polluted land, and promoting mixed-use development.[2]

Cities are also the core of the U.S. economy—most high-value economic activity is clustered in metropolitan areas. So, if cities are the source of most carbon emissions and economic activity, it makes sense to harness the innovative capacity of cities to solve the climate problem. And if new, sustainable economic activity results, this is a green bonus.

Yet this aspect of urban sustainability and climate change strategies—their connection to "green" economic development—has not received much attention. The potential for cities to build new clean technology industry clusters, improve the efficiency of production in existing manufacturing processes, and create well-paying green jobs in construction, manufacturing, and advanced technology sectors is enormous. And so is the opportunity to connect social and economic justice to the sustainability/climate change agenda. Achieving green economic growth with justice is the challenge of the century.

SECTORAL STRATEGIES FOR GREEN DEVELOPMENT

Sectoral strategies are a well-established approach to economic development. The terms sectoral and cluster strategies are often used interchangeably, although sectoral strategies typically focus more on job creation, while cluster strategies focus on economic development.[3] A sector or cluster is a geographic concentration of companies that are interconnected by the markets they serve, the products they produce, their suppliers, and their workforce needs.[4] The idea is for a city to identify its strengths and target sectors that are likely to take hold and grow. The goal is to capture as much of the supply chain as possible to a city, state, or region. For example, a city focusing on solar energy would want to manufacture the solar systems (including component parts) as well as design and install solar systems. In addition to the usual economic development tools—helping companies with facility siting, infrastructure development, and financing—sectoral strategies may include workforce training, technology adoption, and upgrading manufacturing practices.[5] This comprehensive approach to economic development requires the participation of many stakeholders, including city and/or regional economic and workforce development offices, employers, community and technical colleges, community organizations, unions, and so on.

Sectoral strategies can also incorporate a social justice agenda. In the nonprofit and foundation world, the focus of sectoral strategies is on creating employment opportunities for low-income people and bringing about systemic change in how labor markets work for low-income groups.[6] With 78 million Americans (26 percent of the population) living in poverty and city mayors reporting that poverty rates have stayed the same or increased over the last decade, sectoral strategies hold promise for alleviating urban poverty.[7] As we'll see later in the chapter, community groups and city governments see green jobs as the next big opportunity for employing low-income individuals. The possibility is real; University of Massachusetts economist Robert Pollin and colleagues estimate that 870,000 of the potential 1.7 million green jobs that could be created over the next decade can be filled by those with a high school diploma or less.[8]

While a sectoral strategy sounds like a recipe for customizing a city's economic development strategy, in fact cities and states tend to run in packs when it comes to sectoral strategies. In the 1980s and '90s, most cities were trying to attract information technology industries. For the last decade, many cities and regions have been attempting to become biotechnology or bio-manufacturing centers. Currently, the number of cities that are pinning their hopes on "green jobs" is increasing. But just as all cities can't become biotechnology centers, not all cities, regardless of their commitment to sustainability or climate change, will become players in any green economic sectors.

City planners implementing a sectoral strategy need to strategically assess their economic strengths and determine how to build on them.[9] But cities also have to look outward. In order to determine the likelihood of building a new sector or transforming an existing one, economic development practitioners need to understand trends in its growth internationally and nationally, the spatial organization of production and supply chains, industry concentration, occupations and their skill requirements, and workforce needs. It is through this often neglected process that a city figures out which sectors are reasonable targets.

Sectoral strategies aren't so much about picking winners as about creating them by investing in research, development, and infrastructure and creating demand.[10] Targeting a sector is based on a realistic assessment of a city's competitive advantages. Detroit is not likely to become a player in solar energy, but it could be in hybrid and electric cars. And in green or clean technologies the winners will not necessarily be high-tech centers. As we'll see in chapter 3, Toledo is becoming a player in solar energy because of its historical advantage in glass technology. Cleveland and Milwaukee may be able to exploit their location on the Great Lakes to develop offshore wind capacity. Pittsburgh may be able to transform its building supply industry to serve the burgeoning green building and retrofitting market.

New competitive advantages can also be created. As we learned in the introduction, Germany used smart government policy to become a leader in solar and wind technology despite having little of either resource. Los Angeles is targeting several potential clean-tech sectors and is coordinating land use and waste management policies to attract new companies. Seattle is linking its public transportation strategy to biofuels production throughout the state. Portland is manufacturing streetcars.

In this book, I explore opportunities for sectoral economic development in five areas: renewable energy, energy efficiency, green building, waste management and transportation. Each of these areas can be broadly understood as an economic sector that can connect development goals to environmental ones.

Renewable energy, such as solar or wind, employs people in research, system design, manufacturing, installation, and maintenance. Ongoing research in renewable energy is developing new technologies that will be commercialized over the coming decades. *Energy efficiency* includes all forms of conservation and reduction of energy use, including manufacturing of the products that go into retrofitted existing buildings and new *green buildings*. There are also lots of jobs involved in energy audits and installation of efficiency upgrades such as insulation, windows, heating and cooling systems, etc. *Waste management* employs those who take away and process trash and recyclable materials and is an increasingly important sector as cities seek to improve their recycling rates. *Transportation* includes jobs associated with making, selling, and repairing cars, buses, and subway, light rail, and trolley cars and with building and maintaining roadways and railways. Transportation, married to environmental goals, is also a source of new technologies. The effort to produce a zero-emission car will entail a revolution in industrial design and production.

To what extent can these green sectors be the target of economic development strategies? How are cities creating economic development opportunities in these areas? What has worked and why? To answer these questions, we need to understand how cities might go about creating or expanding a green economic sector. I have identified three strategies a city can pursue to create jobs and economic development in green economy sectors (see table 2.1).

Linking strategies connect sustainability or climate change initiatives to economic development goals such as creating workforce development programs to train residents for green jobs. The programs may target groups that have difficulty connecting to the labor market, such as unemployed out-of-school youth and ex-offenders. A linking strategy may also involve the city in assisting existing businesses in becoming more profitable by adopting renewable energy sources, making their operations more energy-efficient or less polluting, and related efforts. Linking strategies typically aren't about creating new jobs but assisting businesses already in place or training residents who are having difficulty finding a place in the local labor market. The idea is to assess a city's existing assets and identify ways to link them to a green development opportunity.

Transformational strategies identify ways that existing businesses can expand into green markets or services. Many of the possibilities here are in retooling manufacturing. Take the wind industry. Wind turbines have more than 8,000 parts. Local manufacturers could become suppliers to the turbine manufacturers that are springing up across the country. The possibilities for suppliers of building products are extensive. A producer of window shades can expand into thermal shades. Air-conditioning producers are developing energy-efficient products that replace Freon with a refrigerant that produces no greenhouse gas emissions. A few plastics producers have developed a biodegradable carbon dioxide–based plastic that decomposes in less than a year. Transformational strategies create growth opportunities for existing businesses and additional indirect growth in the local economy.

Leapfrogging strategies attempt to create an entirely new sector in a green technology. Several cities are trying to become centers of renewable energy, waste processing, and transportation technologies. This is the boldest step a city can take, and one that requires considerable understanding of the sector. As we shall see in chapter 3, Cleveland's attempt to use Lake Erie to become a leader in offshore wind production, manufacturing, and research illustrates a bold leapfrogging strategy. Because leapfrogging strategies often involve untested technologies, they may not always succeed.

What is common to all of the initiatives is that they are innovative experiments from which we can learn. But not all of the cases I present

TABLE 2.1. Framework for Linking Sustainability Strategies to Economic Development

Strategy	Sector			
	Renewable Energy	Green Building/Energy Efficiency*	Recycling/Waste-to-Energy	Transportation
Linking strategies create connections between elements of sustainability strategies and economic or workforce development.	**Berkeley, CA** Berkeley FIRST Financing residents to go solar **Richmond, CA** Solar Richmond Training disadvantaged youth for jobs in solar installation	**Los Angeles, CA** Linking efficiency retrofitting to work-needy residents **Milwaukee, WI** Me2, energy efficiency retrofitting	**Chicago, IL** Waste to Profit Network **United Kingdom** National Industrial Symbiosis Programme	**Denver, CO** Transit-oriented development **Los Angeles, CA** The Coalition for Clean and Safe Ports
Transformational strategies attempt to transform or "green" existing economic sectors or strengths.	**Toledo, OH** From glass to solar panels	**Pittsburgh, PA** Green Building Alliance **Syracuse, NY** Growing an indoor environmental quality sector **New York City** NYC Green Manufacturing Initiative	**Bronx, NYC** Sustainable South Bronx	**Portland, OR** Building local streetcars
Leapfrogging strategies attempt to build entirely new green sectors and jobs.	**Austin, TX** Creating a solar industry **Cleveland, OH region** Creating a wind industry		**Los Angeles, CA** RENEW LA	**King County/(Seattle, WA** Biowaste to biodiesel **Portland, OR** Supporting a niche bicycle industry

*Because energy efficiency and green building are, by definition, rooted in construction-related industries that exist everywhere, initiatives in this area, either link to existing industries or transform them.

are "best practice" examples in terms of achieving their intended outcomes. Some of the initiatives have not achieved their goals or turned out as planned. I believe, however, that we learn more from understanding why a particular strategy worked in one place but not in another than we do from focusing only on successes. One goal in telling the stories of these cities is to illustrate a range of approaches to building a green economy and where they have worked and why. Another is to examine the link between being a leader in sustainability or climate change and pursuing a green economic development strategy. Some cities that aren't at all focused on sustainable development or climate change are leaders in trying to develop a green economy. Some cities have an explicit social justice agenda linked to green economic development, while for others it is implicit, being negotiated, or nonexistent. What every case does reveal, however, is that cities can't do it alone—a host of state and federal policies are needed if the United States is going to become an economic leader in the energy-climate era.

Why some cities are successful and others are not in developing a new economic sector is due partly to their economic and locational strengths, partly to choosing effective strategies, and partly to how the policies are carried out. Practitioners engage in numerous activities to attract new business growth or maintain and build on existing strengths. Whether in pursuit of a linking, transformational, or leap-frogging strategy, the activities will include some combination of the following:[11]

- Identifying firms in the targeted sector that could expand or locate in the area;
- Strengthening existing firms in the sector in the local economy (e.g., technical assistance in adopting up-to-date technologies, expanding into new product lines, coordinated purchasing);
- Facilitating cooperation among university researchers and businesses in developing new technologies or products;
- Developing financing mechanisms to fill capital needs not met by conventional financing sources;
- Creating employment and training programs to assure an adequately skilled workforce;
- Helping firms respond to environmental and other regulations;
- Expanding markets through the city's purchasing power; and
- Addressing local competitiveness weaknesses (e.g., transportation

inadequacy, outdated land use regulations, high energy costs).

These activities are the nuts and bolts of economic development planning. We will see them all in action in the chapters that follow.

CITIES, SUSTAINABILITY, AND SOCIAL JUSTICE

The term "sustainable development" has become so widely used as to be almost meaningless.[12] It is most commonly defined as development that meets the needs of the present without compromising the ability of future generations to meet their needs—in other words, development that doesn't degrade the planet or impose disproportionate costs on our descendants.[13] Some advocates like to define sustainable development in terms of the "three E's":

- *Economy*—Creating economic activity in order to create decent jobs, income, and a tax base.
- *Ecology*—Protecting and building the city's natural assets and creating a less polluting environment.
- *Equity*—Ensuring that all residents have access to economic opportunity and are not exposed to environmental harm based on social class.[14]

The idea of sustainable development is now mainstream (who is going to advocate for unsustainable development?). The widespread adoption of sustainability typically ignores a tacit radicalism—the sustainability agenda is a political critique of the inherent ecological damage and economic inequality created by free-market capitalism.[15] As such, a sustainability agenda should embrace the idea of linking environmental goals to broader social justice goals as in the "three E's." The environmental justice movement, a concept first articulated in 1982, points out that low-income people and communities of color are often the targets of every kind of environmental assault from toxic waste dumps to elevated levels of ambient lead. By the same token, lower-income workers and minorities are more frequently subjected to workplace hazards, less likely to be protected by collective bargaining agreements, and more frequently in irregular forms of employment that have none of the normal protections such as OSHA inspections. These are injustices that an urban sustainability agenda should seek to redress. At an international level, the equity aspect of sustainability calls for serious efforts to reduce poverty and a belief that doing so requires both greater government regulation and dramatic changes in lifestyles, particularly in the case of wealthier countries.[16]

This political critique, however, is typically glossed over in working definitions such as that in the American Planning Association's *Policy Guide on Planning for Sustainability*: "the capability to equitably meet the vital human needs of the present without compromising the ability of future generations to meet their own needs by preserving and protecting the area's ecosystems and natural resources. This concept of sustainability describes a condition in which human use of natural resources, required for the continuation of life, is in balance with Nature's ability to replenish them."[17]

While this definition emphasizes the ecological component to the exclusion of the other two, most urban policies promoted under the rubric of sustainability focus on the economic leg of the stool, paying only lip service to the ecological/environmental aspect. In *Taking Sustainable Cities Seriously*, Kent Portney points out that sustainability, as defined by the city's 1996 Sustainable Boston initiative, took a backseat to traditional economic development, mainly because the linkages weren't obvious.[18] Boston is certainly no exception in this regard.[19] Few U.S. cities mention social or environmental justice as a component of their sustainability agenda.[20] In fact, the two are often at odds. There is a long history of social justice and community organizations criticizing and pressuring city governments to include the urban poor as beneficiaries of their economic development agendas.[21] Occidental College professor of politics Peter Dreier chronicles the successes of these grassroots movements in achieving gains such as living-wage ordinances (now adopted by more than 200 cities), community-benefits agreements, and more accountability when offering tax abatements and other subsidies.[22] Historically, the environmental justice community has expressed mistrust of the sustainability movement, noting that sustainability advocates worry more about future generations than those being exposed to environmental harms now.[23] Tufts University professor and environmental justice advocate Julian Agyeman calls for a refocusing on what he defines as "just sustainability"—"the need to ensure a better quality of life for all, now and into the future, in a just and equitable manner, whilst living within the limits of supporting ecosystems."[24] Agyeman reminds us that "sustainability is at least as much about politics, injustice, and inequality as it is about science or the environment."[25]

In recent years, the sustainability agenda has shifted to focus more on climate change as evidenced by the U.S. Conference of Mayors Climate Protection Agreement signed by more than 970 cities, the C40 Climate Leadership Group, an organization of the world's largest cities committed to tackling climate change, ICLEI-Local Governments for Sustainability, an association of local governments committed to advancing climate protection and sustainable development with 550 member cities in the United States and more than 1,000 cities worldwide, and numerous other organizations.[26] Is it possible that focusing more on climate change rather than sustainability could more effectively redirect the urban agenda toward accomplishing environmental, equity, and economic goals? One might not think so, since most cities see sustainability and climate change as part and parcel of the same agenda. Many cities that have created offices of sustainable development or have sustainability plans list reducing greenhouse gas emissions as key priorities (e.g., Austin, Los Angeles, Oakland, Minneapolis, New York, Portland, Philadelphia, Seattle).[27] But because climate change activities—promoting renewable energy and energy efficiency, reducing waste, and increasing public transportation—have employment opportunities associated with them, this new addition to the agenda has catalyzed a movement to connect the economic and equity aspects of this environmental agenda. The climate change movement is gaining traction at the city, state, and national level (see text box below).

Local Action Alone Will Not Solve the Climate Change Problem

Scientific evidence of global warming has been gathering since the late 1980s.[a] Since the first report of the Intergovernmental Panel on Climate Change (IPCC) in 1990, more and more scientists and the National Academy of Sciences have joined a consensus that human activity is the cause of global warming.[b] The most hard-hitting evidence that global warming is very likely created by human activity and not the result of natural variability was released in late 2007 in the fourth report of the IPCC. The report details the effects of global warming on natural and human systems, many of which will be "abrupt, unpredictable, and

(*continued*)

irreversible." The IPCC estimates that CO_2 emissions would have to fall by 50–85 percent by 2050 to avert disaster—defined by global temperatures rising more than 2 degrees Celsius. The IPCC predicts that average worldwide temperatures will increase by 4.5 degrees Fahrenheit (2.5 degrees Celsius) by 2100. In May 2009, scientists at MIT's Joint Program on the Science and Policy of Global Change released results from the most comprehensive modeling yet carried out on climate change impacts, which found the effects will be about twice as severe as predicted. The researchers predict an end-of-century temperature rise of at least 9 degrees Fahrenheit. The computer simulation found that in addition to greenhouse gases rising at a higher rate than expected, several mitigating factors were not as strong as expected.[c]

As the world's largest emitter of greenhouse gases (overtaken by China in 2009), the United States has a need and an obligation to address the problem. Instead, while the rest of the world was taking action, the Bush administration questioned the evidence.[d] The United States is not one of the 180 countries that have ratified the Kyoto Protocol, the international agreement that sets binding targets for 37 industrialized countries and the European Union to reduce greenhouse gas emissions to an average of 5 percent against 1990 levels by 2012.[e] Only Norway, Switzerland, and Iceland have come close to meeting the targets, with the European Union extending the deadline to 2020. The G-8 Climate Scorecard released in July 2008 warned that none of the world's eight largest economies are doing enough to prevent catastrophe.[f] The United States ranked last among the eight countries for its efforts. In fact, the United States and Russia are the only G-8 countries that haven't endorsed the goal of reducing their emissions by half.

The price of dramatically reducing emissions will be high, but significant reductions can be made without compromising economic growth. The definitive analysis of the economics of climate change was led by Lord Nicholas Stern, then head of the U.K.'s Government Economic Service and former chief economist at the World Bank. The 2006 Stern Report notes that "Emissions have been, and continue to be, driven by economic growth; yet stabilisation of greenhouse-gas concentrations is feasible and consistent with continued growth."[g] Although the Stern Report estimates that the cost of mitigation would be about 1 percent of gross world product, the cost of not acting is even higher. Stern estimates that inaction could reduce economic output from 5 to 20 percent as it plays out over the century.

Most experts agree that nations need to put a price on carbon in order to stimulate the new climate-friendly technological revolution needed in the

(continued)

Local Action Alone Will Not Solve the Climate Change Problem   (cont.)

energy-climate era. The normally conservative International Energy Agency estimates that the price of emitting CO_2 would have to be $200 a ton to avert global warming and stimulate the needed technology revolution.[h] No country has established a price even close to this. The European trading scheme established in 2008 sets the price of carbon at $43 per ton. The American Clean Energy and Security Act that passed in the House of Representatives in June 2009 sets the initial price at $13 a ton. It also establishes a cap and trade program that sets mandatory caps on 87 percent of U.S. greenhouse gas emissions, mostly directed at the electric power, oil, and gas producers and other heavy industries. Total U.S. greenhouse emissions would be reduced, as a result, by 15 percent below 2005 levels by 2020.

[a]See The Heat Is Online, http://www.heatisonline.org/contentserver/objecthandlers/index.cfm?id=3458&method=full, for a concise summary of scientific evidence on climate change.

[b]Romm, 2007: 12. The IPCC is an offshoot of the United Nations Environment Programme and the World Meteorological Society.

[c]See http://web.mit.edu/newsoffice/2009/roulette-0519.html (accessed May 28, 2009).

[d]On this point, see Ross Gelbspan's well-documented analyses in *The Heat Is On* (1997) and *Boiling Point* (2004), which describe how the coal and oil industries have funded a small group of climate change skeptics to refute the evidence on climate change. The media fed our nation's reluctance to respond by treating the skeptics as equals in an ongoing debate rather than the fringe of the scientific community that they were. Also see Romm, 2007: 216–221.

[e]The Kyoto Protocol is linked to the United Nations Framework Convention on Climate Change. It was signed in Kyoto, Japan, in December 1997, and countries became bound to its limits in February 2005. See http://unfccc.int/kyoto_protocol/items/2830.php (accessed July 12, 2008).

[f]Britain, Canada, Japan, France, Germany, Italy, Russia, and the United States.

[g]Stern, 2006: 11.

[h]The International Energy Agency (IEA) is the energy policy advisor to 27 countries, including the United States. It was started during the 1973–74 oil crisis to help member countries provide reliable, affordable, and clean energy for their citizens. The "three E's" guiding the IEA are energy security, economic development, and environmental protection. See http://www.iea.org/.

Politically, the traditional environmental movement has gained two important new allies that could help create a broader coalition for linking environmental, economic development, and equity goals: the labor movement and the movement for social and environmental justice. This is a significant change. Historically, the environmental movement has been mostly white and upper-middle-class. Labor unions were skeptical, since the early programs aimed at creating a cleaner environment seemed to come at the expense of traditional polluting industries and hence jobs. Advocates for low-income groups and minorities saw little in the environmental movement that helped their constituency. However, in the past decade, trade unions have come together with environmentalists to pursue job opportunities in new, green industries through labor-environmental coalitions such as the Blue-Green Alliance and the Apollo Alliance. And environmental justice advocates have moved beyond demands for safer and cleaner low-income neighborhoods to efforts to organize on behalf of green jobs.

The Apollo Alliance has been front and center nationally in linking climate change action with a social justice and labor agenda. The Apollo Alliance is a coalition of labor unions, environmental and community organizations, and business leaders focused on moving the nation toward energy efficiency and independence; it claims that in the process the nation can create about 3.3 million good jobs, stimulating $1.4 trillion in new GDP and creating $284 billion in net energy cost savings.[28] It was organized in 2003 with the idea that a national commitment of the magnitude of the Apollo space mission is necessary to achieving these goals, with an investment of $300 billion over ten years (the cost being repaid in full through increased federal tax revenues and earnings). The Apollo Alliance now has affiliates in nine states and five cities, each charged with building political support for policies and programs to create green-collar jobs, defined as well-paid, career-track jobs that contribute directly to preserving or enhancing environmental quality (see text box on pp. 28–30).

Consider the work of Apollo affiliate Green for All, an organization focused on building a green economy that creates opportunity for poor people. The group was founded by social justice and eco-equity superstar Van Jones. This national organization and its founder got their start in Oakland, California, where Jones started the Ella Baker Center for Human Rights in 1996.

The Center, named for a civil rights leader of the 1950s and '60s, had as its original focus alternatives to violence and incarceration for inner-city youth. One of the key alternatives Jones identified was good job opportunities, and the center launched several programs to connect youth with jobs. By 2005, green jobs were seen as a source of employment for inner-city youth. Jones and staffer Ian Kim worked on the social justice and climate change/sustainability plank of Ron Dellums' mayoral campaign in 2006. And during the six months between his

election and taking office, they worked with the new mayor on craft-
ing a strategy for transforming Oakland from a declining manufacturing city to a leader in the green economy. In October 2007, the
Oakland City Council created the Oil Independent Oakland by 2020
Task Force, which drew on local, regional, and national experts to
make recommendations for reducing the city's greenhouse gas emissions and becoming a national leader in the green economy and green
jobs creation.[29]

While working with city government, Jones and Kim were
also creating the program that would become the Green-Collar
Jobs Campaign at the Ella Baker Center. The key initiative of the
campaign was a green job training program, the Oakland Green
Jobs Corps, which would target the city's at-risk youth, the under-
employed, the formerly incarcerated, and others with barriers to
employment. A year later the Oakland City Council appropriated
$250,000 of city funds from a class action settlement against out-
of-state energy suppliers that was required to be used to promote
renewable energy and energy efficiency.[30] The program started in
October 2008 with 40 participants, all low-income young adults.
The students receive training in solar installation, green construction, and energy efficiency as part of a construction training program. After seven months of classes delivered by a community
college and hands-on training, the students get paid work experience with local employers. The first class graduated in June 2009.[31]
The Ella Baker Center worked with the Oakland mayor's office and
other allies to assemble a unique Green Employer Council of 15
green-collar firms who have agreed to provide paid work experience and on-the-job training for graduates. These firms include
solar installers, green construction contractors, and energy efficiency contractors.

Although this is not a large number of jobs, it is a promising
approach for linking environmental, economic, and equity objectives. A social and environmental justice organization helped shape
the city's focus on sustainability and climate change and worked
with the mayor to make sure the agenda was well connected to job
creation that targeted inner-city youth. The follow-up act was to
create national green jobs legislation.

During a discussion in San Francisco hosted by U.S. Speaker
of the House Nancy Pelosi, who was building toward the 2007
omnibus energy bill, Jones had the opportunity to present his green

job training idea. Pelosi had also just established the House Select Committee on Energy Independence and Global Warming to develop an energy policy to enhance national security, reduce greenhouse gas emissions, and move the country toward energy independence. Agreeing that the addition of green job training would enhance the legislation, Pelosi directed Jones to work on a green jobs bill with Representative Hilda Solis (D-CA, now U.S. Secretary of Labor), a longtime advocate for environmental justice issues, who was appointed to the Select Committee by Pelosi.

While the Ella Baker Center worked with Solis and others in the House, a close national ally, the Apollo Alliance, had initiated a similar bill on the Senate side with Senators Bernard Sanders and Hillary Clinton. The two bills were reconciled to form the Green Jobs Act, which authorized $125 million per year for the Department of Labor to create an Energy Efficiency and Renewable Energy Worker Training Program, including $25 million set aside for pilot programs providing "green pathways out of poverty," such as the Oakland Green Jobs Corps. A coalition consisting of the Ella Baker Center, the Apollo Alliance, the Workforce Alliance, and many others emerged to back the bill. Solis placed special emphasis on the "pathways out of poverty" section of the bill, and worked particularly hard on developing and keeping that section intact as the bill made its way through committees.

In December 2007, Congress passed the Green Jobs Act as part of the omnibus Energy Independence and Security Act of 2007. Funds have not been appropriated, but the 2009 American Recovery and Reinvestment Act (President Obama's "stimulus package") included $500 million in green job training funds inspired directly by the Green Jobs Act.

With the national spotlight on Jones, the time was ripe for taking the green jobs and social justice agenda to a national scale. Jones created a nationwide group, Green for All, while Kim stayed on to lead the local green jobs campaigns and to organize the California Green Stimulus Coalition to press the agenda at the state level. The coalition comprises about 45 labor, social justice, environmental justice, and community organizations that are helping the state legislature to develop a plan for using federal stimulus funds to create green jobs and provide the training to fill them.[32] In April 2008, Governor Arnold Schwarzenegger announced he was using $10 million of $74 million in discretionary stimulus funds to launch a California Green Jobs Corps that basically replicates the Oakland program statewide. The Governor's Green Corps will serve 1,000 at-risk youth (ages 16–24) through 10 grants of $1 million throughout the state. Existing training providers and community colleges will implement the program, which will include paid internships in renewable energy and energy efficiency occupations.

In addition to uniting the three E's, what we see in this story is a new unification of unions, environmentalists, environmental justice activists, and community and social justice organizations around an economic development and climate change agenda. This case also illustrates how these organizations can influence city, state, and even national policy. As we will see in later chapters, Oakland is one of many examples. With President Obama committed to a green jobs agenda, we have a unique opportunity to move the green urban agenda forward with national policy. This opportunity has been shaped by cities and will further shape what cities can do.

OBSERVATIONS ON STRATEGY AND SCALE

A tour of cities, and their efforts to link sustainability and climate change strategies to economic development and jobs, leads to some inescapable conclusions about national policies. First, cities can be innovators, but the influence of individual city policies on consumer and industrial demand for many green products, whether solar energy, subway cars, or green-building products, is too limited, for the most part, to create large-scale markets for renewable energy sources. Federal standards and policies to induce demand are required. Second, we will find that cities can try—and occasionally succeed—in their efforts to link sustainability policies to economic development spin-offs. But again, this is a national economy. Few cities can stimulate enough demand for a given product to build an industry, the goal of many import substitution strategies. Many cities will find that they can specialize in different sectors of the green economy. Third, this is also a global economy. Industries and jobs stimulated by energy policies will not necessarily be located domestically in the absence of national industrial and trade policies.

Fourth, the competition among cities and states to lure green businesses with subsidies is heating up. Cities (and states) have a history of providing incentives to lure industries that goes back to the 1930s.[33] Sometimes these produce short-term gains, but they often subsidize activities that would take place anyway and merely spend taxpayer dollars to influence location decisions at the margin.[34] Absent industrial policies to develop these new industries, the desire to attract green businesses is just the latest variant on a familiar zero-sum game of smokestack-chasing. As we shall see, if the United States wants to get serious about capturing or recapturing clean energy production such as wind and solar, or reviving modern versions of traditional industries such as streetcar and subway-car system production we have to get over our aversion to industrial policy. City-led economic development strategies can't do it alone. Cities can make modest progress on their own in achieving sustainability and greenhouse gas reduction—or they could be constituent elements in a national transformation. Much of the potential for green cities will be determined by the energy, climate, and related industrial policy of the Obama administration.

Finally, we will see that not all green jobs are good jobs. Achieving economic justice goals by improving job quality requires regulatory and labor-market policies at all levels of government. Whether green jobs actually turn out to be well-paying jobs with decent benefits is less a function of technology than of the labor-market policies we pursue.

In the chapters that follow, we examine the strategies that cities are using to develop a green economic sector and the extent to which their strategies link to sustainability and social justice. Although the link is not made in every example, the potential is there. While I am optimistic about the ability of cities to create good green jobs, we will see that not all cities will be able to capture much economic activity as they pursue sustainability and climate change agendas. And even when it all works, a city's efforts may not create local jobs. We'll see that Austin, Texas, has implemented policies to develop solar energy that other cities are trying to replicate. But try as they may, elected officials and planners have not been able to create a solar manufacturing industry in place. Seattle sets a great example for how a city that wasn't developed with a public transportation infrastructure can create one. Seattle is the nation's leading city in changing over to hybrid electric buses—but bus production won't take place there. From the perspective of an individual city or region, capturing green jobs is important, but we must not lose perspective—sustainability and climate change activities are of the utmost importance in their own right.

How Many Green Jobs, Really?

There is a lot of enthusiasm about the green economy, but not much agreement on exactly how many jobs it includes. Researchers define the green economy in different ways. They don't agree on what industries to include, and some focus on occupations rather than industries. Researchers also disagree on how to measure the green job potential (some measure existing jobs and others potential future jobs). The most common method is the use of input-output models. These models analyze the job potential of an output, say a wind turbine, by estimating how an increase in demand will create jobs—not only in producing the actual turbine, but in the industries producing the inputs. Direct jobs are those created in the turbine factory. Indirect jobs are those created from producing the inputs. There is also a multiplier effect, via the jobs in other sectors that result from the increased production of the output—the workers in the new wind production facility will require housing, groceries, schools, etc.

Some studies estimate the number of jobs that would be created with a certain dollar amount of investment in the technology, while others estimate based on the amount of the technology produced (e.g., jobs per megawatt installed in the case of renewable energy). There is agreement that not all green jobs will be new jobs. Many, if not most, will be existing jobs, but workers will be producing different products or services (e.g., changing their output from gas guzzlers to hybrid cars, from products made with new inputs to products made with recycled inputs, from auto glass to solar panels, from inefficient to efficient buildings). And all agree that there will be job losses in some sectors as green sectors grow (e.g., jobs in the coal industry or domestic oil industry will decline). As the world searches for clean technologies, new products and processes for producing them are being invented. Some of the clean technologies that will drive the economy may not even exist yet, which is part of why it is so difficult to define their job creation potential.

The broadest framing of the scope of green jobs is "clean tech," defined as goods and services that promote conservation of natural resources and provide cost savings to the end user. Cleantech Group identifies ten economic sectors, with jobs in each ranging from manufacturing to research and development. They include agriculture and nutrition, air quality, enabling technologies (e.g., manufacturing process technologies), energy technology (clean energy generation, storage,

(continued)

efficiency, and infrastructure), environmental information technology, materials and nanotechnology, materials recovery and recycling, manufacturing/industrial, transportation and logistics, and water purification and management.[a] There are several other definitions of clean tech, and the term is often used interchangeably with green tech. While clean tech helps us understand the technologies that will drive the economy in the energy/climate era, it does not lend itself to a good accounting of net job creation. Employment data are collected by industry and occupation, and these categories are neither.

Many of the green job studies focus on renewable energy. The United Nations Environmental Programme estimates that 2.3 million people are employed directly in renewable energy worldwide. Of these, 400,000 are in wind, 170,000 are in solar photovoltaics, 624,000 in solar thermal, and more than 1 million in biomass and biofuels.[b]

In an effort to sift through studies using different methodologies and different units of employment (e.g., jobs per kilowatt hour, full-time job equivalents, person-years of employment) in the United States, Daniel Kammen and his colleagues at the University of California, Berkeley analyzed 13 recent studies of the job creation potential of renewable energy. What is particularly valuable about Kammen's analysis is that it estimates the number of jobs that would be created through 2020 under several policy scenarios (in this case different national renewable portfolio standards). The most optimistic scenario estimates total U.S. employment in renewable energy at 188,018 by 2020, with a 20 percent renewable portfolio standard by 2020 (met 40% by biomass, 55% by wind energy, and 5% by solar).[c] If the United States were producing for an export market, employment could increase as much as 16 times these estimates.

The Renewable Energy Policy Project (REPP) uses a "calculator" to estimate the number of jobs that could result from renewable energy development under different renewable portfolio standards or other programs to accelerate renewable energy development. The calculator is based on a survey of industry practices in manufacturing, installation, and operating and maintaining practices for each renewable energy technology analyzed (solar, wind, biomass, and geothermal). The calculator estimates the number and types of jobs for each renewable technology by year per installed megawatt of capacity, assuming that most inputs would be produced in the United States.[d] The reports assume that many of the component parts of domestic manufacturers producing wind turbines and solar panels in the United States will be domestic, an

(*continued*)

How Many Green Jobs, Really? (*cont.*)

assumption that hasn't held up in practice. If the United States committed to producing 25 percent of our electricity from renewable sources by 2025, more than 850,000 manufacturing jobs would be created.[e]

The green economy goes far beyond renewable energy, but these jobs are easier to estimate than for, say, energy efficiency endeavors. For these, researchers must establish criteria of what is sufficiently efficient to meet a threshold above which economic activity and related jobs can be considered green. Most agree that efficiency-related jobs are likely to vastly outweigh jobs in renewable energy, particularly over the next five years.

Casting the net even wider, Robert Pollin and colleagues at the Political Economy Research Institute at the University of Massachusetts Amherst estimated that 1.7 million net new jobs could be created over two years with $150 billion of funding on green infrastructure in six areas: retrofitting buildings, expanding mass transit and freight rail, building a smart electric grid, wind power, solar power, and next-generation biofuels. The report identifies occupations within these areas that would experience employment demand. Although many of these jobs would put laid-off workers back to work, some would be new jobs.[f]

Whether counting direct, indirect, or induced jobs, determining what a green job is and calculating exactly how many of them there are is not an exact science. What is evident is that green investments create jobs—all kinds of jobs. How many? Even by the most conservative estimates, we're talking about hundreds of thousands of new jobs—and maybe millions. The actual number will depend on the policy we put in place.

[a]Cleantech Group does not include traditional environmental technologies such as air pollution control, remediation, and hazardous waste management, making a distinction between technologies that remediate existing pollution and complying with state or federal regulations and clean-tech products and services, which are developed to avoid these problems to begin with.

[b]Renner, Sweeeney, and Kubit, 2008.

[c]Kammen, Kapadia, and Fripp, 2004 (updated 2006).

[d]Several REPP reports are referenced in this chapter.

[e]Blue-Green Alliance, 2009.

[f]Pollin, Heintz, and Garrett-Peltier, 2009; Pollin, Wicks-Lim, and Garrett-Peltier, 2009. The $150 billion includes $100 billion from the stimulus and $50 billion from the proposed American Clean Energy and Security Act (passed by the House in 2009). The model used estimates that it takes $60,000 to create one clean-energy job, including direct, indirect, and induced effects.

3

Renewable Cities

WITH THE RIGHT MIX OF POLICIES AND INCENTIVES, renewable energy could supply 40 percent of America's electricity needs by 2030.[1] It could also create a world-class 21st-century renewable energy industry, with $700 billion in economic activity and, according to some, three million estimated domestic jobs.[2] Unfortunately, the United States has gone from being a leader in renewable energy technology research and development to a consumer of technology designed and produced elsewhere. Although we still have some research and production, it will take a lot of investment and a comprehensive national policy for the United States to become a leading producer of solar and wind energy. In the absence of national policy, many states have been implementing their own policies and programs to promote renewable energy. And cities also have been promoting renewable energy—from high-tech cities where innovation is expected to older manufacturing cities seeking paths to revitalization. In this chapter, we examine cities as the locus of economic development for renewable energy, notably solar and wind.

Cities are taking different paths to promote renewable energy, which is what we'd expect given that each area of the country has different natural resources. There is plenty that cities can do to promote use of renewable energy use, but becoming a solar or wind production center is not a goal a city can fully achieve in the absence of state and national policy. This chapter explores a range of efforts in cities to create jobs and economic development in renewable energy.

Our tour starts with Berkeley and Richmond in California's East Bay area. The focus here is on Berkeley, which has developed a unique financing model, Berkeley FIRST, to make it easy for residents and businesses to convert to solar. While Berkeley holds no illusions about becoming a production center, part of the plan is to link solar energy adoption to jobs in solar design and installation. Berkeley FIRST links to a training program targeting inner-city youth in nearby Richmond. The next stop is Austin, where the city-owned utility has made a sizable investment in wind and solar energy. Austin is also attempting to be a leader in solar manufacturing. We then move to the Midwest and Toledo, a rust belt city with high unemployment that claims the nation's largest producer of thin-film solar panels. Toledo's economic development specialists are helping the area's high-tech glass producers retool for producing solar panels to turn around an economy dependent on the auto industry. Cleveland hopes to revitalize its manufacturing industry by becoming a center for offshore wind research and production, and the whole region is focusing on supplying numerous wind turbine companies throughout the Midwest. But first, we turn to a brief summary of the state of global solar and wind industries today. Is solar energy too expensive to be practical? Can wind overcome transmission and variability problems? What is the future of these promising technologies? Can they really create millions of jobs? And which cities, states, and nations will be the winners?

A QUICK PRIMER ON THE SOLAR AND WIND INDUSTRIES

With average annual growth of 48 percent per year since 2002, grid-connected solar photovoltaic power (PV) is the world's fastest-growing energy technology.[3] At present, solar supplies only half of 1 percent of the nation's energy needs, but that has the potential to grow to 35 percent of all energy (and 69 percent of electricity) by 2050.[4] The average cost of producing a PV module has dropped from almost $100 per watt in 1975 to about $4 per watt in 2009 (although First Solar thin-film has hit $1 per watt). Most experts suggest solar has to consistently reach about $1 a watt to compete with coal-fired electricity.[5] Prices may drop even more, as the cost of silicon could decline by more than 40 percent due to new production capacity coming on board, according to the research firm New Energy Finance. Solar thin-film will likely be at $1 per watt by 2010.[6] Thin-film solar's share of the market will expand, and could be as much as 40 percent by 2012.[7]

Solar and Wind Glossary

Watt (W): The metric unit for measuring power, defined as energy per time unit, i.e., joules per second. It is frequently used to measure the rate of energy production, transfer, or consumption of various machines and devices, such as lightbulbs, cars, power plants, etc. In electricity, one watt is alternatively defined as an electrical current of one ampere flowing under an electrical potential difference of one volt.

Kilowatt (kW): A standard unit of electrical power equal to 1,000 watts. This scale is suitable for devices with relatively small electric engines, such as home electrical heaters or ten 100-watt lightbulbs (exactly 1 kW). The energy consumption rate of an average car is measured in tens of kW.

Megawatt (MW): A standard unit of electrical power equal to one million watts. This scale is useful for describing the energy consumption of large electric motors, such as in airplanes or locomotives. The energy produced in a small power plant is measured in hundreds of MW.

Gigawatt (GW): A standard unit of electrical power equal to one billion watts. The GW is most commonly used for large systems such as wind turbines or coal, natural gas, and nuclear plants.

Kilowatt-hour (kWh): A unit of energy defined as one kilowatt used or produced over one hour. An average U.S. household uses about 10,000 kilowatt-hours (kWh) of electricity each year. One megawatt of wind or solar energy can generate between 2.4 million and 3 million kWh annually—enough to power 240 to 300 households.[a]

Solar energy is produced by harnessing the sun's energy. Solar technologies absorb the photons from electromagnetic radiation (e.g., visible light, infrared, ultraviolet, radio, microwave) and convert their energy into a utilizable form. In a solar photovoltaic (PV) cell, photons pass through two or more thin layers of semiconducting material (usually silicon). The electrical charges generated are conducted away by metal contacts as direct current. Multiple cells are connected and encapsulated (usually behind glass) to form a module or panel. Thin-film solar technologies use non-silicon semiconductor materials and are produced using a roll-to-roll manufacturing process that is similar to printing paper. Thin-film is cheaper to produce, but has lower efficiency at present.[b] A different form of utilizing sunlight is solar thermal energy, which

(continued)

Solar and Wind Glossary (*cont.*)

concentrates light and heat from the sun with mirrors to produce heat. On a small scale, this technology is used in buildings to heat water or small spaces. On a larger scale, it can be used to boil large quantities of water, which can then be converted into electricity through steam engines.[c]

Wind energy is produced by harnessing the power of wind using turbines that spin when wind blows through them. Air has mass, and when it is in motion, it contains the energy of that motion—"kinetic energy." Some portion of that energy can be converted into mechanical or electrical energy. Some locations are more suitable for wind energy due to higher levels of wind regularity and velocity.[d]

[a]Adapted from Massachusetts Technology Collaborative. Available at http://www.mtpc.org/cleanenergy/energy/glossaryenergymeas.htm (accessed November 16, 2008).

[b]Adapted from http://www.electricityforum.com/solar-electricity.html (accessed November 16, 2008).

[c]Energy Information Administration. 2008. Renewable Energy Trends in Consumption and Electricity 2006. U.S. Department of Energy. 23–25. Available at http://www.eia.doe.gov/cneaf/solar.renewables/page/trends/trends.pdf (accessed December 2, 2008).

[d]American Wind Energy Association, Wind Power 101. Available at http://www.ifnotwind.org/we101/wind-energy-basics.shtml (accessed November 16, 2008).

The cost of wind is considerably less than solar; the production cost has declined from 30 cents per kilowatt-hour in the early 1980s to less than 5 cents per kilowatt-hour with the federal production tax credit. Installed capacity of wind energy grew by more than 5,000 megawatts

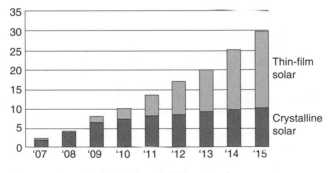

FIGURE 3.1 Global Solar Cell Demand.
Source: Mizuho Securities, Nikkei Microdevices.

in 2007—a 45 percent expansion in just one year, representing more than $9 billion in investment.[8] Tight credit markets starting in late 2008 have slowed or stopped some projects and caused some solar and wind companies to lay off workers.[9] Worldwide, investment in renewable energy dropped by $13.3 billion in the first quarter of 2009, a decrease of 53 percent from the same period in 2008.[10] Despite the slowdown, Clean Edge predicts continued mid- to long-term growth in both solar and wind energy, particularly with new government spending and policies to promote it.[11]

While solar and wind production are expanding in the United States, we have squandered their economic development opportunity. Twenty-five years ago, we were the world leader in both technologies—now we are playing catch-up with other countries that have had policies in place to drive demand and bring the cost of production down. While Germany, Japan, and other European countries were investing in renewable energy research, in 2003 the Bush administration provided $27 billion in subsidies for coal oil, and nuclear technology, with only token subsidies for renewables.[12] The good news is that we can catch up—but only with public policy and investment that explicitly focuses on economic development and job creation. What we see in both wind and solar is that the location of manufacturing matters. The overwhelming majority of jobs in both sectors are in manufacturing, not design, installation, and operation.

Only two U.S. manufacturers are among the world's top 20 producers of solar panels, and the fastest-growing is China (table 3.1).[13] The United States has lost its status as a wind producer as well. We had more than half of the world's wind production in the 1980s, with California alone producing 90 percent of the world's wind power in 1988 (now it produces less than 4 percent). With the exception of G.E., the top wind turbine companies are from Europe and Asia. This represents quite a missed opportunity, as global wind capacity has increased, on average, more than 25 percent a year over the last decade to a current level of 60,000 MW, 40,000 of which is in Europe.[14] Although short-term growth has been slowed due to the world financial crisis, the long-term growth trajectory for both wind and solar is quite positive.[15]

Why isn't the United States a leader in solar and wind production? The simple answer is lack of investment and lack of public policy to promote it (figure 3.2). Recall the role of Germany's feed-in tariff in building an export industry. Yet only a few states are just now considering feed-in tariffs and as we'll see later in the chapter, just over half

TABLE 3.1. Top 10 Photovoltaic and Wind Turbine Manufacturers, 2008

	Solar			Wind		
Company	Country of Origin	Cell Technology	Capacity 2008 (announced)	Company	Country of Origin	Capacity 2007 (in MW)
Sharp Electronics	Japan	Crystalline	870	Vestas	Denmark	4,512
Q-Cells	Germany	Crystalline	834	GE Wind	United States	3,285
Suntech Power Holdings	China	Crystalline	590	Gamesa	Spain	3,048
First Solar	United States	Thin-film	484	Enercon	Germany	2,771
SolarWorld	Germany	Crystalline	460	Suzlon	India	2,078
Sanyo	Japan	Crystalline	365	Siemens	Denmark/Germany	1,405
BP Solar	UK	Crystalline	480	Acciona	Spain	871
Kyocera	Japan	Crystalline	300	Goldwind	China	831
Motech Industries	Taiwan	Crystalline	330	Nordex	Germany	673
Solarfun Power Holdings	China	Crystalline	360	Sinovel	China	673
Total (in MW)			8,012	Total (in MW)		19,791
Total for Top 10			5,073	Total for Top 10		20,147

Source: Electronics, Design, Strategy News, 2008; U.S. Department of Energy, 2008; BTM Consult ApS, International Wind Energy Development, World Market Update 2007, March 2008, p. 23.

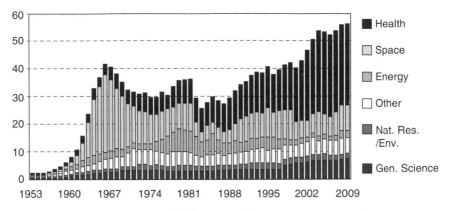

FIGURE 3.2 Trends on Nondefense R&D by Function, 1953–2009 (outlays for the conduct of R&D, billions of constant FY 2008 dollars). *Source:* American Wind Energy Association, 2008.

the states are requiring utilities to purchase more renewable energy through a renewable portfolio standard (see text box on pp. 50–51), which requires a set proportion of energy to be purchased by utilities from renewable sources. Although cities and states are trying to increase demand for renewable energy, there is no consistent industrial policy to expand supply. And funding for renewable energy research has been declining since the early 1980s, with a corresponding decline in innovation.[16] This could change with the Obama administration.

The main federal incentive to renewable energy production, the Federal Production Tax Credit, rather than being a long-term assurance, has typically been renewed by Congress on an annual or biannual basis, and has even lapsed for periods since it was initiated (figure 3.3). It was about to lapse again at the end of 2008, but was saved when supporters in Congress were able to add an eight-year renewal onto the $780 billion Emergency Economic Stabilization Act of 2009.[17] While this continuation is important, both the American Wind Energy Association and the Solar Energy Industries Association argue that to be effective in the current economic climate of lower tax liabilities, the tax credit should be refundable, as similar credits are for biodiesel and other alternative transportation fuels.

The countries that invested in research and implemented policies to promote shifts to renewable usage are also the ones now producing solar and wind technology for domestic use and for export. Foreign solar and wind companies have also begun locating in the United States to meet the growing demand for wind and solar energy. While these companies are creating some U.S. manufacturing jobs in producing panels and turbines, we are missing out on an even greater economic development opportunity in producing the parts that go into the final products and in future rounds of innovation.

Leaders in both industries have been vertically integrating their supply chains, purchasing all of, or controlling interests in, their suppliers.[18] As a result, both industries have become highly concentrated, which puts the United States at a disadvantage, since few of them are located here. In solar, the top five silicon cell companies control 59.9 percent of the market.[19] The top five largest wind turbine manufacturers control 82.2 percent of the world market. Only recently have the European companies located in the United States started using U.S. suppliers. Spanish-owned Gamesa, which has 28 percent of its turbine manufacturing capacity in the United States, has been importing its major components from overseas because U.S. capacity is lacking. Likewise, the new Vestas turbine plant in Colorado imported almost all its component parts as of 2007. But this is changing. In 2007 and the first quarter of 2008, at least 17 U.S. manufacturing facilities

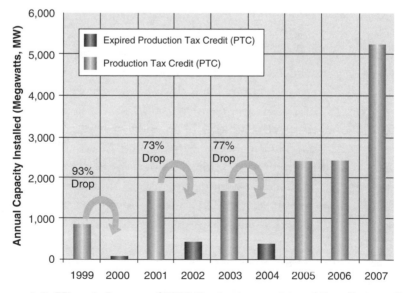

FIGURE 3.3 Historic Impact of PTC Expiration on Annual Installation of Wind Capacity. *Source:* American Wind Energy Association, 2008.

have been opened or expanded to supply the wind industry, creating more than 4,000 jobs and $500 million in manufacturing investment.[20] As shortages of many of the major wind turbine parts (e.g., gearboxes, machined parts, bearings, forgings) and transportation costs increase, more European wind companies in the United States will be looking for American suppliers.[21]

Currently, only about 16,000 people in the United States are employed directly in the wind industry and 7,600 in solar (table 3.2). These jobs generate another 30,800 indirect jobs in other sectors, and with the right policy in place the number of jobs could expand dramatically.[22] Navigant Consulting and the Solar Energy Industries Association estimate that an eight-year extension of the federal tax credit will drive 19,000 solar energy installations, with total increased investment of $232 billion, and create 276,000 direct jobs (440,000 combined direct and indirect) between 2009 and 2016.[23]

We could create hundreds of thousands more if we build the supply chains—about 4.85 jobs per megawatt of installed wind and about 30 per milliwatt of installed solar capacity. But it will take more than a federal tax credit. Ideally, federal policy would promote both the production and consumption of renewable energy, through regulation as well as subsidy, to require or incentivize local utilities to use green power sources. These national policy changes may be coming. But in the meantime, there's much to be learned from city and state initiatives.

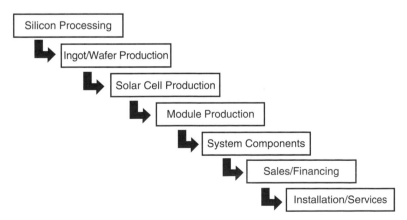

FIGURE 3.4 The Solar PV Industry Value Chain. *Source:* Centers of Excellence, 2008.

TABLE 3.2. The Renewable Energy Industry in the United States, 2006

Industry Segment	Revenues/Budgets (billions)	Direct Jobs	Total Jobs Created (direct plus indirect)
Wind	$3.00	16,000	36,800
Photovoltaics	1	6,800	15,700
Solar Thermal	0.1	800	1,900
Hydroelectric Power	4	8,000	19,000
Geothermal	2	9,000	21,000
Biomass			
Ethanol	6.3	67,000	154,000
Biodiesel	0.3	2,750	6,300
Biomass Power	17	66,000	152,000
Fuel Cells	0.9	4,800	11,100
Hydrogen	0.8	4,000	9,200
Total, Private Industry	**35.4**	**185,150**	**427,000**
Federal Government	0.5	800*	1,850
DOE Laboratories	1.8	3,600**	8,300
State and Local Government	0.9	2,500	5,750
Total Government	**3.2**	**6,900**	**15,870**
Trade and Professional Associations and NGOs	0.6	1,500	3,450
TOTAL, ALL SECTORS	**$39.20**	**193,550**	**446,320**

*Includes federal employees and direct support contractors.
Source: Bolinger, 2007.

Jump-Starting Solar in Berkeley

At the state level, California is the nation's leader in promoting conversion to solar, and some of the Golden State's cities have pioneered the most ingenious strategies (see text box on pp. 45–46). Politically liberal Berkeley, where progressives usually control city government, has pioneered a system that uses the local government to finance consumers' up-front costs of investing in solar. A local ballot initiative enacted in 2007, Measure G, requires Berkeley to reduce its greenhouse gas emissions by 80 percent by 2050. A broad shift to solar-powered homes is the logical way to achieve this goal, but cost is a deterrent. The typical cost of installing a home solar electricity system is in the range of $15,000 to $25,000, depending on the size of the house.

To jump-start the process, Cisco DeVries, Mayor Tom Bates's then chief of staff, masterminded the Berkeley Financing Initiative for Renewable Energy, or Berkeley FIRST, as it is known.[24] Several cities provide direct rebates to home and business owners, but this financing scheme overcomes the problem of having to invest a lot of money up front to achieve long-term savings, a problem that dissuades most consumers from investing in solar systems whose initial cost will be paid back in energy savings only over decades.

The Berkeley strategy is brilliantly simple. Homeowners pay no money up front to finance conversion to solar energy. The city sends approved solar installers to homes and businesses to assess what type of system they need and then to install it. Once the property owner signs a contract, the city pays for the system and adds a charge to the property tax bill, with the cost repaid over time. The charge is calculated so that the increase in property tax is roughly netted out by the energy savings. The homeowner breaks even until the cost of installation is amortized over 20 years, and then reaps permanent savings on energy bills. Berkeley FIRST contracts with a third-party administrator, Renewable Funding, to oversee the financing provided by the city. This approach, therefore, does not require tapping into home equity or credit, which is important in today's tight credit markets.

The city's initial costs were financed by the sale of bonds. The fees and below-market interest the city pays are passed on to the consumer. For a typical $22,000 solar system, homeowners will pay about $180 a month in additional property taxes, but homeowners receive a rebate from the utility company that ranges from $2,000 to $15,000 and a federal tax credit that allows them to deduct 30 percent of the system's cost from their tax bill.[25] Consumers are able to take advantage of these tax breaks because they are essentially the ones "buying" the solar system through a loan from the city, a loan that they pay back via their increased property tax bill.

Like other property taxes, the Berkeley FIRST special tax is secured by a lien on the property that ranks above the first mortgage. Failure to pay any property tax can lead to foreclosure of the property in order to collect delinquent taxes.[26] From the city's perspective, the beauty of the scheme is that it is self-financing. From the homeowner's perspective, it makes installing a solar system affordable, and since the assessment stays with the property, homeowners don't have to worry about staying long enough for the system to pay for itself. While renewable financing programs have been offered by utilities, the advantage of a city government program is that the tax-exempt, low-interest bond financing reduces costs significantly.

Berkeley's linking strategy was motivated mainly by the city's desire to be a leader in clean energy consumption. Jobs were a secondary goal. The program will generate some employment, mostly in sales and financing, system design, installation, and maintenance. When I asked DeVries whether the city would be using solar panels made in California, he didn't hesitate in responding that most are made in Asia. "But," he said, "the jobs in installation and design can't be shipped overseas."[27] True, and jobs in installation pay fairly well—entry-level installers start at about $15 per hour with full health benefits, and foremen earn close to $30 hourly.[28] But there aren't that many of them.

There was no attempt to use Berkeley's increased local demand for solar energy systems to generate new local industry as trends in solar production were rightly seen as beyond the city's control. While other communities have attempted a direct link between increased demand and the incubation of new industries, it's clear that we live in a national (and international) economy, and every locality that uses solar energy cannot also be a solar producer.

California's solar industry employed 17,000 in 770 companies in 2007. Of these businesses, about 93 percent are design and installation companies and 7 percent are in manufacturing. A recent study by the San Francisco Bay and Greater Silicon Valley Centers of Excellence predicts that the state will need 5,700 new solar installers, 1,800 system designers and engineers, and 1,600 project managers and foremen. Bay Area design and installation companies employ a little over 1,400 workers (table 3.3).

In nearby Richmond, just north of Berkeley, we find another linking strategy. Richmond is a poor community, with high rates of youth unemployment. Like the Ella Baker Center's Green Jobs Corps in Oakland ten miles to the south, Richmond Build's construction training program seeks to reduce crime and violence by increasing employability. The idea was to create a pool of qualified applicants for contractors obligated to hire locally; a Richmond ordinance requires that public works projects valued at greater than $100,000 use Richmond residents for 20 percent of the work hours and that 20 percent of new hires be Richmond residents.[29] The 12-week construction preapprenticeship training program has a solar component. After the first six weeks of training, another partner, Solar Richmond, steps in to deliver a five-week segment in solar PV and solar thermal installation. As part

TABLE 3.3. Bay-Silicon Valley Region Solar Employers

Company*	City	Products/Services	Employees
Sun Power Corp.	San Jose	Manufacturing, design and installation	350
Nanosolar	San Jose	Manufacturing (thin-film PV)	250
Solar City	Foster City	Design/engineering, installation, financing	215
Akeena Solar	Los Gatos	Design/engineering, installation, financing	200
Miasole	Santa Clara	Manufacturing (thin-film PV)	175
Borrego Solar Systems	Berkeley	Design/engineering, installation, financing	130
Sun Light & Power	Berkeley	Design and install solar PV and solar thermal	52
Regrid Power	Campbell	Design/engineering, installation, financing	50

*Several of the companies that design, finance, install, and monitor solar systems operate in several states.
Source: Centers of Excellence, San Francisco Bay, April 2008.

of the solar training, each cohort installs two solar systems on low-income residences in Richmond. Another partner, Rising Sun Energy Center, helped Richmond Build develop a one-week energy efficiency training component that began in May 2009.

Funding for Richmond Build indicates a commitment on the part of state and city government to give the disadvantaged a chance in the green economy. The initiative received $300,000 per year for two years to train 150 people in 2006 from the governor's 15 percent discretionary fund. Corporate sponsors have stepped in since the state funding expired. Chevron is contributing $450,000 per year for six years to Richmond Build as part of a $61 million community benefits package it agreed to provide to the city in exchange for city council approval of an expansion of its refinery to process dirtier crude oil.[30] Other corporate sponsors include several construction-related companies. In addition, the Richmond Housing Authority provided Richmond Build with a building for its training programs.

Until the recession hit, employers were having trouble finding qualified workers. Now there is less hiring, which is taking a toll on Richmond Build. Since taking in its first cohort in April 2007, Richmond Build has graduated 180 students, 40 of whom have been placed in green-collar jobs. About half of those employed are working for a company that does energy efficiency and weatherizing work; the other half are working as solar installers in a variety of companies. A few graduates have found jobs working in the trades or in the city's public works department. The hourly pay rate of those working is between $15 and $19, but not all are employed full-time. Recent graduates have had an even more difficult time—of the most recent cohort of 21 graduates, only four have found full-time work, while four others are doing apprenticeships with trade unions.

Even in the best of times, training programs working with youth who often have juvenile records and other barriers to employment find it difficult to find employers willing to hire them. Richmond Build's response was to provide an incentive for employers to give its students a try. If an employer hires a graduate, Richmond Build will pay half of the worker's salary for the first 90 days of employment. Of the 14 Richmond Build workers who have participated in this on-the-job training opportunity, six are still working.

Gary Gerber, president and CEO of Sun Light & Power, a leading design and installation company of custom and other renewable systems in the Bay Area, has hired a few Richmond Build graduates and has had to supplement their training. He hires them because "it's the right thing to do," adding that it is not unusual for him to get college graduates applying for installation jobs. He is also skeptical of how much career advancement will be possible for installers with only short-term training. While several people have worked their way through the ranks of his company from installer to crew leader and even project manager, the number of positions drops dramatically at each rung of the career ladder. While Gerber speaks positively about what programs like Richmond Build are trying to do, he notes that the industry hasn't yet established training standards. As president of the California Solar Industry Association, Gerber has made a priority of working with the North American Board of Certified Energy Practitioners to develop a standard curriculum for preparation for PV installer certification. His advice: "If you want to get a job in the design and installation side of the solar industry, become an electrician."[31]

That's the story unions are telling as well. Across the United States, various locals of the International Brotherhood of Electrical Workers (IBEW) are providing training and apprenticeships in solar and other renewable energy jobs. For example, IBEW Local 292 in Minneapolis, Minnesota, has a training center that features a solar lab and its own solar system. Half of Minnesota's solar installers who have achieved the North American Board of Certified Energy Practitioners' qualifications are IBEW Local 292 members. There is a waiting list of prospective candidates for the five-year comprehensive apprenticeship focusing on renewable energy.[32] Boston's Local 103 includes solar in its apprenticeship training program and journey-level update classes. Similar curricula are being rolled out by other IBEW locals.[33] Proponents argue that training workers in a variety of renewable energy projects leaves them better prepared for potential ebbs and flows in demand. The business representative of IBEW Local 292 noted that better-trained workers are "far more recession-proof than workers trained exclusively on renewable installations."[34]

It's hard to determine whether a lot more demand for solar installers would occur if we weren't in a recession. But if the high level of investment in places like the Bay Area can't stimulate more than a couple of thousand design and installation jobs, it is unlikely that many cities will be able to do so either. Of course, cities should expand incentives for

---

California's Energy Efficiency, Renewable Energy, and Global Warming Policies

Title 24: Energy Efficiency Standards for Residential and Nonresidential Buildings (1978) A legislative mandate requiring California to reduce energy consumption in buildings. The standards are occasionally updated.[a]

Title 20: Appliance Efficiency Program (1976) The program establishes efficiency standards for refrigerators, air conditioners, furnaces, hot water tanks, and other appliances.[b]

Net Metering (1996) The law requires utilities to offer net metering for solar and wind energy systems. Residential customers can bank credits for later use if they produce more electricity than they use, but must use the credits within a year. Customers cannot sell surplus energy back to the grid.[c]

Renewable Portfolio Standard (2002) Updated in 2006, this standard requires utilities to increase power produced by renewable sources 1 percent per year to 20 percent by 2010.[d] An Executive Order signed

(continued)

California's Energy Efficiency, Renewable Energy, and Global Warming Policies (*cont.*)

by Governor Schwarzenegger in 2008 raised the RPS to 33 percent by 2020.[e]

Green Wave Environmental Initiative (2004) Started by then State Treasurer Phil Angelides, this program calls on the state's two largest public pension funds to invest $1.5 billion in environmental technology and in environmentally responsible companies.[f]

Million Solar Roofs, which became California Solar Initiative (January 2006), provides more than $3 billion in incentives for solar power. The goal is to generate 3,000 megawatts of new solar power statewide by 2017.

Global Warming Solutions Act of 2006 (AB32) requires a 25 percent reduction in carbon emissions by 2020. It has the potential to create 89,000 jobs.

Green Collar Jobs Act (AB3108) assesses workforce development needs and creates education and training programs.

Feed-in tariff (AB 1069) (2008) California is the first state to use feed-in tariffs to motivate more renewable energy installations. The idea is to create a stronger development incentive than net metering and other incentives in place.[g] The California feed-in tariff allows for selling power back to the grid, but differs from that of Germany and other European countries in that customers are paid market rates, not a highly subsidized rate. Further, receiving a feed-in payment precludes receiving other state renewable energy incentives.[h] Once solar prices come down to grid parity, the government subsidy will be eliminated.

[a]See http://www.energy.ca.gov/title24/
[b]See http://www.energy.ca.gov/appliances/
[c]See http://www.sdge.com/business/netMetering.shtml
[d]See http://www.cpuc.ca.gov/PUC/energy/Renewables/index.htm
[e]See http://www.gov.ca.gov/executive-order/11072/
[f]See http://www.treasurer.ca.gov/greenwave/020304_enviro.pdf
[g]See p. 184, http://www.energy.ca.gov/2007publications/CEC-100–2007–008/CEC-100–2007–008-CTF.PDF, http://www.renewableenergyworld.com/rea/news/story?id=50748
[h]See http://www.cpuc.ca.gov/PUC/energy/electric/RenewableEnergy/different.htm

solar energy to achieve greenhouse gas reductions, but these efforts will create only a relatively small number of jobs.

AUSTIN: A WHOLE LESS THAN THE SUM OF ITS PARTS

All the elements are seemingly in place to make Austin, Texas, a pioneer in the use of renewable energy as a catalyst for economic development. They include strong and supportive political leadership, a renewables-friendly city-owned utility, and citizen groups pressing for even more aggressive action. The University of Texas, Austin has a clean technology research program. A well-educated workforce and a base of high-tech industries make Austin attractive to green-tech companies. Financial incentives for locally produced solar panels are in place. Even the local business community is on board, with the Chamber of Commerce leading a green economic development initiative. Yet the Austin story also illustrates that even when they do everything right, cities are only one link in the policy chain needed to create jobs in renewable energy. Austin's experience reveals that not all cities, even with active policy in place, have what it takes for renewable energy to be an economic driver. Despite valiant efforts, it remains to be seen whether Austin can capture much of the manufacturing part of the solar value chain.

Renewable Energy Policy in Austin

I think this program makes a very important point to cities across America and around the world that the sum of all local policy is global policy. If we will simply take action in our own communities to reduce our carbon footprint, we can truly change the fate of the planet. This kind of leadership makes me very proud to be an Austinite.
—Austin Councilman Lee Leffingwell[35]

When the Austin city council passed a renewable energy resolution in 1999 calling for Austin Energy (AE), the city-owned electric utility, to obtain 5 percent of its energy from renewable resources by the end of 2004, Austin became one of a handful of cities with what's known as a renewable portfolio standard (RPS)—a hard requirement that a set percentage of energy be purchased from renewable sources (see text box). Within just two years, AE was obtaining 6 percent of its power from wind farms in western Texas. This impressive gain was in part due to AE's highly successful GreenChoice program, which allows customers to choose to obtain their power from renewable sources. Customers agree to pay a slightly higher rate that has been negotiated by the utility with a renewable provider.[36] Both the city council and Austin Energy were satisfied with their progress in adopting renewable energy, though with a fairly modest initial target.

But they would be prodded to take bolder steps by the Resource Management Commission (RMC), an advisory body to the city council on renewable energy. RMC Commissioner Michael Kuhn, also president and CEO of Imagine Solar, recalls that commission members wanted to link renewable energy to economic development and thought that a stronger RPS was needed to attract solar companies.[37] Evidence was on their side; at the time, California-based solar system integrator PowerLight was considering locating in Austin and told city officials the potential market in Texas would have to be at least 6 megawatts for it to locate there. And with unemployment rising and the city's tax base declining since 2000, the city needed a new focus for economic development.[38] Although not explicitly tied to economic development, the RMC prepared a development plan recommending an RPS requiring 20 percent renewable energy by 2020 and adding solar rebates to the program mix to reach the goal.

It was a bold step that the city council wasn't prepared to take because it was thought to be prohibitively expensive. A campaign was organized by Public Citizen, a nonprofit public interest organization whose Texas branch was promoting increased investment in renewable energy. Public Citizen launched a new initiative and organization, Solar Austin, to advocate for the RPS. Solar Austin organized a coalition of renewable energy businesses and advocates, urban planners, and residents to make the case for the RPS to the city council. The campaign's timing was fortunate. Will Wynn was running for mayor and decided to make solar energy his defining campaign issue, declaring he would make Austin the clean energy capital of the world. He supported the RPS and was elected in May 2003. The RPS (along with a measure to increase energy efficiency by 15 percent) passed the city council by the end of the year. The council also approved a recommendation of the RMC plan to fund clean energy economic development initiatives.[39] Austin now had the political will, the policy, and the commitment from all players—the mayor, the city council, AE, nonprofit organizations, and the public—to support solar energy and to use it as an economic development driver for the region.

The management of AE was initially not enthusiastic about the new RPS because of the high cost of solar energy. AE general manager Roger Duncan (then deputy general manager) argued that it would be more prudent to wait until new and cheaper thin-film technologies were on the market rather than making huge investments in more expensive PV systems. The point of difference between AE and Solar Austin and other groups promoting solar energy was not so much around the "20 by 20" goal but the schedule of implementation. Solar Austin and other groups advocated for adding 10 MW a year, while Duncan wanted to backload the adoption of 100 MW of solar, arguing that it would allow for installation of next-generation thin-film and even nanosolar as they commercialized. As he puts it, "I didn't want to fill rooftops with old technology."[40] Local solar activists saw his position as backing down on the commitment to develop solar energy. After defending the utility's position at several heated town meetings, in December 2003 Duncan surprised the group by announcing the ambitious goal of developing 15 megawatts of solar generating capacity by 2007, increasing to 100 megawatts by 2020.[41]

Once the decision was made, AE began offering the nation's highest solar rebate, $5.00 a watt, to encourage solar adoption. For a $15,000 3-kilowatt rooftop system, Austin Energy pays between 50 and 65 percent of capital costs. And with net metering (see text box), AE pays for solar energy fed back into the grid. But despite the incentives, by mid-2005 AE had achieved less than 7 percent of the 2007 15-megawatt solar goal, mostly because of the high cost of solar. Then in 2008 AE announced plans to build a 30-megawatt solar farm—the nation's largest—on a 300-acre parcel on city-owned land in nearby Webberville. AE signed a contract with San Francisco–based Gemini Solar Development Company to build the facility and has agreed to a 25-year power purchase agreement that will cost $10 million a year. The price for PV will be 16.5 cents per kilowatt hour, or about four times the cost of natural gas. In addition, AE plans on adding close to 600 megawatts of wind energy to its current portfolio of 439 megawatts, and 12 megawatts from landfill methane gas, toward the goal of achieving 30 percent of its total energy from renewables by 2020.

AE is also a leader in developing smart-grid technology to support wind and solar power. By the end of summer 2009, almost all of the city's 397,000 customers had smart meters installed. The two-

Renewable Portfolio Standards

Renewable portfolio standards (RPS) require utilities or suppliers to provide a specified percentage of electricity from renewable sources by a given year. At least 43 countries, 29 U.S. states, and a few cities have enacted RPS laws. The goal of an RPS is to create a market for electricity by specifying amounts to be used, with generators of renewable energy competing to supply it. For example, California's RPS stipulates that utilities must purchase 20 percent of their electricity from renewable sources by 2010. The premise is that market competition will drive down costs. States vary in the extent to which they specify specific types of renewable energy to be included.[a] Berkeley Lab estimates that about half of the wind power capacity built in the United States between 2001 and 2006 was partly motivated by state RPS and up to 60 percent for 2006 installations.[b]

Many portfolio standards use renewable energy credits or certificates (RECs) as proof that one kWh of electricity has been generated by a renewable source. In some states, such as Texas, suppliers that do not meet requirements to purchase renewable energy credits are penalized.

The United States does not have a national portfolio standard. Compare this to the European Union, which has a 12 percent renewable standard for electricity production by 2010 in addition to standards in place in 25 member countries. The American Council on Renewable Energy estimates that a national portfolio standard could create $700 billion in economic activity and five million jobs by 2025.[c] The Union of Concerned Scientists estimates that about 45 gigawatts of new renewable energy capacity will be needed by 2020 to fulfill current state RPS policies, while Global Energy Advisors estimates that more than 52 gigawatts would be required, amounting to approximately 3 percent of 2020 U.S. electric sales. While seemingly modest, reaching this goal would nearly double the percentage of non-hydro renewable energy generation currently in the United States.[d]

The RPS is too new and varied a policy instrument to evaluate its impact definitively. Modeling wind capacity growth in states with different types of policy against states with no policy suggests that having an RPS in place does stimulate the early development of wind production.[e] Preliminary evaluations suggest that successful RPS laws include clear targets for in-state production, political support and regulatory commitment, predictable long-term purchase obligations, auto-

(*continued*)

matic enforcement penalties,[f] flexibility mechanisms, certificate trading, and development of adequate transmission capacity.[g]

[a]See Rabe, 2006 and 2003.
[b]Wiser and Bolinger, 2007.
[c]American Council on Renewable Energy, 2007.
[d]Wiser et al., 2007: 10.
[e]Blair et al., 2006; Menz and Vachon, 2006.
[f]Blair et al. suggest penalties must be at the level of $20 per MW to be effective. Texas has one of the strictest of current penalties at the lesser of 5 cents per missing kWh or 200 percent of the mean trade value of certificates in the current compliance period (Deyette and Clemmer, 2005: 8).
[g]See Wiser, Porter, and Grace, 2004; Wiser and Langniss, 2001.

way meters are capable of sending and receiving information to reward consumers who reduce energy use during peak demand periods. In addition, AE, the Environmental Defense Fund, Austin Chamber of Commerce, Austin Technology Incubator, and other local partners started the Pecan Street Project to, according to its mission statement, "make Austin America's clean energy laboratory and to develop a model for urban power system of the future." The project will test prototypes for storing and distributing renewable energy and will be the nation's first project of its type for testing smart-grid technologies. Texas is uniquely suited for this type of research because the state has its own grid, meaning that modifications can be made without going through federal regulatory channels as other states must.

Austin's Clean Energy Incubator, launched in 2001 by the Austin Technology Incubator at the University of Texas and the U.S. Department of Energy's National Renewable Energy Laboratory, provides space and technical assistance to clean energy start-up companies. So far, the Clean Energy Incubator has housed 18 companies, with six currently in residence. Among incubator companies' products and services are energy storage devices, evaluation of solar system performance, and pollution- and runoff-reducing irrigation systems.

Another initiative is the Texas Clean Energy Park. With $600,000 in start-up funding from the Texas Workforce Commission and additional support from AE, the Austin Technology Incubator, and the IC2 Institute at the University of Texas, it will start with a research park, which will be followed by a business park. In December 2007, HelioVolt chose the park over California, Pennsylvania, and New York locations as the site of a manufacturing facility to test and produce thin-film solar power cells.[42] The company was founded in 2001 in Texas, but entertained competitive offers from the other states when it decided to build a new manufacturing facility. In addition to $101 million in private venture capital funding, HelioVolt received a 60 percent tax abatement for ten years for locating in Austin and $1 million from the Texas Enterprise Fund, a business incentive fund. The company

---

How Net Metering Works

Net metering enables consumers who generate electricity to profit from generation exceeding their own energy needs. This is typically done by "turning back" their electric meters when they generate electricity that exceeds their demand; they then receive retail prices for the excess electricity generated.[a] Customers, in essence, "bank" their energy so that they can use it at a different time than it is produced. This is particularly beneficial to customers who live in areas where wind and solar energy production is sporadic; net metering allows them to benefit throughout the year from the energy they generate without having to go to the expense of storing it in batteries.

Net metering is an easy-to-administer, low-cost incentive for consumers to generate their own energy. Consumers are able to use their own standard kilowatt-hour meter, and thus don't incur any additional costs. Net metering also benefits utilities to the extent that it decreases load on the system during peak usage times.[b] The money utilities "lose" due to forgone revenues (because consumers are banking electricity at retail prices instead of selling it at wholesale) is partially made up for in savings on administrative costs associated with other forms of buying excess energy generated by consumers.[c]

The U.S. Energy Policy Act of 2005 requires all public electric utilities to offer net metering to customers upon request; additionally, each state regulatory authority and nonregulated electric utility was to "consider" net metering and decide whether to enact a policy on it within three years of the act's passage. As of February 2009, 43 states plus the District of Columbia offered some form of net metering.[d] State policies vary by utility types allowed and size limits on individual systems. New Jersey and Colorado are considered to have exemplary policies because they allow systems up to 2 MW to use net metering; Minnesota's program is lauded because customers actually receive a

(continued)

check at the end of each month for the retail amount of excess electricity generated.[e]

[a]The true definition of net metering entails use of one meter and purchase of excess energy at retail prices; however, this definition varies in some states.

[b]See http://apps3.eere.energy.gov/greenpower/markets/netmetering.shtml

[c]See http://www.awea.org/pubs/factsheets/netmetfin_fs.PDF

[d]See http://www.dsireusa.org/library/includes/topic.cfm?TopicCategoryID=6&CurrentPageID=10

[e]See http://www.newrules.org/electricity/nmeter.html

will invest $80 million in the facility and create 150 jobs. Another coup was landing DT Solar, a New Jersey–based developer of large-scale solar facilities that located its Southwest headquarters in Austin. The office will only create about 25 jobs, but will have significant impact as it starts to develop solar projects in the $30 million to $300 million range.

But even with all these initiatives in place, Austin is not seeing the hoped-for development of a solar manufacturing industry.[43] To date, HelioVolt is the only company in the area producing solar panels. Most of the solar employment growth in the Austin area has been in system design and installation. This is not trivial, but only provides a couple of thousand jobs.[44] And Gemini Solar Development Company, which is building Austin Energy's 30-megawatt farm, uses Suntech modules made in China and assembled in the United States. The $10 million cost could have been invested in an actual facility in Austin but for the fact that electric rates can float the power purchase agreement but not an up-front capital investment.

The reality for Austin is that cities and states are entering into a competitive frenzy in attracting renewable energy companies, and the price keeps going up. While nearly every locality can shift to renewable energy and gain installation jobs, every state and city cannot be a national production center. Texas and Austin were early movers in promoting renewable energy. However, neighboring New Mexico and Colorado, as well as other states, have started aggressively courting renewable energy companies with attractive incentive packages, and companies happily play one off against the other.

Solar Array, a company incubated in Austin with local subsidies, is looking to locate its first production facility to produce large-scale and industrial thin-film solar panels. The company's VP for Marketing,

John Merritt, told me that New Mexico and New York are offering more attractive financial packages. And New Mexico is offering to pay the wages of workers for the first 60 days of employment while they are attending training programs designed by the community colleges (Austin Community College offers renewable energy certificates and degrees, but Texas does not offer a similar training incentive). Merritt notes that locating close to markets is also important and adds that Ontario's feed-in tariff is creating demand that could be filled with a New York facility.[45] In April 2009, the company announced that it had chosen Bernalillo County, New Mexico, as the site for a 225,000-square-foot manufacturing plant that will employ 225 workers by the end of 2010 and could employ up to 1,000 in five years.[46]

Solar Array isn't the first renewable company Austin has lost. After nine years in the Austin area, wind farm developer Renewable Energy Systems Americas moved its headquarters to Colorado, where the company is developing a large wind farm. RES took 70 full-time employees along and plans to add 70 more workers in Colorado. Company officials cite a more diverse economy and labor market base as a key factor in the move, along with Denver International Airport being served by more airlines.

The competition will only get stiffer as the federal stimulus package adds more incentives for development of renewable energy. This is why a new coalition of business, policy, and advocacy groups, the Catalyst Project, is calling for Texas to be more aggressive in advancing renewable energy as an economic development opportunity. Catalyst Project members note that while the portfolio standard led the state to its top position in wind generation, it didn't catalyze the development of wind turbine manufacturing, turbine maintenance, or research and development in wind technology. The project's 2008 report, *Igniting Texas' New Energy Economy*, calls for the state's Emerging Technology and Enterprise Funds to target grants to renewable companies, develop a new energy incentive package and green jobs education and training programs, and create a high-level point person on the state's energy strategy.[47] As the slow development of solar companies in Austin suggests, Mayor Wynn's goal of making Austin the clean energy capital of the world can only be achieved if the state gets on board with a solar economic development agenda too. A 2009 bill in the state legislature for a $500 million rebate program for solar installations, estimated to create 250 to 500 megawatts of solar power in Texas, did not pass. Solar energy advocates are concerned that this legislative failure will further erode the state's position as a manufacturing location.[48]

Despite a state agenda on developing a renewable manufacturing sector and the disappointing results in solar manufacturing, Mayor Wynn seeks to keep Austin competitive in several green technologies, while still moving the city to adopt more renewable energy. The city's 2007 climate protection plan increases the RPS to 30 percent and calls for reducing CO_2 emissions from municipal activities to zero by 2020. Wynn notes that Austin has consistently been cited by *Forbes* as one of the nation's top metropolitan economies and is consistently in the top ten of various green-city lists. He hopes to capitalize on the indirect benefits of being perceived as a national leader in the climate change movement and to keep the momentum going with the city's involvement in research on peak load management, renewables, water conservation, and other green technologies. "There will be setbacks and missteps," he notes, "but pursuing innovation will keep Austin on the short list of cities implementing policy that is having an impact."[49]

TOLEDO: AN UNLIKELY CENTER OF SOLAR TECHNOLOGY

If building a solar industry is difficult in environmentally conscious places like the Bay Area and Austin, one might conclude that it would be impossible in Toledo. Yet the nation's largest thin-film solar panel manufacturer is located there, and the metropolitan area employs more than 6,000 people in businesses contributing to the solar industry in 15 companies and institutions. And if Steve Weathers, president and CEO of the Regional Growth Partnership, has his way, the area will witness 100 new high-tech and advanced manufacturing start-ups by 2010.

The secret is Toledo's capacity to build on a traditional source of manufacturing strength—glass technology and manufacture. With one-third of its manufacturing jobs lost since 2000, Toledo hopes to transform its glass industry to produce thin-film solar panels. The transition from specialized glass to solar is not as far-fetched as one might think. Solar panels—whether PV or thin-film—are primarily a glass product. The most advanced auto glass uses the same thin-film technology to deposit microscopically thin layers of materials between layers of glass, which, for example, allows a windshield to respond to changes in glare. There's a wind connection too; 70 percent of the raw material that makes up a wind turbine is made by Toledo-based Owens Corning, which also produces building-integrated solar products.

Solar isn't new to Toledo. The University of Toledo conducted research for 25 years before officially creating the Wright Center for Photovoltaics Innovation and Commercialization with an influx of funds from the state in 2007. Hoping to stem the tide of 200,000 manufacturing jobs lost since 2000, the Ohio Department of Development invested $18.6 million in university solar research centers, about half of which went to the University of Toledo. With an additional $30 million in contributions from federal agencies and industrial partners, the university was able to dramatically advance its research and solar incubator activities. To date, the center's alternative energy incubator has spun off seven solar start-ups.

The jewel in the crown is First Solar, which began as Glasstech Solar in 1984 and survived on 15 years of patient U.S. Department of Energy cost share support while the company perfected its thin-film manufacturing process. Today, it is a national leader in production of solar panels. Started by local glass entrepreneur Harold McMaster working with University of Toledo researchers, it became Solar Cells, which in turn was purchased by Phoenix-based investment firm True North Partners (partially owned by Wal-Mart's John Walton) and became First Solar in 1999.[50] Walton invested $30 million in the project and eventually put in double that amount to get the product into production. All told, it took about $150 million in public and private funding to develop the product and manufacturing process. In 2000, First Solar built a $16 million factory outside of Toledo, the world's largest solar panel factory at the time. The company has been on quite a growth trajectory since then—annual production has increased by 800 percent and revenues grew from $6 million to more than $500 million by 2007, while production costs have been reduced from $3.00 to $1.12 per watt.[51] First Solar's technological advantage is a thin-film semiconductor production process that has lower raw material costs than traditional crystalline manufacturing processes. The process allows the company to sell panels for the commercial and industrial market at a 35 percent lower cost than most companies.

The company already produces more panels than any other U.S. producer, and in late 2008 First Solar executives announced an expansion that will add 134 employees to the current workforce of 700. Recently, First Solar invested $25 million in SolarCity, a Bay Area design and installation company. First Solar will sell SolarCity

1.4 million solar panels that will be produced in Ohio. The expansion marks the company's move into the residential market. This partnership allows SolarCity to expand into East Coast markets and First Solar into the rapidly growing residential market.[52] The two companies had been discussing the deal for over a year, but it was finalized only when the renewal of a 30 percent federal tax credit that was part of the federal financial rescue package made future growth enough of a reality for First Solar to seal the deal.

Like First Solar, many high-tech start-ups need business assistance, and the Regional Growth Partnership (RGP), a privately funded nonprofit economic development corporation, has stepped up to provide it in northwestern Ohio. Until recently, the RGP followed an attraction, retention, and marketing-based approach to economic development typical of such organizations. In 2005, Steve Weathers was recruited to replicate the innovation-based approach to economic development he pursued in San Diego as the vice president of the San Diego Economic Development Corporation. Under his leadership, the RGP now focuses on commercialization and start-ups. The RGP offers business assistance to start-up companies seeking to develop their technology and obtain venture capital funding for commercialization. The goal is to accelerate the time from conception to production. The partnership also started northwestern Ohio's only venture capital fund for high-tech and renewable energy companies. In the last year and a half, RGP has launched 40 companies, with a total of 90 alternative energy, advanced manufacturing, and biotech companies in the pipeline.

One of its stellar success stories is a start-up called Xunlight. RGP director Weathers recalls that when University of Toledo professor Xunming Deng and his wife, Liwei Xu, walked into his office, they had a scientific paper and an idea about producing flexible solar panels that could be integrated into roofing material. With RGP's assistance, the company wrote a business plan and a funding proposal that produced almost $60 million in venture capital, a $2 million loan from Lucas County, and almost $1 million from the state's Third Frontier program to improve product yield in its manufacturing process.

Deng and Xu had been developing the technology since 1996, started Xunlight in 2002, opened a facility in 2007, and began shipping product in late 2009. Eighty people are employed in research and production on the 25-megawatt pilot line. Their goal is to tap European and U.S. markets, particularly in California, Ohio, and New Jersey.[53]

Another success story is Solargystics, whose flexible thin-film cells can be integrated into building materials. As with Xunlight, RGP helped the company develop a business plan and proposal that netted a $1 million grant from the Third Frontier program and $50,000 from RGP to perfect its prototype and develop its manufacturing process. Researchers on the Solargystics team started out in Michigan, but relocated in Toledo because of the university's research facilities and Ohio's Third Frontier program, says CEO Jeff Culver.[54] As a member of the university's Wright Center, company researchers have access to testing equipment that they couldn't procure on their own. Culver's goal is to bring production costs down to 50 cents per watt—half of what industry leader First Solar is doing.

In the summer of 2009, Toledo announced the opening of two more renewable energy companies. Sphere Renewable Energy, incorporated in Ohio as Buckeye Silicon, is investing $50 million in a plant to make polycrystalline silicon for the solar industry. The company, currently housed at the University of Toledo, seeks to perfect a process that produces silicon at half the cost of other manufacturers by using a waste product of phosphate fertilizer production as its input. An advantage of the company's process is that it is encapsulated and does not require the same environmentally harmful chemicals normally used in silicon production, and also requires much less electricity. When it reaches full production, Buckeye will produce 5000 metric tons of silicon annually and employ between 100 and 150 people at salaries between $36,000 and $60,000. The second company, SuGanit Systems, is also housed at the University of Toledo while it commercializes a new process for producing ethanol from cellulosic waste materials (e.g., leaves, grass clippings, cornstalks, wood chips). The new plant will be built on the Toledo port to freight in the waste. Private waste haulers are currently negotiating to deliver yard waste to SuGanit. Over the summer Toledo is testing the 10 percent ethanol blend for efficiency and emissions. The pilot plant will create 20–25 jobs and once in full production of 20 million gallons of fuel annually. Eventually the plant will employ 100–150 workers. SuGanit has received funds from the Third Frontier program for testing and perfecting its production processes.

Ohio's governor, Ted Strickland, enthusiastically supports state programs to catalyze growth in the renewable energy industry. In addition to Third Frontier, the Ohio Department of Development's Green

Places Initiative supports local green energy and technology initiatives. A key program is the Advanced Energy Jobs Stimulus Fund, which is injecting $150 million over three years into advanced energy development. Of that, $28 million a year for three years will provide support for advanced energy projects in the commercialization and later stages. The fund also provides incentives to companies that are retooling to add workers or repurpose their equipment to supply the wind and solar market.

Like Austin, Toledo has all of the policies in place to succeed—a university research program, an economic development organization focused on fostering start-ups, and several state government programs that provide various types of assistance. More importantly, Toledo had a manufacturing infrastructure in advanced glass technologies that could easily be retooled for thin-film solar production. The 6,000 jobs are a good start, but can Toledo continue to spin off companies, and will the ones they have stay? First Solar has built plants in Malaysia and Germany and Solar Fields was purchased by German-based Q-Cells, after all. But Weathers doesn't see these as negative developments. In fact, Weathers predicts that Xunlight also will open factories in Asia and Europe. Like longtime Toledo presence Owens Corning and new-comer First Solar, Weathers maintains that successful companies have to locate plants all over the world to compete in international markets. His plan is to create as many successful new companies as he can, knowing that some will stay, some will have a presence in Toledo while expanding elsewhere, and some will fail.[55] The goal is to innovate and stay ahead of the game by assisting in new start-ups.

CLEVELAND: THE NEXT WINDY CITY?

We can become the Silicon Valley of alternative energy.
—U.S. Senator Sherrod Brown

Although he may not have been the first person to think of exploring the potential of developing offshore wind on Lake Erie, Ronn Richard was one of the first in a position to shape that vision into a reality. Richard joined the Cleveland Foundation as president and CEO in the summer of 2003 and that fall participated in Leadership Cleveland, a yearlong development program for Cleveland-area professionals in influential positions in the public, private, and nonprofit sectors. The program's focus that year was on how to transform Cleveland's economy. Richard thought of the offshore wind turbines near Copenhagen and set the group to examining whether Lake Erie would be a good site for producing wind power. Most of the city's leaders didn't take the idea seriously, but Richard persisted. The Cleveland Foundation contracted with Green Energy Ohio (GEO), a statewide nonprofit organization that promotes sustainable energy policy, to install wind-measuring equipment three miles offshore to assess the economic viability of generating electricity from wind turbines there. GEO began measuring wind in September 2005 and in January 2008 issued the results, showing that the wind resource on Lake Erie was stronger than at any of the ten land sites tested in Ohio.[56] These encouraging results, along with studies that estimated anywhere from 12,000 to 26,000 jobs could be created in Ohio through an increased focus on the manufacturing of wind turbines and their components, generated enthusiasm for moving forward.[57]

In early 2006, the foundation hired Richard Steubi, who had two decades of experience as an executive, consultant, and entrepreneur in the energy industry, as a fellow to lead the foundation's initiative to develop an advanced energy cluster in northeastern Ohio, with a particular focus on wind energy manufacturing. The foundation provided $200,000 to the Cuyahoga County Commissioners to charter a regional energy task force comprised of various public, private, and nonprofit interests. Led by Cuyahoga County prosecutor Bill Mason, the Cuyahoga Regional Energy Development Task Force examined the legal, technical, environmental, and financial factors that would have to be addressed to develop offshore wind farms on Lake Erie. In February 2007, the Task Force outlined a plan for developing an offshore wind cluster in the region's economy, proposing the Great Lakes Wind Energy Center (GLWEC).

The GLWEC was envisioned to have two components. The first would be a small offshore project to establish regulatory precedents and to identify the engineering issues associated with icing in a freshwater environment (all of the world's preexisting wind farms are in salt water and are not subject to freezing). The pilot wind project would also, the Task Force hoped, make a bold statement to wind companies and residents that Cleveland is committed to being a leader in the wind industry. The second component of the GLWEC would be to establish the region as a major player in research and development of next-generation wind technology. The Task Force believes that Cleveland's leadership can accelerate the pace at which offshore wind energy can become economically viable, thereby positioning the region to capture the economic development benefits.

Wind energy advocates got a boost when Governor Ted Strickland released the state's Energy, Jobs and Progress plan, which outlined the adoption of an RPS. Less than a year later, in May 2008, Ohio became the 26th state to pass an RPS, requiring that at least 25 percent of all electricity sold in the state be from "advanced" sources by 2025.[58] Half of this requirement must be generated by renewable sources (such as wind, solar, hydropower, geothermal, or biomass) and the rest by third-generation nuclear power, fuel cells, and clean coal technology. Utilities can meet the requirements by generating the power or by buying, selling, and trading credits using a renewable energy credit (REC) tracking system, but at least half of the renewable energy must be generated in-state.[59] The legislation also requires that the Ohio Public Utilities Commission (PUC) develop rules for decoupling profits from sales. Like those of Illinois and other Midwestern states, the RPS was a political compromise. It would have been impossible to pass an RPS without any provisions for coal, given the state's coal resources and the industry's political influence. A sweetener for the industry is a provision that RPS compliance can be reduced to ensure that utilities do not experience wholesale power cost increases of more than 3 percent. Nevertheless, the RPS was a victory for renewable energy that could stimulate as much as 7,000 MW of new wind energy by 2025, and capital expenditures of up to $14 billion dollars, perhaps $9 billion of that for component parts produced in Ohio.[60] That would be a big expansion—the Ohio Wind Energy Working Group estimated that in 2006, the wind industry accounted for $250 million in revenue and 1,700 direct and indirect jobs in the state.

With a skeletal vision that included the GLWEC and a statewide RPS, the Task Force decided it was time to have a consultant from the wind industry conduct a more detailed investigation on whether offshore wind energy was financially viable—and if so, how it should be pursued. Over $1 million was raised from various civic partners, including Cuyahoga County, the City of Cleveland, the Cleveland Foundation, Case Western Reserve University, and the Cleveland-Cuyahoga Port Authority, to conduct an economic development feasibility study and implementation plan. The Task Force selected a consulting team led by German companies juwi (a wind developer) and Germanischer

Lloyd to complete the study in April 2009; it did not identify any deal breakers.

The study did, however, find that the costs of offshore wind would be considerable. Renewable energy expert George Sterzinger calculates that building out this industry could require between $50 billion and $100 billion of investment per year over a ten-year period, which would be primarily financed by long-term contracts for selling the power produced from the installations.[61] Federal funding would also be needed for pilot tests. But the potential is huge—the National Renewable Energy Lab estimates that it is theoretically possible to develop over 100,000 megawatts of wind power on the Great Lakes.

The generally positive findings of the feasibility reports have given increased credibility to the idea of offshore wind in the eyes of state and federal government, the media, and local actors needed to move the project forward. The next step is to pursue and complete the pilot offshore wind project in Lake Erie. The Cuyahoga Regional Energy Development Task Force is working to obtain permitting for a site and is talking to several wind manufacturers and developers to establish a partnership to develop the project. Proposals for very different types and sizes of turbines are being considered. In addition to cost, the pilot project will determine the extent to which technical concerns such as icing will be problematic for subsequent large-scale deployment.

In December 2008, Governor Strickland announced that Spanish-owned MTorres Group was considering locating a wind turbine plant in Cleveland that could employ up to 200 people, and as many as 3,000 if it could supply a broader U.S. market, for the assembly and deployment of offshore wind turbines, initially on Lake Erie. In January 2009, Cuyahoga County officials requested $28 million in federal stimulus funds to support the development of a pilot wind turbine project in Lake Erie, representing about half of the estimated cost of building six to eight turbines and connecting them to the grid. One month later, the city requested $26.5 million in federal and state stimulus funds to renovate docks and warehouses to accommodate a facility for the assembly and erection of offshore wind turbines (of this, $20.2 million would be for a new manufacturing warehouse and renovation of an existing one to handle railcars). The port applied for $13 million from the state under its $1.57 billion job-stimulus plan. The port is expected to apply for $13.5 million in money from the

Economic Development Administration, under the U.S. Department of Commerce.[62]

While the technical details of offshore wind are being examined, parallel efforts to strengthen the wind energy supply chain in the Cleveland region are under way. In 2007, Cleveland's Westside Industrial Retention and Expansion Network (WIRE-Net) organized the Great Lakes WIND Network to connect potential parts suppliers in Northeast Ohio to original equipment manufacturers. With an $850,000 grant from the Ohio Department of Development, WIRE-Net has been holding supply chain workshops throughout the state so potential suppliers can discover opportunities and learn what they have to do to become qualified by potential customers. Ed Weston, director of the Great Lakes WIND Network, explains that turbine producers approach him with a list of the components they are looking to source and he gives them introductions and referrals. To date, WIRE-Net has identified more than 50 manufacturers of castings, machining, bearings, gears, and other components in the Cleveland region that could supply wind turbine producers. To support the effort, the Ohio Department of Development has started a program to assist manufacturers in expanding their facilities and developing their workforces in order to meet wind production demands. WIRE-Net is creating a Web site and information-management system for suppliers, marketing the supply chain, and sending leads on new business to state development officials. WIRE-Net has identified about 80 companies that are supplying parts to wind turbine producers and has visited 180 companies interested in becoming suppliers. Weston estimates that about one-third of the companies he has met with are taking the next steps to find a supply chain role in wind.[63]

Retooling existing manufacturing companies to serve the wind industry will take time. While attending a supply chain workshop in Chicago, I talked to a manufacturer who was eager to start producing gearbox parts for the wind industry, but he is on an 18-month waiting list for the German machine tools he needs to start production. And once the machinery is in place, it takes 12 to 18 months to qualify with the turbine manufacturer. Wind turbine parts require very high precision and quality expectations are very high, so manufacturers won't sign an order without the suppliers demonstrating that they can meet the standards.[64] The Great Lakes Wind Network is working with companies on gearing up to meet the requirements.

Decoupling

Decoupling refers to the severing of a utility's profits from its sales and revenues in order to remove the disincentive to promote energy consumption. With decoupling, utilities can promote energy efficiency without worrying that it will affect their bottom line. Under conventional utility regulation, companies earn profits based on the amount of energy they sell. Typically, public utility commissions set rates by predicting energy costs and adding a certain profit margin. In times of lower-than-expected energy use (e.g., mild weather), utilities have to ride out the period of lower revenues until conditions change or rates are adjusted. Decoupling breaks the link between recovering fixed costs from sales volume.

Currently, at least 12 states have decoupling in place, and another 26 states are considering it.[a] A number of other states may soon adopt decoupling in order to receive extra energy-related federal stimulus funds.[b] While methods of decoupling vary, they usually involve companies offering programs that promote energy efficiency and, in exchange for doing so, recouping some of their losses by adjusting their rates to meet certain revenue targets. In one model, if sales are less than projected over a certain period of time, rates are adjusted slightly upward, typically no more than 2 to 3 percent.[c] Idaho offers a form of this where customers can get a credit on future energy bills if their utility's revenues exceed a set amount over a defined time period. The most controversial model uses flat-rate billing (like a cable bill) rather than usage-based billing.[d] It is problematical because it is regressive—poorer families using less energy are charged the same as wealthier households consuming more energy—and because flat-rate billing may actually encourage higher consumption.

[a]See http://online.wsj.com/article/SB123378473766549301.html

[b]While the federal stimulus bill, signed in February 2009, does not require states to adopt decoupling, it encourages it. See http://www.nytimes.com/gwire/2009/02/24/24 greenwire-stimulus-does-not-require-decoupling—markey-9846.html?scp=5&sq= decoupling%202009&st=cse; http://www.motherjones.com/politics/2009/02/gops-misguided-energy (accessed April 8, 2009).

[c]See http://www.progressivestates.org/content/671/utility-decoupling-giving-utilities-incentives-to-promote-energy-efficiency

[d]See http://online.wsj.com/article/SB123378473766549301.html

A shortage of skilled labor is another obstacle. Weston notes that most of the machine shops and foundries he visits report that they would like to become suppliers to wind turbine companies if they could find the workers. The problem isn't simply a shortage of training, but that companies can't find applicants who are willing to participate in the on-the-job training and schooling needed for skilled manufacturing positions. Even when the companies pay tuition, transportation, and provide time off for school, they can't find takers. Despite relatively high pay, benefits, and good working conditions, too few young people are willing to commit to the training required for a skilled job in manufacturing, even if the promise is a green job. This could be the result of a generation having witnessed mass factory layoffs and concluding that manufacturing jobs are just not secure, or it could reflect the greater prestige of white-collar jobs. But in a region of the country endeavoring to rebuild itself around advanced manufacturing, the shortage of skills is a serious impediment.

Neither wind nor any other single industry will turn around Cleveland's economy. But to the extent the region can position itself at the center of an offshore wind power hub, it could become a significant source of employment. In the interim, if more local companies can become suppliers to the wind industry, they will help in revitalizing the region's manufacturing sector.

CITIES, WIND, AND PORTS

While the bulk of the economic development potential of wind is in manufacturing, several port cities are capitalizing on importing foreign turbines. The combination of the eight-year extension of the federal production tax credit and state portfolio standards has resulted in more foreign manufacturers shipping turbines and parts to the United States. Among them are Longview and Vancouver, Washington, on the West Coast, Corpus Christi on the Gulf Coast, and Duluth-Superior, Minnesota, on the Great Lakes.[65] Several of these cities are making sizable investments in improving their ports to accommodate wind turbines that can be 150 feet long and parts such as nacelles that weigh about 85 tons.

In Washington, the Port of Longview has been handling turbine parts from Korea and China since 2005. It helps to make up for the loss of business in its former specialty, importing raw logs, which is in decline. Port Director Ken O'Hollaren calculates that importation of turbine parts now accounts for one-fourth of the port's revenue.[66] A 2007 contract made the city the exclusive importer of turbines and other parts for Danish Siemens Power Generation, and in that year alone 37 ships carrying 127 Vestas turbines came through the port.[67] To handle the increased trade, the port has been installing new equipment such as a $3.2 million mobile harbor crane and a custom-built transporter and dolly system.[68] The number of longshoremen employed has been rising gradually since 2005.

In February 2009, the Port of Vancouver signed a three-year contract extension with Vestas and added a two-year contract with Siemens. Port officials expect these agreements to create 235 new jobs and generate $20 million in city revenue.[69]

Duluth-Superior, Minnesota, began as a port of entry for wind turbines in 2005, and traffic has been picking up at a fast pace since then; in 2008, the port handled 2,000 wind turbine components totaling 307,000 freight tons. The parts are loaded onto custom-designed semitruck caravans and sent off throughout the upper Midwest and Canada.[70] To give a sense of the scale, the port accepted a shipment from Siemens for a 76-turbine wind farm in Adair, Iowa, that took six ships and more than 500 semitrucks to deliver, according to the *Minneapolis-St. Paul Star Tribune*. A new development is that foreign-owned factories in the United States are beginning to export from the port.

Corpus Christi, Texas, hopes to translate its increased port traffic in wind turbines into a broader wind-related economic development sector. The port began receiving turbines in 2006 and is now developing its own 35-megawatt offshore wind farm, to be developed by Colorado-based Revolution Energy. Furthermore, a $20 million U.S. Department of Energy wind-energy research and blade-testing facility, the world's largest, recently opened in fall 2008. The hope is that the University of Houston–run facility will attract manufacturers to the area.[71]

Promising as developments are for these cities, it may be likely that imports will not grow significantly over the long term. As wind technology advances, the trend is toward larger turbines that will be difficult to import. James G. P. Dehlsen, founder and chair of Clipper Windpower, believes that production of blades and towers will expand faster than imports because even land-based turbines are moving toward the 5–6 megawatt size and will be cumbersome and expensive to ship. He thinks the industry will move to hybrid towers that are fabricated on site.[72] Although importing may be good news for a few port cities, the national economy would benefit more from increased wind turbine production and a supply chain to support it.

THE ROLE OF PUBLIC POLICY IN DEVELOPING
A RENEWABLE ENERGY ECONOMY

What we see in the city and state policy to develop renewable energy are standard economic development strategies. The idea is to catalyze the development of new companies and attract big players in order to develop new sectors or clusters of economic activity. But cities can't do it alone. Some cities, with the support of state policy, can. But most importantly, developing a renewable energy economy in the United States needs federal support. Here's what we need to do.

Stimulate Demand

Germany and other countries with feed-in tariffs demonstrate that government policy is essential for creating demand for renewable energy. It bears repeating that Germany has achieved its exporter status with relatively low solar and wind resources by using the feed-in tariff to allow renewable energy to compete with fossil fuels on a fairer playing field. The feed-in tariff has created the stable investment environment that has allowed companies to innovate to reduce production costs. In February 2009, the German Renewable Energy Federation announced that Germany's renewable energy sector would triple its share of power generation to 47 percent by 2020 with continued feed-in subsidies. Even though some manufacturing jobs are being moved to Asia, the goal is to keep the core of the industry in Germany as innovation continues.

Germany's success with the feed-in tariff does not necessarily mean we should adopt it on a national level in the United States. The costs would be staggering. And feed-in tariffs only apply to distributed generation, not centralized solar plants (such as the one Austin is building), which will be needed to reach the solar adoption goals of many state portfolio standards. While the feed-in tariff was effective in jump-starting the solar industry in its infancy, some argue that

Germany's solar feed-in tariff now is pouring too much money into existing technologies that are being surpassed by new ones (e.g., thin-film and nanosolar), creating an inefficient and expensive sector with little incentive to innovate (although the German Economy Ministry released a plan in February 2009 that will increase investment in renewable energy research).[73] Further, Adam Browning, executive director of Vote Solar, argues that "at high levels of market penetration a feed-in tariff will inevitably result in paying too much for electricity of lower value (e.g., off-peak wind) and not offering enough to develop less mature resources that have additional value to offer (e.g., tidal, solar with storage)."[74]

The United States has taken a different path with the portfolio standard and net metering, which are, to date, state-level policies. At last count, 29 states had portfolio standards and at least 35 had net metering. In both policies, the devil is in the details in terms of how much demand they will stimulate. Even when both are done right, they don't guarantee the development of a domestic renewable energy industry. Meeting the most ambitious state portfolio standards will be difficult. California enacted a feed-in tariff partly because the state is not on track for meeting its RPS requirements. The California Public Utilities Commission reports that the state has acquired only 400 of the 5,900 MW needed to be on schedule with the 20 percent by 2010 RPS goal. Although the RPS contains fines for missing targets, utilities have yet to pay them. The percentage of electricity from renewables has actually declined from 14 to 12.7 percent from the time the RPS was enacted in 2003 to 2007, according to a Center for Energy Efficiency and Renewable Technologies report.[75] John White, executive director of the Center for Energy Efficiency and Renewable Technology in Sacramento, points out that California has installed 16 times as much capacity from natural gas plants as from renewable energy since the 2002 RPS was passed.[76] California is not alone—Maine, New York, Massachusetts, and Minnesota have all missed their goals for adding renewable capacity.

Stimulating demand requires long-term purchasing contracts for renewable producers, usually from the electric utility. The developer pays the up-front costs in exchange for a long-term purchasing agreement. Having such a contract ensures the annual revenue needed to obtain bank financing for projects. A power purchase agreement was part of Gamesa's deal in locating in Pennsylvania and of the deal for the solar farm being developed in Austin. Energy analysts predict that power purchase agreements will drive 75 percent of commercial and industrial solar sales in 2008 and 2009.

No matter what policies the United States enacts, we will be playing catch-up in a rapidly shifting landscape. China is quickly overtaking Germany in production of solar, wind, and other clean technology due to aggressive policies to promote them with subsidies, below-market lending, closed supply chains, and below-market pricing. Another spur to development is a policy implemented in 2007 requiring large utilities to produce 3 percent of their power from renewable sources by 2010 and 8 percent by 2020, excluding hydroelectric. China's five-year plan that starts in 2011 will include even higher standards and subsidies to support clean energy development.[77] And China is spending $221 billion of its $586 billion 2009 stimulus package on renewable energy and other clean technologies.

Following European producers, China's largest solar panel producer, Suntech Power Holdings, will soon build a plant in the United States. The company plans on selling panels at below cost in order to build market share. The *New York Times* reports that the factory, which will employ between 75 and 150 workers, will be located in the Southwest.[78] Other Chinese manufacturers will follow. States will no doubt compete in offering subsidies for the location of these plants.

Fast-Track Ongoing Research

Federal funding for renewable technologies could be freed up by reducing subsidies to the fossil fuel industry. Cleantech estimates that the oil and gas industries receive between $15 and $35 billion annually in the form of low-interest loans and bonds, tax breaks, royalty relief, and research and development.[79]

Many in the field think the future of solar is in thin-film, organics, and nanosolar. Thin-film is moving forward right now, but organics and nanosolar are several years away from commercialization. Considerable investment in research will be needed in these technologies. The United States has sufficient wind resource to meet the U.S. Department of Energy's goal of achieving 20 percent of the nation's electricity from wind energy,[80] and the U.S. House Science and Technology Committee passed the Wind Energy Research and Development Act of 2009 that would provide $220 million annually for four years on research to improve the energy efficiency, reliability, and capability of wind turbines. The American Recovery and Reinvestment Act of 2009 (ARRA) stimulus plan invests $112 billion in various green technologies, and earmarks $2 billion for renewable energy research. President Obama proposes to add another $15 billion annually in renewable energy research, to be funded by a cap-and-trade system.[81] Meanwhile, China is spending $221 billion of its $586 billion 2009 stimulus package on renewable energy and other clean technologies, and has already followed Germany's policy path to overtake Germany and Japan to become the largest alternative energy producer in the world in installed generating capacity. While investment in renewable energy research has increased substantially in the United States, we have a lot of competition that is further along.

Build More Transmission Capacity and a Smarter Grid

Portfolio standards and other policies to increase demand for renewables will ultimately face transmission capacity limits. Rapid growth of wind power in Germany has caused overloads and shortages because its transmission system had not been updated to integrate this intermittent power source.[82] Texas leads the nation in wind-generating capacity (at just over 8,000 megawatts, or 2.9 percent of consumed power) but has reached the point where transmission prevents further development. Texas has experienced grid destabilization due to the intermittent nature of wind generation. In one event, wind deceleration caused a dramatic drop in the amount of electricity feeding into the system. Because sufficient generation from other sources could not be brought on board quickly enough, ERCOT, the agency that runs the Texas grid, came close to instituting emergency procedures to retain sufficient power. In response, in January 2009 the Texas Public Utility Commission awarded nine companies rights to build $5 billion in new electric transmission lines, which will double renewable energy supply to urban areas in the state. The expansion will add 2,900 miles of new power lines and could allow up to 18,500 megawatts of additional wind generation. ERCOT is also expanding its nonspin generation (generation that can come up in 30 minutes) reserve requirements to guard against potential grid destabilization from sharp drops in wind generation, at a cost of about $30 million a year.

Meeting existing state RPS requirements (and hopefully adding a national RPS) will require a major investment in new transmission lines to transport renewable energy from rural to urban locations. Opposition from environmental organizations has already emerged, and has heated up since the stimulus bill was passed. Some environmentalists fear that the construction of new transmission towers will mar pristine landscapes. Activists are protesting plans in California to developing utility-scale solar farms in the Mojave Desert that would require new grid development to get the power to cities.[83]

Finding acceptable locations is essential, as permission for transmission lines takes seven to ten years, particularly if they cross cities, counties, or states.[84] The energy bill that is currently being framed by Congress may include measures to make the regulatory process more streamlined. The Natural Resources Defense Council (NRDC) is working with Google Earth to develop maps of possible project sites that take into account environmental considerations. NRDC is also facilitating conversations between utilities, environmental groups, and local communities to reach agreements on where transmission lines can go. And Interior Secretary Ken Salazar has created a task force to identify sites for adding transmission lines.[85] This process, however, will likely slow down President Obama's goal of doubling renewable energy generation in the next three years.[86]

In addition to new transmission lines, we need to create storage capacity to handle the variable capacity of wind and solar and transform a "dumb" one-way system into a "smart" two-way system that can monitor and manage demand.[87] In a House subcommittee hearing, Tom Casey, CEO of a smart-grid software and analysis company, described a smart grid as being "…like an Internet for electricity, a network of devices that are monitored and managed with real-time communications and computer intelligence."[88] Smart-grid technologies could reduce peak demand by nearly 27 percent, which would free additional transmission capacity and allow for integration of more renewable energy.[89]

It won't be cheap. The National Renewable Energy Laboratory estimates that reaching a 20 percent renewable goal by 2020 would require a $60 billion investment in grid infrastructure. ARRA appropriates approximately $11 billion for research and development, pilot projects, and federal matching funds for the U.S. Department of Energy's Smart Grid Investment Program. But even if we decide to make this massive investment, there are technical constraints in addition to political ones. Since so much is unknown about the technology, some experts suggest the $4.5 billion should be used to test a few small-scale smart-grid pilot projects, while others argue it should be used to install smart meters on as many homes as possible. Both the Senate and House have held hearings to discuss how to proceed. Several smart-grid projects are already under way, each employing different technologies. So rather than a system we have several technologies that often don't work across states. Policies and standards will need to be established by the Federal Energy Regulatory Commission and the National Institute of Standards and Technology to integrate systems before utilities will be willing to make huge investments.

Invest in Manufacturing

Low levels of national investment in research and development in renewable energy have meant that the United States has not been a technology leader and has missed out on related job creation in manufacturing. We are now paying the price of this neglect. The real economic development potential in renewable energy is in manufacturing, which comprises 70 percent of the employment in wind energy and 70–75 percent in solar, depending on the type of system.[90] Much of this is in supplying the parts for the wind turbines and solar panels. Having let critical machine-tooling and other manufacturing strengths go, we will now have to rebuild these industries to establish job-creating supply chains. The United States can no longer afford to think of manufacturing as yesterday's industry. It employs more than 13 million Americans in well-paying jobs with benefits (particularly if unionized) and accounts for more than 80 percent of U.S. exports and about two-thirds of U.S. research and development.[91]

George Sterzinger, executive director of the Renewable Energy Policy Project, makes a strong case that federal and state policies to develop renewable energy projects will not translate into manufacturing jobs without an explicit policy to invest in retooling and modernizing. Sterzinger advocates for extending the Clean Renewable Energy Bonds (CREBs) that were authorized in the 2005 Energy Policy Act for manufacturers of renewable energy and other clean technologies. Government-qualified CREBs would offer bond purchasers a tax credit in lieu of an interest payment.[92] CREBs to this point have only been available for public bodies that sell bonds and use the proceeds to finance renewable energy projects, but could be expanded to support renewable manufacturing. And they could be expanded so that individuals could invest in them. Sterzinger recommends marketing them as Green Victory Bonds, with every dollar of tax credits resulting in about two dollars invested in domestic manufacturing. Bond purchasers would be repaid the principal from the participating firms, and the interest would be paid through a tax credit.[93]

Additional options for financing retooling of manufacturing have been proposed as part of the stimulus package. After holding community roundtables in several Ohio cities, Senator Sherrod Brown proposed a green-energy manufacturing bill as part of ARRA that, if included, would have created a Green Technology Manufacturing Corporation and Green Technology Investment Corporation to administer a loan program for research and development and commercialization of green products and processes and purchasing equipment for green technology development and production and related uses. In 2009, Brown and several other senators sponsored legislation to provide federal funding for manufacturers to retool plants for energy efficiency. A federal investment corporation to provide loans, tax breaks, and grants for manufacturing is essential to catching up in renewable production capacity. Phil Mattera of Good Jobs First, an organization that tracks corporate subsidies, has revealed that some of the manufacturers of renewable technology are using federal, state, and local subsidies, yet are paying wages below the manufacturing average. Any government funding should be tied to providing prevailing wages to ensure that the jobs created are good ones.

As to technical assistance to companies in retooling for renewable energy and other emerging technologies, the U.S. Department of Commerce Manufacturing Extension Program (MEP) has a 20-plus-year history of providing it. A recent strategic plan refocuses MEP on helping firms accelerate technology adoption and keeping suppliers to high-technology companies abreast of the latest needs of industries and how to adapt to them.[94] Increased funding for MEP is needed to help more U.S. firms become original equipment manufacturers and suppliers in the renewable energy industry.

Link Economic Development to Workforce Development

Solar installation is a green job that is generating a lot of enthusiasm among youth. Richmond Build is one of several programs across the country hoping to create well-paying jobs for inner-city youth and adults in installation and other green jobs. While these programs offer much promise, they will need to broaden their focus. Richmond Build includes solar installation as one component of a broader pre-apprenticeship program. There will not be enough installation jobs, even in cities such as those in the Bay Area, to support all of the trainees being produced. Further, there is little room for advancement into the considerably smaller number of supervisory jobs. Jobs in system design take at least a college degree. Programs like Richmond Build have their place, but for the most part should bridge to programs that offer certifications and other credentials. The best bet for inner-city youth with a high school diploma or less is to enroll in a construction or electrical pre-apprenticeship that provides a broader range of employment skills. The skill sets needed in installation differ widely, so the efforts to standardize through NAPCEP and the International Brotherhood of Electrical Workers will be important for ensuring that people who enter into training programs leave with the right credentials.

As to manufacturing, the answer to the skills gap problem is not simply investing more in education and training programs. The answer is to find more young workers to fill the positions opening up because of retirements. Employers that are willing to train workers on their own can't find workers interested in training for skilled manufacturing positions. We need to channel some of the youth enthusiasm about green jobs into manufacturing—a tough task, as a generation growing up with computers, cell phones, and BlackBerrys just isn't interested in manufacturing jobs.

Dan Swinney, executive director of the Chicago Manufacturing Renaissance Council and founder of the Austin Polytechnic Academy on Chicago's West Side, is up for the task. The failing neighborhood high school, one of Chicago's worst, was closed, underwent a $31 million dollar renovation, and reopened to 145 students in fall 2007. The goal is to prepare students for jobs in science, engineering, and advanced manufacturing. The academy uses nationally recognized applied science, mathematics, and pre-engineering curriculum. At least 50 manufacturing partners offer students paid summer internships. Swinney envisions a Renewable Energy Innovation Park operating in conjunction with the school as the next step. He notes, "If we want to have an economy that is environmentally, ethically, and economically sustainable, what would you have? High value-added, advanced manu-facturing. The environmental crisis, for instance, will have to be solved at the point of production. The next generation of environmentalists need to be industrial engineers."[95]

Use Smart Subsidies

The competition among cities and states has already heated up. Sub-sidies abound for solar and wind companies seeking U.S. locations. The question is whether they are smart subsidies or just a new round of the beggar-thy-neighbor strategies that characterize so much state and local economic development practice. As we saw, New Mexico and Colorado are luring companies from Texas. Pennsylvania com-peted with Texas and other states for Gamesa. Companies are shop-ping around for the best subsidies.

Good Jobs First has identified hundreds of millions in subsidies going to wind and solar companies and questions whether cities and states are placing adequate strings on public dollars. The Arkansas leg-islature passed a bill to exempt the LM Glasfiber wind blade plant from state income taxes for 27 years as part of a $33,800,000 subsidy pack-age. The company laid off 150 workers in January. In Iowa another wind blade producer, TPI, received $2 million in state subsidies under the condition that it pay workers at least $13.40 per hour, a require-ment that was later waived.[96]

These stories don't count the millions in research support that some companies have received while developing technology. Toledo's First Solar received more than $150 million in government support and private before building its first U.S. plant. For a company to build plants in other countries to serve foreign markets is one thing, but the United States should benefit more in terms of jobs and economic development from companies that benefit from significant public investment. First Solar's plants in Malaysia and Europe employ three times more workers than the Toledo facility.

These and other stories of subsidies granted to companies that pay relatively low wages and are hostile to unions suggest that more requirements need to be placed on public subsidies. To ensure that these green jobs are good jobs, cities and states should stipulate job-quality standards in exchange for subsidies and enforce them with clawbacks that take away subsidies when businesses receiving them don't comply.

Good Jobs First offers advice and sample contract language for doing this on its Web site.

Be Realistic

While the solar and wind industries are growing dramatically, the transition away from fossil fuels will take decades. The reasons are economic, political, and technical. Of California's big utilities, San Diego Gas & Electric obtains 6 percent of electricity from renewable sources, Pacific Gas & Electric is at 14 percent, and Southern California Edison has reached 15.7 percent. Although utilities are subject to fines for not reaching the RPS goals, the wording of the regulation makes it unlikely that they will be imposed. Among the reasons the utilities cite for failing to meet the goals are inconsistency of the federal renewable tax, unreliability of suppliers, difficulty of getting permission for solar and wind farms, and need for new transmission lines.[97] Although large solar and wind farms are necessary to reach goals in California and other places, considerable opposition to them is emerging among environmentalists.

While Germany produces 14 percent of its energy from renewable sources, energy import dependence is at 62 percent and growing.[98] And Germany's focus on expanding production of renewable energy doesn't mean the country isn't investing in nonrenewable sources, particularly coal. Currently, 26 coal-fired power plants are under construction or being planned. Although some will use more efficient technologies, these coal plants will more than erase any CO_2 savings from expanded use of solar and wind energy. Germany's coal industry has opposed expansion of renewable energy—and won federal subsidies to maintain operations at nonprofitable mines in negotiations when the 2003 RPS of 12.5 percent by 2010 was passed. While acknowledging Germany's success in developing renewable energy, EU environmental commissioner Stavros Dimas publicly commented that Germany is lagging in meeting its greenhouse gas reduction goals.[99]

In the United States, the utility that is adopting more renewable energy than any other utility in the nation, Austin Energy, will still rely on coal, natural gas, and nuclear for most of its electricity over the next decades. AE is paying three times the price of natural gas for its solar electricity. Herein is a core problem. Capacity added now is expensive and may become outdated as thin-film technologies and nanosolar technologies are commercialized. Nonetheless, AE general manager

Roger Duncan explains that Austin Energy is making the investment to promote solar energy expansion and to hasten its competitive development. "I have no doubt that in the future solar will be the dominant source of energy in the world," Duncan says.[100]

The future for renewable energy is bright. But the production landscape is shifting rapidly and the winners and losers in terms of economic development will shift as well. Germany and other European countries that invested heavily to become production leaders are now ceding this position to China, which has more than 100 solar companies that account for one-third of global solar component production. The United States will continue to expand renewable energy generation, but it is likely that China and other low-wage countries will be formidable competitors in manufacturing capacity.

4

Building the Energy-Efficient City

CITIES ARE PRIMARILY MADE UP OF BUILDINGS. AND BUILDINGS consume 71 percent of the nation's electric power and 39 percent of all power, and create 39 percent of the nation's CO_2 emissions.[1] Clearly, improving the energy efficiency of buildings would have a big impact on reducing greenhouse gas emissions. Cities have two options in increasing building efficiency—setting efficiency standards for new buildings and undertaking initiatives to improve the efficiency of existing buildings. A focus on new buildings is important.

While most buildings in any given year are preexisting, by 2030 half of all buildings in the United States will have been built after 2000.[2] For the most part, however, cities are making rather slow progress on establishing standards and incentives for energy-efficient new construction.

While standards for new buildings are increasingly important over time, cities can have a much bigger and immediate impact on reducing greenhouse gas emissions by focusing on standards for existing buildings. Even if we project new building through 2030, the majority of energy use and carbon emissions will be from buildings that exist today. Improving the energy efficiency of buildings is the single most important move a city can make to reduce its greenhouse gas emissions.

A secondary benefit of a green building strategy is economic development and jobs. The jobs in efficiency and green building, however, differ in character. Most of the jobs in improving the energy efficiency

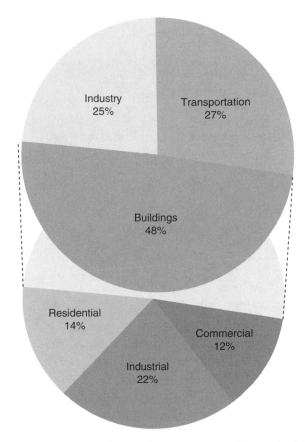

FIGURE 4.1 *Sources of Greenhouse Gas Emissions. Source:* Architecture 2030 and the American Institute of Architects. Data published by the AIA in collaboration with Edward Mazria of Architecture 2030, based on statistics gathered by the U.S. Energy Information Administration (http://www.architecture2030.org/news/resources/AIA-Arch2030FactSheet.pdf; http://www.architecture2030.org/current_situation/building_sector.html).

of existing structures are in retrofitting. Every $1 million invested in energy efficiency in buildings creates between 12 and 15 direct and indirect jobs—many in well-paying unionized construction trades.[3]

In the case of efficiency retrofitting, these workers include energy auditors who determine the most cost-effective improvements and various types of construction and home improvement workers who do the retrofits, such as replacing inefficient systems and appliances, adding insulation, replacing windows and doors, etc. In both retrofitting and new green building there are jobs in manufacturing efficient appliances, heating systems, insulation, and other products. McGraw-Hill Construction projects that the green-building market will increase from $10 billion in 2005 to more than $50 billion by 2010.[4]

It's hard to obtain precise estimates of the net employment impact of this activity, as some of these products would be manufactured anyway (the same worker would be employed whether producing an energy-efficient product or an inefficient one). To the extent that energy efficiency initiatives increase demand for energy-efficient appliances due to faster replacement, a certain number of jobs over and above those already employed producing these appliances will be created. And appliance efficiency standards promote product innovation among producers, creating higher profits, more jobs, and even more efficient appliances.[5]

Another aspect of the efficiency jobs story is the redirection of income saved on utility bills. In 1970, the California Public Utilities Commission authorized utilities to use ratepayer funds to administer energy efficiency programs. An aggressive set of efficiency standards for appliances and buildings was put in place and has been adjusted periodically since then. Between 1972 and 2006, consumers have saved $56 billion on their energy bills as a result of these programs. The redirection of these savings toward other goods and services has created 1.5 million full-time equivalent jobs with a payroll of $45 billion. Although jobs have been lost in the oil, gas, and electric power sectors as a result of efficiency standards, every loss was compensated by 50 new jobs being created in other sectors.[6]

Clearly, energy efficiency and green building can create considerable economic activity. This chapter examines what cities are doing to promote building energy efficiency in both existing buildings and new construction and addresses two questions: Are cities doing enough to promote energy efficiency in buildings? And how are they linking these efforts to economic development opportunities?

A few U.S. cities are attempting citywide energy efficiency initiatives. They offer new financing models that allow property owners to retrofit without paying the costs up front. For the most part, these initiatives are being pursued as energy/environment policy and are not linked to economic development. Los Angeles was the first city to implement strict efficiency standards and a citywide retrofitting program that is explicitly linked to an economic justice goal of employing low-income city residents. We examine this program and the organization that has worked with city government to make it happen. We then explore initiatives in Cambridge, Milwaukee, and Portland that are testing new funding models to make it easier for residents and business owners to invest in energy efficiency. These programs illustrate different strategies for linking climate change goals to job creation, some more explicitly than others.

We then turn to cities and regions that have started initiatives to expand manufacturing of green building inputs. Interestingly, in two of the three cases presented here, Pittsburgh and New York City, these initiatives come not from city government but from nonprofit organizations that have had to push city government to focus on the economic development potential of green building. In the third case, Syracuse, a focus on green manufacturing preceded the city's efforts to promote green building. These cities illustrate the transformative strategy of helping existing manufacturers retool by adding green products into their mix.

BUILDING EFFICIENCY AS ECONOMIC DEVELOPMENT

Cities are the Saudi Arabia of energy efficiency.
—Douglas I. Foy, energy efficiency consultant
and former Massachusetts secretary of
commonwealth development[7]

A negawatt, a term coined by Amory Lovins, is a unit of conserved energy. It's the cheapest source of energy available—every dollar spent on using less electricity saves $2.00 in investment in increasing electric supply. We could realize a 20–30 percent savings in electricity use simply by installing more and better insulation, lighting, and heating and air-conditioning systems.[8] McKinsey Global Institute estimates that almost 40 percent of U.S. carbon emissions reduction potential by 2030 is through energy efficiency efforts that could be achieved with existing technologies.[9] The United States would have to spend $38 billion through 2020 on energy efficiency measures to achieve this 50 percent goal, which would realize energy savings of $900 billion by 2020.[10] While the investment required is huge, so is the payoff—in reducing carbon emissions, in preventing the need for new power plant construction, in cash savings to consumers, and in creating jobs that cannot be exported to other countries.

We can get a sense of the employment impact a serious national energy efficiency initiative would have by looking at Germany. An initiative was started in 1999 with the dual goal of increasing energy efficiency and stimulating employment in the lagging construction sector, and it has achieved impressive results. Between 2001 and 2006 a public investment of €3.8 billion (€5.2 billion as of June 2009) stimulated €15.2 billion in investment and retrofitted 342,000 apartments and houses.[11] The initiative created 25,000 full-time jobs and saved 116,000 jobs in the construction sector. It also has created €4 billion in new tax revenues and savings in unemployment benefits and reduced annual building emissions by 2 percent. Further, the initiative has created a market for new technologies that are being produced in Germany, including low-temperature heating boilers, fuel cells, photovoltaic and solar thermal systems, heat exchangers for ventilation systems, triple-glazed windows with inert gas, and thermal insulation material.[12]

At the start of 2006, the CO_2 Building Retrofit Program (*Gebäudesanierungsprogramm*) was expanded with €1.4 billion yearly, to be allocated through a reduced-interest credit system, subsidies, and tax credits for the period of 2006–2008. In addition, through the first stimulus program from November 2008 (*1. Konjunkturprogramm*), the government has allocated an additional €3 billion for the period 2009–2011.[13] Accompanying these investments, the government has set the goal of doubling energy productivity in 2020 relative to 1990[14] and adding 200,000 jobs by 2020 as part of the national energy efficiency plan.[15] According to Environment Minister Sigmar Gabriel, the green jobs sector employs about 1.8 million, which is a 50 percent increase in just three years.[16]

Until President Obama's stimulus package was passed, it was left to U.S. cities and states to attempt on a local scale what Germany has been doing at a national level.[17] A few U.S. cities are experimenting with different strategies to encourage private investment in efficiency upgrades, and to varying degrees they are providing energy audits that help consumers make cost-effective decisions, identifying trustworthy vendors, verifying that the anticipated savings are realized, and ensuring that enough qualified workers are trained to conduct the work.[18] These programs are just getting under way, but they seem to hold much promise for reducing energy usage, greenhouse gas emissions, and consumer spending on energy, and perhaps for job creation.

Cities are expected to receive $1.9 billion of $3.2 billion in block grants under the U.S. Department of Energy (DOE) Energy Efficiency and Conservation Block Grant Program, from the 2009 American Recovery and Reinvestment Act. Funds can be used for energy audits and upgrades to residential and commercial buildings, installing renewable energy systems on state or local government buildings, developing and implementing building codes and inspections, and creating financing mechanisms for energy conservation programs.[19] To be eligible for this funding, states must submit an energy efficiency and conservation strategy and plan and agree to pay prevailing wages.[20] States wanting to allocate more than the base funding for efficiency initiatives must move toward adopting stronger energy codes.[21] Another $3.1 billion will go to the Department of Energy's State Energy Program for both energy efficiency and renewable energy programs. States accepting these funds have to agree to decouple utility profits from sales to create incentives for them to embrace energy efficiency (see text box on decoupling, chapter 3). These funding streams will give a big boost to state and city efficiency programs already under way and allow new ones to begin.

A FOCUS ON GREEN BUILDINGS

While they are retrofitting buildings, cities also need to ensure that new construction is more energy-efficient. Unfortunately, most cities are moving at glacial speed in regulating efficiency in new construction. Only 92 U.S. cities have enacted ordinances requiring some new buildings to reach a sustainability standard, the most common of which is the U.S. Green Building Council's Leadership in Energy and Environmental Design (LEED) green building rating system.[22] In addition, or independently, some cities are offering tax incentives, expedited permitting, grants and loans, and technical assistance to encourage green building.[23] A few of these cities are hoping that green building can generate enough demand to create economic development and employment opportunities in green building products.

The LEED rating system is based on earning points in five areas of sustainable construction: the site, water efficiency, energy and atmosphere, materials and resources, and indoor environmental quality. The more points, the higher the rating—it goes from basic certification to

TABLE 4.1. Sample of City Green Building Ordinances

City	Ordinance	Applies to	Standard	LEED-Certified 2000–2008*	Building Permits Issued in 2007**
Austin	Green Building Program (2004), Green Building Resolution (2007)	All municipal projects >5,000SF and renovations costing $2 million or more	LEED silver. Also uses Austin Energy Green Building rating system, which allocates up to five stars.	6 certified 7 silver 8 gold 2 platinum	3,548
Boston	Green Building Ordinance (2004, 2007)	Municipal buildings Projects > 50,000SF	LEED silver, but projects are not required to register with LEED LEED certification	10 certified 11 silver 8 gold 1 platinum	150
Chicago	Sustainable Building Policy (2002, 2004)	All city-funded projects (new construction and renovation)	LEED silver. Also uses the Chicago Standard for municipal facilities, which is based on selected points from LEED.	22 certified 18 silver 22 gold 5 platinum	1,679
New York	Local Law 86 (2005)	All buildings receiving public funds valued at $10 million or more than 50 percent of construction or reconstruction costs.	LEED silver	2 certified 8 silver 15 gold 3 platinum	5,765
Oakland	Green Building Ordinance (2005)	City building projects that equal or exceed $3 million in construction costs.	LEED silver	1 certified 3 silver 3 gold 2 platinum	293

City	Ordinance	Scope	LEED Requirement	Certification	Permits**
Portland	Green Building Resolution (2009) updates previous ordinances (1999, 2005)	All municipally owned or occupied new construction and renovation projects over 5,000 square feet with a total construction cost of more than $250,000, and all new city-funded private construction and renovation projects over 10,000 square feet with a total construction cost of $250,000	LEED silver and achieve the minimum LEED Optimize Energy Performance points required to meet the targets of the Architecture 2030 Challenge (see p. 87).	8 certified 19 silver 30 gold 6 platinum	1,384
San Francisco	Resource Efficiency Requirements and Standards (2004)	>5,000 sq. ft. city-owned new construction, renovation, and additions	LEED silver	9 certified 9 silver 15 gold 3 platinum	155
	Green Building Ordinance (2008)	Most new commercial and residential high-rises (public and private)	LEED certification for large projects; medium projects use GreenPoint rating system.		
Seattle	Seattle Green Building Policy (2000)	City-funded projects and renovations > 5,000 square feet	LEED silver	16 certified 19 silver 17 gold 1 platinum	1,538
	King County Green Building and Sustainable Development Ordinance (2008) updates previous ordinances (2001, 2005)	All King County-owned and county-financed projects	LEED gold		

* As reported by the U.S. Green Building Council.
** U.S. Bureau of the Census, Building Permits by Place.

silver, gold, and platinum. Since it was created in 1998, LEED has
certified more than 3,648 certified projects in 91 countries and has
more than 17,000 projects registered (awaiting certification).[24] Since
green design and construction requires a new knowledge base, the
U.S. Green Building Council credentials practitioners, from architects
to contractors, to become LEED-certified.

City LEED ordinances vary in the types of construction covered
under the ordinances and in the levels of certification required (table
4.1). Most of the LEED requirements cover a small percentage of
new construction, either because they apply only to buildings above
a certain size or only to certain types of projects. Many cities only
apply LEED requirements to projects of 50,000 square feet or more.
Given that 95 percent of commercial buildings are under this limit,[25]
such ordinances will not have much impact on reducing a city's carbon footprint. But even if LEED ordinances covered the majority of new construction, this would represent a small percentage of
total building. The number of LEED-certified buildings relative to
new buildings constructed is quite small. Nationwide, there are only
3,457 LEED-certified buildings, and only 142 of these are at the
platinum level—the level at which significant energy efficiency differences occur. A 2008 study commissioned by the U.S. Green Building Council estimates that LEED buildings deliver energy savings
of 25–35 percent above the national average, but building scientist
Henry Gifford argues that by failing to compare LEED buildings'
energy use against that of other buildings constructed during the
same time period, the savings are overestimated. Gifford finds that
LEED buildings used more energy than that used by a comparable
set of projects of similar building types during the same periods of
construction.[26]

Having an impact on energy efficiency will require more than
stronger LEED ordinances. Even if more cities used the highest
LEED standards for all new construction, critics have noted several
problems with the system, the most important being that it doesn't
address energy efficiency sufficiently to have much impact on energy
efficiency and greenhouse gas emissions.[27] In fairness, LEED is the
first national standard for green building and has evolved to correct
this weakness. In 2005 LEED was revised to include two mandatory
energy efficiency points that could decrease a building's energy consumption by as much as 14 percent in new buildings and by half as

much in existing buildings.[28] And LEED 2009 has gone even further by giving energy efficiency more than one-third of total points.

Part of what LEED has achieved is making green building mainstream in architecture and construction by starting with the innovators. The strategy has worked; demand for green buildings has been steadily increasing. The first national large-scale analysis, conducted by researchers at the University of California, Berkeley, finds that green buildings command about 2 percent more per square foot in rent than traditional buildings matched for location. Consumers are attracted to the lower water and energy costs of green building and amenities such as more even and comfortable temperatures, more natural light, and surfaces and products that do not emit harmful chemicals. As the effectiveness of different building systems and construction practices is documented, LEED has laid the groundwork for the building codes that follow—and only by adopting stricter building codes can cities significantly impact building energy efficiency.

Ed Mazria, founder of Architecture 2030, an organization for advocating strategies to dramatically reduce greenhouse gas emissions through building efficiency, recognizes the importance of LEED in addressing all aspects of green buildings, but argues it doesn't address the urgency of climate change. Mazria developed the Architecture 2030 Challenge as a way for cities to take on more dramatic reductions in emissions. The Architecture 2030 Challenge calls for fossil fuel use reductions for all new buildings of 60 percent in 2010, 70 percent in 2015, and 90 percent in 2025, and carbon neutrality by 2030. It has been adopted by the U.S. Conference of Mayors, the U.S. Green Building Council, ICLEI-Local Governments for Sustainability, the National Association of Counties, the Congress for New Urbanism, and other organizations.[29] But signing on only means that a city will include the emissions reductions goals in its climate action plan—there is no formal mechanism that requires cities to meet the goals.

Ultimately, we will need to see wide-scale adoption and enforcement of stringent building codes to have a significant impact on energy efficiency.[30] A model building energy code is being developed by the American Society of Heating, Refrigerating and Air-Conditioning Engineers (ASHRAE), the organization that writes the national codes for building mechanical systems, which in turn set minimum standards for state and city building energy codes.[31] Working with the American Institute of Architects and the U.S. Green Building Council, ASHRAE is developing the Advanced Energy Design Guidelines (Standard 189), to be released in mid-2009. Standard 189 will require buildings to be 30 percent more efficient than the existing national code by 2012 and net zero by 2030.[32]

Through the guidelines, former ASHRAE president Kent Peterson, who started the Standard 189 process, comments, "We're showing the marketplace that technology exists today to build much more efficient buildings than code requires." While the demonstration aspect of the standards is important, adoption of Standard 189 is voluntary, which limits its impact. Only two states, California and Florida, have adopted the latest and strictest ASHRAE commercial and residential codes, which suggests that we have a long way to go before stringent building efficiency requirements are the norm. In August 2009, California adopted new building energy efficiency standards that moved the state toward net zero for residential development by 2020 and commercial development by 2030. It sets targets for reducing building energy use by 15 percent and landscape water use by 50 percent starting in 2010. It is 50 percent more stringent than the International Energy Efficiency Code and exceeds the Architecture 2030 Challenge. The value of this precedent-setting state building code is that cities can adopt it or even more stringent codes rather than undertaking their own processes of code reevaluation.[33]

Federal standards are needed to force quicker adoption of energy efficiency in new construction. To that end, the American Clean Energy and Security Act of 2009, which passed the House and is being considered by the Senate, requires updating national building energy codes to be 30 percent below baseline energy code by 2010, 50 percent by 2015, and to achieve additional 5 percent reductions every three years through 2030. Comparing these targets to a call in Congress to build 100 new nuclear power plants to achieve energy independence and significant GHG emissions reductions, Architecture 2030's Mazria calculates that the energy savings achieved would eliminate the need for the plants, while achieving six times the emissions reductions of 100 nuclear plants at much less cost.

Peterson suggests that the next step in promoting efficiency will be to require building energy labeling, so that a building's energy performance is public knowledge.[34] Already, California has passed legislation mandating that any property sold must reveal its Energy Star rating.[35] The legislation requires nonresidential building owners or operators to disclose Energy Star ratings and energy use data from the previous year to potential buyers beginning in 2010.[36]

CITIES, SOCIAL JUSTICE, AND ENERGY EFFICIENCY

Several U.S. cities have implemented citywide energy efficiency programs. One such program in Babylon, New York—Long Island Green Homes—is open to all residents who want to make improvements to increase their home's energy efficiency without paying upfront costs. A benefit assessment is determined based on pre-improvement utility bills. After the improvements have been made, the costs are paid from the savings on the customer's utility bill.[37] A similar program has been highly successful in Hays, Kansas.

Cambridge, Massachusetts, has not yet had the same success in implementing utility-based funding. In 2008, Cambridge launched the Cambridge Energy Alliance—an initiative that was at the time unprecedented in both its scale—a goal of retrofitting at least half of all buildings in the city in five to seven years—and its funding model— its costs would be derived from the energy savings it produces. The Phase 1 goal of retrofitting half of the city's residential, commercial, and industrial buildings, would reduce the city's total greenhouse gas emissions by 10 percent by 2011, reduce its peak power load by 15 percent, and reduce CO_2 emissions by 150,000 tons a year. Consumers would realize $160 million in savings over ten years.

Here's how it was supposed to work. A nonprofit organization, the Cambridge Energy Alliance, was created to manage the program, starting with about $500,000 in seed money provided by two local foundations and other institutional investors. Working through the local utility, N-Star, the Alliance hired five energy service companies (ESCOs) to conduct efficiency audits, make recommendations for improvements and retrofits, and hire the contractors to complete the work.[38] The ESCOs are paid to do the audits, which are free to building owners, through a system recovery charge levied by the utility company. The model called for creating a privately funded revolving loan fund to offer residents and businesses low-interest loans that would be paid back through savings on utility bills. The goal was to raise $100 million to create the revolving loan fund.

But then the economy tanked. Deborah Donovan, the Alliance's executive director, explains that in the current economic environment potential backers don't want to make unsecured consumer loans. So, although the audits are still free, consumers have to secure their own financing for retrofits. With energy prices dropping and financing drying up, only a handful of residents are requesting audits, let alone investing in retrofits. The model was diminished further when the participating utility, N-Star, decided it was not willing to support the utility-bill payback plan. This decision was a real blow to the program as it addresses a major problem with energy efficiency programs— landlords who aren't interested in efficiency because their tenants pay utilities. Under a utility-bill based model, landlords have no up-front costs and the charge is on the utility bill. Property owners essentially get improvements that are covered through the savings on their tenants' utility bills. Renters benefit from lower utility bills.

So the Cambridge Energy Alliance is left with no carrots to motivate home and business owners to invest in efficiency retrofits. The other benefit offered by the Alliance is marketing. Donovan notes that there was a threefold increase in the number of audits requested from N-Star in the past year due to the Alliance's marketing of the program.[39] But now the audit requests are down as well, as customers aren't likely to request audits if they can't afford the follow-up. While the city decides how to allocate its federal energy efficiency dollars, the Alliance will have to develop a new financial model to attract residents and businesses to invest in efficiency upgrades.

To date, none of these programs incorporate a social justice component—focusing on creating access to these good jobs for the unemployed and low-skill, low-wage workers. Both Los Angeles and Milwaukee are attempting to make this link.

LOS ANGELES: CONNECTING CITYWIDE RETROFITTING TO JOBS FOR CITY RESIDENTS

For most people Los Angeles conjures up images of smog and cars, not sustainability. But that is changing fast. The city's ambitious 2007 GREEN LA plan aims to reduce greenhouse gas emissions by 35 percent below 1990 levels by 2030. LA's green building ordinance, passed on Earth Day, April 22, 2008, is also one of the nation's boldest, and it builds on the nation's largest green building program, discussed below. Most recently, the Los Angeles Green Retrofits Ordinance, passed in April 2009, commits the city to installing energy efficiency upgrades on all city-owned buildings larger than 7,500 square feet or built before 1978. The goal is to get them to LEED silver certification. And because of the commitment of Mayor Antonio Villaraigosa and the involvement of the Los Angeles Apollo Alliance in drafting the ordinance, it has a clear commitment to social justice in the form of prioritizing buildings in low-income communities for retrofitting and providing residents of these communities access to the jobs that will be created. The city also agreed to support local minority- and women-owned green business development as part of the initiative and to link retrofitting to purchasing local green products. Thus, this initiative represents a linking of sustainability not only with economic development but with social and economic justice goals as well.

The organization that convenes the Los Angeles Apollo Alliance, Strategic Concepts in Organizing and Policy Education (SCOPE), has been in existence since 1993, working to remove barriers to social and economic opportunities for poor and disenfranchised communities. SCOPE created several initiatives that have linked inner-city residents to training and jobs with advancement opportunity in the entertainment and health care industries before turning to green jobs. In many cities, social and economic justice organizations are viewed as a thorn in the side of elected officials. Not in LA; when SCOPE signed on as the Apollo convener in 2006, Mayor Villaraigosa, City Council President Eric Garcetti, and City Councilman Herb J. Wesson Jr. supported the organization and its ambition of creating a green economic and workforce development strategy. SCOPE worked on two fronts, drafting the efficiency ordinance and launching the Green Retrofit Workforce Initiative to prepare a cadre of workers once it was passed.

To support the worker training aspect of the initiative, the Regional Economic Development Institute at Los Angeles Trade Technical College organized the LA Infrastructure and Sustainable Jobs Collaborative. SCOPE, the City of Los Angeles, and other public, private, union, and community partners are involved in developing comprehensive training programs to connect low-income disadvantaged populations to livable-wage jobs in the energy utility and energy efficiency initiatives.[40] Depending on the sector, participants will be placed in union apprenticeship or community college training programs.

Like other cities, Los Angeles is cobbling together funds for its comprehensive energy efficiency initiative. Federal stimulus dollars will be used along with funds from the city's Department of Water and Power energy efficiency budget. Some of the additional funding for the efficiency initiative will be derived from a pool of $42.7 billion in state infrastructure bond funds passed by California voters in 2006.

Los Angeles Community College Build Green Program

In 2002, the Los Angeles Community College District (LACCD), one of the largest community college districts in the nation, began the nation's largest green building initiative. Voters approved Propositions A and AA, totaling $2.2 billion, in 2001 and 2003 to fund a major expansion and modernization of the city's nine community colleges. A third proposition, Measure J, passed in November 2008, adding $3.5 billion to the initiative. Under the District's sustainability policy, 90 new buildings must meet or exceed basic LEED certification (some of the buildings will meet higher levels) and emphasize elements particularly important to the geographical area, such as water-saving technologies and low-water, native-plant landscaping. A solar energy aspect of the program is intended to bring each of the campuses enough renewable energy to meet all of its electrical needs (about 1 megawatt per campus).[41] In the future, excess electric power will be converted to hydrogen to power fuel cells.[42] In this LA story, too, we see a linkage between sustainability, economic development, and education and training.

The educational goal of the program is to create a pool of LEED-certified architects, engineers, and contractors to expand green building throughout the LA region. LACCD is creating a sustainable development curriculum that includes classroom instruction and internships. Although this program is not fully developed, students currently participate in an internship program with placements in firms that provide products and services to LACCD under the Proposition A/AA Bond Program. LACCD asked businesses working under the program to provide internships for students. To date, more than 721 students from the nine colleges in the District have been placed in internships paying the Los Angeles County living wage of $11.25 per hour. Of these, 75 have been hired as permanent staff by local architecture, design, information technology, and engineering firms.[43]

By the end of 2010, 28 buildings will have been completed. The job creation impact of Green Build has been considerable. LACCD is creating thousands of construction jobs. An economic analysis of Measure J projects that the $3.5 billion bond measure alone will create close to 50,000 jobs in the region.[44]

LA's efficiency and green building programs illustrate how the sustainability, job creation, and social justice goals can be realized in tandem. What they haven't addressed is how to make it affordable for individual homeowners and businesses to invest in energy efficiency.

MILWAUKEE AND BEYOND: FINDING THE FUNDING FOR ENERGY EFFICIENCY

For energy efficiency to have a big impact on reducing greenhouse gas emissions, it has to be undertaken on a very wide scale. Even though consumers know they could save money in the long run by making their homes or businesses more energy-efficient, they are often unable to make an up-front investment that will take several years to pay off. Several cities are testing different financing models to overcome this obstacle, including Babylon and Cambridge, mentioned above. Milwaukee, with the assistance of the Center on Wisconsin Strategy (COWS), a University of Wisconsin–based "think and do" tank that supports economic development strategies that promote living wages, environmental sustainability, and strong communities, is starting a citywide efficiency program that attempts to create career pathways for the unemployed and low-skill workers.

COWS and the City of Milwaukee developed Milwaukee Energy Efficiency (Me2), which has managed to find work-arounds to some of the funding problems encountered in Cambridge. The original goal was to raise $5 million for a private capital fund to finance retrofits that would be paid back over ten years from the energy savings realized; this pilot would then be extended citywide with potentially hundreds of millions of dollars of efficiency opportunities. Consumers would pay nothing up front—payments would be made out of savings on the utility bill.[45] A pilot phase of the program focused on residential and commercial retrofits was to start in the fall of 2008.

COWS and the city worked for some time to initiate the pilot with Focus on Energy, a state program that provides efficiency services with utility money under Public Service Commission jurisdiction. Eventually, Focus on Energy launched its own pilot to investigate some aspects of Me2, including community-based marketing, but not the no-up-front-cash offer. The pilot will get started later in 2009 once the stimulus money makes it way to Milwaukee. Cities can use up to 20 percent of their energy efficiency block grants for revolving loan funds to finance retrofits and the Department of Energy supports city's using funds in this way. So, Me2 will have $1.6 million for the pilot. Eric Sundquist, a policy analyst at COWS working with the program, says the goal is that a successful pilot will allow them to raise other public and private funds for the revolving loan program.[46]

With unemployment high in Milwaukee and Wisconsin and more than 20 percent of the state's workers in poverty-wage jobs, COWS is hoping to place workers in living-wage jobs through Me2.[47] To that end, COWS is working with the state's technical college system to create "on ramps"—short-term remedial programs to prepare for entering training and apprenticeship programs in construction and related trades.

As in Cambridge, Milwaukee encountered some problems in initiating utility-based billing, despite some promising discussions with the local investor-owned utility, We Energies. The state's Public Service Commission, which oversees public utilities, has argued that it doesn't have sufficient authority to authorize the needed tariff, and it has proposed language to provide that authority. A bill is pending. In the meantime, the Me2 solution is to bill through the city's trash bill, secured by the user's property tax. The repayment obligation is attached to the property rather than the property owner (as in the Berkeley FIRST program discussed in chapter 3), eliminating any disincentive to retrofitting owners might have if they think they might relocate or move. This proved to violate a state statute against cities collecting installment payments on municipal services bills, but the legislature amended that statute in a bill facilitating stimulus-related programs. With this hurdle to the pilot overcome, Me2 is moving ahead both in Milwaukee and with a very similar program in nearby Racine.

With stimulus block grant funding in place, many more cities will be developing energy efficiency programs. Motivated by a 2009 Climate Action Plan that calls for reducing greenhouse gas emissions 80 percent below 1990 levels by 2050, Portland is about to launch a pilot energy efficiency project.[48] Like Milwaukee's program, it will allow consumers to pay back low-interest loans for improvements over a 20–30 year period, and so far it appears that it will be through their utility bills. The pilot will pay for home energy audits, weatherization, upgrading heating, air-conditioning and ventilation systems, and related undertakings. The $5 million to $10 million program will begin in one neighborhood, offering about $6,000 to each property owner for upgrades. The pilot will retrofit between 500 to 1,000 homes a year, depending on the cost. In addition to stimulus funding, the city is creating a new clean energy investment fund, which will receive funds from the Oregon Department of Energy.[49]

While the current recession has dampened demand for retrofits, ARRA funding should stimulate demand for energy efficiency programs. As cities gear up, they can learn from the problems encountered by other cities. For example, implementation of the projects in Cambridge and Milwaukee was delayed due to unforeseen legislative and institutional barriers to different methods of subsidizing the up-front costs of energy efficiency. Cities just getting started have much to learn from these early innovator programs.

CONNECTING EFFICIENCY AND GREEN BUILDING TO MANUFACTURING

If cities adopted strict green building codes, could they, along with energy efficiency initiatives, create enough demand to revitalize their manufacturing sectors? Can cities help spur the invention of new products? To answer these questions, we examine three regions that are attempting just that. In all three cases, the goal is to transform, or "green," a traditional manufacturing sector. In addition, we see leapfrogging strategies to the extent that completely new green products are being developed. Planners in the Syracuse, New York, region are working with university researchers to build on strengths in indoor environmental-quality systems manufacturing to supply the growing green building industry. In Pittsburgh, it is not city government but a nonprofit organization that is promoting the link between energy efficiency and jobs. The Green Building Alliance focuses on increasing awareness of green building practices among architects, developers, and construction companies. The ultimate goal, however, is to make sure the area's large building supply industry makes the transition to green products. In New York City, it is several nonprofit economic development groups that are leading green manufacturing initiatives.

PITTSBURGH REGION: THE GREEN BUILDING ALLIANCE

Even though it does not produce much of it these days, steel is what most people think of when Pittsburgh is mentioned. Few would guess that Pittsburgh ranks fifth among U.S. cities in the number of green buildings. Nearly 100 green building projects are completed or under way in the area. And it is not just new buildings—Pittsburgh has renovated 155 historic buildings to make them more efficient, four of which are certified green buildings. But all this green building and retrofitting is not the result of city policies or the vision of a mayor; it wasn't until 2007 that Pittsburgh passed an ordinance to provide incentives for green building.[50] And to date, Pittsburgh has not passed an ordinance requiring green certification through LEED or another rating system.[51] Nor has the city thought of connecting all its green building activity to an economic development strategy.

In a city leadership vacuum, the connection between green building and economic development is being made by a nonprofit organization, the Green Building Alliance (GBA), which began in 1993 as an informal coalition of professionals interested in green building. But it wasn't until executive director Rebecca Flora (now with the U.S. Green Building Council) came on board that the organization focused on green building as an economic development driver. Flora personally pitched green building to local developers and corporations. Gary Saulson, director of corporate real estate for PNC Financial Services Group, relates in the *New York Times* how Flora convinced him to make an operations center already under construction a LEED-certified building.[52] Over time, Flora and the GBA convinced other Pittsburgh area companies and developers that green building was cost effective.

A 2006 GBA study identified 1,800 building supply manufacturers in the region, with total employment of more than 68,000.[53] Flora's concern was that most of these companies were unaware of the sea change taking place in their industry.[54] If building products manufacturers are not retooling to make advanced products such as fiber-optic daylighting or pollution-removing systems, or making products from recycled material, she concluded, the United States could actually lose jobs as contractors look to European and Asian suppliers, which are already making the transition.

So Flora launched the GBA's Green Building Product Initiative in November 2006, a strategy to transform western Pennsylvania's building supply industry into a regional center for manufacturing green building products. Aware of the economic development opportunity, the Heinz Endowments granted the initiative $250,000 and the Ben Franklin Technology Development Authority, Pennsylvania's technology-based economic development program, provided another

$1 million.[55] One part of the initiative is the Pennsylvania Green Growth Partnership, formed by GBA and Philadelphia University to help building product manufacturers transition into green products. A research network associated with the partnership, which includes Carnegie Mellon, Drexel, Penn State, Pittsburgh, Temple, and Villanova universities, conducts research to support technological innovation and commercialization of new green products and production methods. The partnership hosts annual forums to connect university researchers to corporate sponsors to commercialize their products.[56]

Through the initiative, the GBA is offering grants to companies, university researchers, and partnerships of both to develop new green building products. Two rounds of grants, totaling $588,000, have been given out to ten projects. The projects represent a wide array of green building products. Recipients of grants include:

- Ductmate GreenSeam II to further develop a product to reduce duct leakage
- Tegrant Corporation and the University of Pittsburgh to test the performance of and production methods for insulated concrete forms
- Villanova University for developing a superlattice solar cell prototype
- Geothermal Energy Systems and Carnegie Mellon University for testing heating and cooling systems for a neighborhood of buildings
- Temple University for ReD, a type of window for large-scale commercial buildings made of a material that shifts from transparent to translucent to maximize light while reducing heat loss and solar heat gains.

In January 2009, a third round of grants was announced, totaling $240,000.[57] In addition to three proof-of-concept grants, the projects funded were:

- $100,000 for commercialization of plastic composites using renewable and recycled raw materials that achieve greater thermal insulation and lower embodied energy, to Bedford Reinforced Plastics and the University of Pittsburgh.
- $80,000 to develop an energy-efficient air-conditioning system that uses a refrigerant that produces no greenhouse gas emissions, to Thar Technologies and Carnegie Mellon University.

To the extent that these and other products prove marketable, the GBA will catalyze an expansion of the rapidly growing green building supply market in western Pennsylvania and throughout the state.

But Pittsburgh itself is not acting aggressively to incentivize green building or energy efficiency. A few small steps include a 2007 ordinance that allows the Pittsburgh Urban Redevelopment Authority (URA) to offer lower interest rates for projects that earn LEED certification on its urban development loan programs. The higher the LEED rating, the bigger the interest rate reduction (up to 2.5 percent). The loan program is part of the URA's Sustainability and Green Design Policy, which applies to its own office operations and to the development of large-scale mixed-use developments. And in November 2007, the City Council approved changes in the city's building code that offer sustainable development density bonuses. Developers of nonresidential projects that earn basic LEED certification can add 20 percent more floor area and 20 percent more height to their projects.[58] To date, Pittsburgh has not passed an ordinance requiring LEED for new construction or changed its building code requirements.

Pittsburgh is the largest city in western Pennsylvania, and no other cities in the western half of the state are undertaking efficiency initiatives or investing in green building, meaning that demand for green building products will have to come from outside the region. In truth, no matter how much green building it does, Pittsburgh isn't large enough to drive markets in green building supply. The city and local nonprofit groups can catalyze invention of new, greener products and technologies, but they need a larger market to expand the green building supply sector. Pittsburgh's geographic location makes it ideal to supply a national green building products market.

Syracuse, New York: Building on Indoor Environmental Quality

In contrast to Pittsburgh, elected officials and city and regional planners in the Syracuse area have focused for some time on green manufacturing as an area with growth potential. But city efforts to stimulate demand in green building have lagged behind the economic development strategy. Syracuse is pursuing a sectoral economic development strategy that supports research partnerships focused on new product development and attracting new companies. So this strategy has elements of both a transformative and a leapfrogging strategy, to the extent that completely new green products are being developed. The city has begun to move on the green building front, but here too, it is not clear how much demand can be stimulated in a region that is largely rural except for the center city of Syracuse. And the one development that could stimulate considerable demand for green products, a proposal for the world's largest green shopping mall, is plagued with fiscal and political problems. But if successful, Syracuse could demonstrate to other rust belt cities how green manufacturing could revitalize their economies.

Mayor Matthew Driscoll wants Syracuse to be the "green capital of the world." Creating a green economy may be a way to help the city stem the loss of manufacturing jobs and reduce the metropolitan area's 16 percent poverty rate. Working to its advantage are a strong economic base in higher education and a number of companies that could be suppliers to green building and retrofitting industries. The goal is to help these old-line companies transform themselves into an integrated 21st-century industry focused on "indoor environmental quality."

In 1996, the Metropolitan Development Association (MDA) of Syracuse and Central New York identified indoor environmental quality as one of seven sectors on which to focus its efforts. Average annual earnings in this sector locally are about $54,000 and usually include benefits, making these relatively well-paying jobs. To get started, the MDA tapped into state government programs to stimulate growth in lagging upstate regions. The first was a $15.9 million grant from the state's Strategically Targeted Academic Research (STAR) program for purchasing equipment or renovations of laboratories conducting research on indoor environmental quality. In 2002, the MDA received funds from the Centers of Excellence, a statewide network of centers created to stimulate economic development in declining upstate regions by supporting research centers in emerging technologies.[59] The centers are charged with facilitating joint industry-university research, technology transfer, and commercialization of products in defined sectors.[60] With an additional $22 million from the federal Environmental Protection Agency, the STAR Center became the Center of Excellence in Environmental Systems. And in 2004, the focus of the Center was expanded to include energy systems and became the Center of Excellence in Environmental and Energy Systems (Syracuse CoE).[61] MDA Director Rob Simpson notes that CoE is the top lab facility in the country for research on indoor environmental quality and only behind one in Denmark in the world.

The Syracuse CoE describes itself as a federation with more than 140 institutional and business members. Several large companies anchor the federation, such as Carrier Corporation, a leader in heating, air-conditioning, and ventilation systems. Although Carrier moved its two Syracuse manufacturing facilities, which employed 1,200 people, to Asia in 2003, it still employs 1,600 in research and development.[62] In 2006, Carrier started a research center, the Indoor Air Quality Key Competency Group, in Syracuse and also contributed $1.5 million to the Syracuse CoE to build and operate a Total Indoor Environmental Quality Laboratory.

Even with high levels of state support and key businesses on board, the MDA is fighting an uphill battle. A 2007 study by consulting firm Battelle revealed that the region is still losing jobs in the targeted sectors. Environmental services (green building and sustainable design, indoor environmental quality, renewable energy, and water quality) employed more than 10,000 people in central upstate New York in 2005, a decline of almost 28 percent since 2001, compared to a 5.6 percent decline nationally (this large loss is due to the Carrier plant closings in 2003). During the same period, employment in green building design declined 16 percent, to 2,500 workers. And Indoor Environmental Quality declined by 43 percent, to 2,400.[63] So, in addition to stemming employment loss, the CoE has to focus on catalyzing new start-up companies and attracting companies into the region.

CoE grants to several start-up companies in the region for product research and development have paid off. HAPcontrol (Syracuse) produces "bio-furniture" that does not release harmful gases, PhytoFilter Technologies (Saratoga Springs) is testing a plant-based system for removing volatile organic compounds from indoor air, and Isolation Systems (Tonawanda) is developing air purification and room air management systems. NuClimate Air Quality Systems in East Syracuse received a Syracuse CoE grant to test and build a prototype for its "Q" Air Terminal, a highly efficient heating, cooling, and ventilation unit for large public buildings such as schools and hospitals.

Several of these and other businesses funded by the CoE have or are seeking certification as eligible products under the LEED rating system, which offers points for commercial interiors that use products and furniture that have no or low emission of volatile organic compounds (VOCs). Other green product start-ups were developed through research at Cornell University, such as e2e Materials, which has an exclusive license to patent materials created with its natural fiber glue, made with a soy resin.[64] The company just developed a particleboard that has the same strength as the traditional product, but only one-third the weight. It is inherently flame-retardant, meaning that it doesn't require the addition of chemicals that release VOCs. Given that more states and cities will follow the lead of California and New York City in banning formaldehyde resin, the product should be in demand once it finds its way into more building materials. A second Cornell-initiated start-up, Novomer, received $6.6 million in venture-capital funding in 2007 for scaling up production of biodegradable plastic made with carbon dioxide that breaks down naturally in as little as six months and is price-competitive with traditional plastic.

While these start-ups offer encouragement that the strategy can work, it's a long-term process—it took Patrick Govang and a Cornell University professor 15 years to develop e2e's natural fiber glue. And there is stiff competition. Two other companies, Metabolix, in Cambridge, Massachusetts, and Minnesota-based NatureWorks, already produce biodegradable plastic, but Novomer hopes that by using a feedstock that is cheaper than the corn-based feedstocks these companies use, it will win market share.[65]

To build a cluster, Syracuse will have to attract a few big players, and to that end the MDA identified 340 U.S. and international companies with potential interest in locating in the area. The MDA and Syracuse CoE have assigned 90 partners (including every economic development agency in the county) to a "green team" that is contacting the companies on the prospect list. A recent catch is BITZER Scroll, a German manufacturer of energy-efficient air compressors for state-of-the-art air-conditioning systems that located near Syracuse in February 2008. Several state and local economic development organizations worked together to attract the company, which was considering sites throughout the world.[66] A skilled workforce and the region's strength in indoor environmental quality research were key factors in the location decision, as were business incentives including $1.4 million from Empire State Development and a $100,000 grant from the Syracuse CoE for a research and development project that will be conducted by faculty and students at Syracuse University. For its part, the company pledged to invest $30 million in its operation and to create 289 jobs over five years at an average annual salary of $60,000.

The MDA and CoE are increasing Syracuse's visibility in green sectors by hosting and attending national and international trade shows and conventions for various clean tech industries. But Syracuse is behind other cities in instituting climate change policies that could support the MDA's economic development efforts. The city didn't pass a green building ordinance until September 2007. And it is weak in that it only requires LEED silver certification, and only for major renovations or new construction of public buildings. On the plus side, the ordinance does include public schools, and Syracuse is just starting on a $927 million, ten-year renovation plan for 35 of the 42 buildings in the Syracuse City School District that will follow the requirements of LEED for Schools.[67]

Syracuse looks to two other developments to stimulate green product demand, the Near West Side Initiative and a controversial green entertainment complex, Destiny USA. The Near West Side initiative is redeveloping three census tracts that are among the poorest in the country. The goal is to transform the area into a green arts and technology corridor.[68]

The revitalization of the Near West Side is well under way. It started with two newcomers moving in: King and King Architects, a 140-year-old local firm, and public television station WCNY, which has broken ground on a $17.5 million building. The Syracuse CoE is building a new green headquarters on a brownfield site in the neighborhood. Syracuse University is also building in the area as part of a broader commitment to revitalizing downtown Syracuse.[69] Finally, Home Headquarters is using a $4.2 million grant from the Syracuse Neighborhood Initiative to retrofit and renovate an eight-block residential area in the Near West Side containing 147 properties.[70]

Although the city's green building ordinance doesn't stipulate it, the MDA is encouraging developers in the area to build to LEED gold standards and has provided some assistance in helping them comply. The Near West Side Initiative project could create more than 800 construction jobs and an additional 300 jobs in five green technology companies that will locate in the district, according to Marilyn Higgins, who chairs the Near West Side Initiative.[71]

Destiny is a proposed $20 billion green regional shopping and entertainment center that includes a $450 million, 1,342-room hotel and conference center, an aquarium, a golf course, and other amenities. It is an expansion of the existing Carousel Center shopping mall, the top tourist attraction in Syracuse. Originally proposed in three phases, it has gone through numerous revisions, the most recent being a proposal for a 1.5-million-square-foot complex that would meet LEED platinum standards and would be powered entirely by renewable energy. Project planners estimate it will create as many as 122,000 construction jobs at an average wage of $31,000 and 250,000 permanent jobs after construction.

But many question both its green credentials and its employment projections. For starters, Destiny is only accessible by car.[72] For many green buildings the additional energy used for cars to reach them exceeds the energy savings realized by about 30 percent.[73] Destiny developer Robert Congel defends the project's "greenness" by emphasizing that the Carousel Center sits on what was a highly polluted brownfield site. He points to support from Rick Fedrizzi, Syracuse native and president of the U.S. Green Building Council, to defend his position. And the U.S. Environmental Protection Agency describes Destiny as "the world's largest structure to be built from recycled industrial materials," referring to the more than 3,000 tons of coal ash that will be incorporated into sidewalks and other concrete elements. Congel says he plans to make Destiny a showcase for green products and to that end will create a green research and development center that he lightheartedly refers to as the "Rehabilitation Center for Petroleum Addiction."[74] Mayor Driscoll also defends the project, saying it, "will be a trigger to development elsewhere in the city" and would help fight sprawl.[75]

Even more controversial is the staggering amount of federal, state, and local subsidies Destiny has received. In addition to a 30-year exemption from city and county property taxes, state tax credits under the state Empire Zone and Brownfield Cleanup programs, and federal Empowerment Zone tax credits, Destiny also is receiving subsidy under a federal program created exclusively for its benefit. A corporate tax cut bill, the American Jobs Creation Act of 2004, authorized up to $2 billion of tax-exempt private "green bonds," a low-cost financing program that allows developers of brownfield sites to borrow billions of dollars at very low interest rates. Funding for the green bond program made its way into the 2004 National Energy Bill as a result of heavy lobbying by senators Hillary Clinton and Charles Schumer, Governor George Pataki, several congressional representatives, and Congel, who contributed heavily to lobbying for the legislation.[76] Only Destiny and three other shopping mall developments in the country fit the green bonds eligibility requirements.[77] Destiny is eligible to borrow up to $1.04 billion through the program. The bill passed, and in January 2006 Destiny became eligible for more than $1 billion in federal green bonds. A year later the Syracuse Industrial

Development Authority issued $323 million in bonds as part of a $540 million financing package for Destiny. Fedrizzi announced that the U.S. Green Building Council would purchase a $50,000 bond to demonstrate support for the project.[78]

Controversy also emerged over the question of whether Destiny's green expansion qualified for tax abatements granted when the Carousel Mall was developed. The state program provides state tax credits of 10 to 22 percent of cleanup costs and redevelopment of polluted brownfield sites, which would realize between $200 and $720 million in state-subsidized tax credits for Destiny.[79] In both cases, the New York Supreme Court ruled that Destiny was entitled to the tax benefits.[80] Citing novel issues regarding interpretation of the law, the State Department of Conservation is seeking to appeal the decision.

What would the region get for its investment? Congel claims Destiny will attract millions of tourists and generate $65 billion in net taxes over 30 years, in addition to the jobs. And Destiny managers claim the huge demand for energy from solar, fuel cells, biodiesel, and wind power created by the project would create large enough economies of scale for renewable energy that it would drive down prices. But it's not clear that even a project as large as Destiny could influence demand for green products or power. Thomas Leyden, a vice president with the solar development firm PowerLight Corporation (which has since been purchased by Sun Power), one of Destiny's potential energy partners, concluded, "It may be the biggest solar installation and renewables project in the world, but there's no way Destiny will move markets to that extent within a decade, or even move markets in any substantial way."[81] Another doubter is state senator John DeFrancisco, who points out that Congel is "legally bound to build only a fraction of the square footage of his plan" and told me that "Congel could reap extraordinary tax benefits without actually meeting his goals."[82] He notes that Phase One was supposed to be done six years ago and is still not enclosed. Given that the proposed mall addition has no tenants to date, DeFrancisco predicts that Destiny will probably never be built.[83]

In fact, Destiny officials announced in May 2009 that the first phase will be ready for occupancy in late July, although tenants still have not been announced. The second phase has been put on hold because of tight credit markets. Should Congel not obtain financing by August 2009, the Syracuse Industrial Development Agency can rescind the tax exemption.[84] It appears that Congel delivered on the promised green construction features, but to date the development has not created noticeable demand for green products.

So Syracuse has had some success with its green sectoral strategy. Several start-up companies are now in business, but their employment impact is small. NuClimate Air Quality Systems, for example, employs only five people and is unlikely to expand, as it subcontracts most of its work.[85] And some of the companies "claimed" as successes are really too far away to be considered part of the Syracuse region. Still, the region has the potential to capture more growth in indoor environmental quality by developing supply chains among clusters of firms. For example, e2e employs only seven people, but president Patrick Govang focuses less on the employment expansion possibilities of his company and more on its becoming part of a regional economic cluster that allows him to realize his triple bottom-line goals.[86] The key input to the glue is soy meal; to obtain it locally, Govang located the company on the property of Empire AgriFuel, a planned soybean and canola crushing and biodiesel production facility in Cortlandville.[87] Soy meal is a by-product of the extraction and crushing process used to obtain soy oil. Govang notes that the by-product of e2e's process could be used for animal feed. Govang is seeking assistance from the MDA in finding a local market for his by-product. His hope is that the MDA will facilitate a regional supply network among businesses in the cluster (see chapter 5, the Chicago Waste to Profit Network).[88] As to Destiny, it is not yet clear whether it is anything more than a giant shopping complex heavily subsidized by the public. The green features (use of recycled inputs, recycling of construction debris, low water usage, renewable energy, LEED rating) do set a standard for retail construction, which is important, but its merits with regard to the area have to be judged on its economic development stimulus impact.

New York City Green Manufacturing Initiative

New York City, by virtue of its density and extensive public transportation network, is already a highly energy-efficient city and Mayor Michael Bloomberg has undertaken several initiatives to further reduce greenhouse gas emissions. Local Law 86, passed in 2005, requires all municipal new construction and major renovation projects costing more than $2 million and all private construction that receives city funds to build to LEED silver certification as of January 2007. It also requires municipal capital projects of $12 million or more in value to be 20 to 30 percent lower in energy costs than a comparable traditional building. And PlaNYC, unveiled in April 2007, is widely acclaimed as one of the nation's most comprehensive plans for reducing a city's carbon footprint. The goal is to reduce the city's greenhouse gas emissions by 30 percent by adding new green housing, increasing green space and public transportation capacity, reducing air and water pollution, increasing recycling, and cleaning up contaminated land.[89] Further, PlaNYC commits the city to spending 10 percent of the city's annual energy budget on efficiency upgrades on municipal buildings ($81.2 million in 2007). And New York is undertaking additional efficiency initiatives under the Clinton Climate Initiative's Energy Efficiency program.[90]

The city estimates that Local Law 86 and PlaNYC initiatives could create 5,000 jobs in retrofitting and impact about $12 billion in construction and renovation through 2017. Missing, however, from PlaNYC and the city's capital program is a strategy to use the investment in green construction and operations to stimulate a green manufacturing sector. Helping local manufacturers meet the green product needs created by Local Law 86 and PlaNYC would maximize the job creation benefits of the public investment.

To bridge this gap, the city council created the Green Manufacturing Initiative to link green building to New York City green product suppliers and granted $75,000 to the New York Industrial Retention Network (NYIRN), a nonprofit economic development organization, and the New York City Apollo Alliance to lead the charge. NYIRN has been advocating for city policy to support manufacturing since 1997 and views it as an important economic driver in its own right, but also as part of an economic justice agenda, since 78 percent of manufacturing employees are people of color, 63 percent are immigrants, and 24 percent are high school dropouts.

NYIRN and the Industrial and Technology Assistance Corporation (ITAC), a nonprofit training and consulting organization, published two studies that revealed a large market for green products and identified 1,500 New York City manufacturers that make building and construction products. The studies called for stepping up publicity and marketing to connect manufacturers to local architects and developers, since many were unaware that local producers existed. As in Pittsburgh, the idea is to help existing companies transform themselves into green building products suppliers. The two groups developed a series of workshops and small tradeshows, Spec It Green, on topics ranging from financing to installing green materials. The Spec It Green events let architects and contractors know of local green building suppliers and promote collaboration among manufacturers. The eight Spec It Green events held so far have attracted over 1,000 participants. Examples of local purchasing that occurred as a result of the Spec It Green networking seminars include:

- Citigroup is now sourcing wall coverings/finishes that are formaldehyde-free from DFB, a manufacturer within walking distance of their new buildings in Queens.
- Bank of America buys IceStone countertops, made from 75 percent recycled glass, by a Brooklyn company.
- Bank of America's One Bryant Park building used wall coverings, arch woodwork, cork, and other products from NYC green suppliers.
- Manufacturers that participated in the Spec It Green program began to sell products and materials to each other.

The Green Manufacturing Initiative received an additional $200,000 over the following year for organizing these activities and developing a Web site, Made in NYC (www.madeinnyc.org). The directory at the Web site lists more than 750 New York City manufacturers making products that could assist in achieving LEED certification and indicates which ones are green with a green apple. The Web site gets about 2,000 hits a month, which NYIRN staff assume are predominantly from contractors and architects searching for locally produced supplies. NYIRN estimates that the city's green manufacturers have increased their sales at a minimum by $2 million as a result of the Green Manufacturing Initiative. Although this only translates into 38 new jobs, NYIRN executive director Adam Friedman estimates that local producers will generate millions more in sales through the long-term relationships that they have facilitated. Friedman points out the importance of the trade shows and tours of the building supply operations: "Architects and contractors want to meet the person running the operation. They want to know they will perform and deliver on time."[91]

Now that NYIRN has built interest within the manufacturing community in greening their operations and products, NYIRN is providing more in-depth technical assistance to help companies upgrade and reposition themselves to enter new markets. This year, NYIRN is organizing workshops for woodworkers to learn about the particularly vigorous requirements for using sustainably harvested woods and opportunities to test wood finishes and adhesives that do not emit harmful chemicals. Other Spec It Green programs provide information on writing product specifications and learning about the various environmental product certifications that now exist.

Through the Green Manufacturing Initiative, NYIRN has strengthened its network of professionals and experts involved in green industry. The Rochester Institute of Technology (RIT) has begun to play a larger role in providing technical assistance to New York City manufacturers. DFB, a Spec It Green participating company, enlisted the expertise of RIT in developing its formaldehyde-free material that is now used in its Sol-R-Shade product. Such resources are critical to manufacturing companies that are seeking out the environmental alternative in their products. For its part, Urban Agenda, the convener of the NYC Apollo Alliance, has reported on job openings and training needs in the area of energy efficiency and has organized the Green Collar Jobs Roundtable to develop strategies for scaling up green-collar job training.

As in Syracuse, those seeking to revitalize manufacturing are fighting an uphill battle. The Green Manufacturing Initiative, as part of NYIRN's broader efforts to maintain New York City's diminishing manufacturing industry, seems to be having some success in filling niche markets for green building products. As demand for products increases, some small firms will be able to expand, creating a small number of good, green jobs.

PUBLIC POLICY FOR CREATING AN
ENERGY-EFFICIENT ECONOMY

President Obama's stimulus package targets $26.6 billion to energy efficiency initiatives.[92] Most experts agree that this is just a down payment on what is needed to dramatically reduce energy consumption. Using the widely agreed-upon 12–15 jobs per million of spending estimate, the stimulus will create between 320,000 and 400,000 jobs. State and city funds will increase the total job creation effect. Although the numbers are difficult to estimate, energy efficiency and green building will also save existing and create new manufacturing jobs.

But energy efficiency and green building are more than job-creation strategies. The primary goal is to reduce the nation's energy consumption and increase energy security. While achieving these goals takes national policy and funding, a lot has to happen on the ground in cities for energy efficiency goals to be achieved. Many mayors are claiming that they are creating the greenest city in America, but few are actually taking the serious steps required. Given the newness of citywide energy efficiency planning, cities need technical assistance on planning and implementation. Good urban planning is the key to success. Planning matters when it comes to achieving both a more energy-efficient and a more just city. In the efficiency and green building arena, attention to the nuts-and-bolts planning of building codes and zoning is essential to improving energy efficiency.

Cities need technical assistance in planning energy efficiency programs. To that end, Living Cities, an organization that promotes integrative approaches to city planning, held a Recovery through Retrofitting boot camp in the summer of 2009.[93] Among the 16 city teams were Babylon, Chicago, and Milwaukee. The boot camp worked with cities on accelerating progress already made and expanding programs to a city scale. The program emphasized driving demand, financing, quality control, and management. More cities need to engage in similar programs to ensure that federal dollars flowing to cities for efficiency efforts are used wisely.[94]

A key planning challenge for cities is figuring out how to scale building efficiency efforts. Two barriers identified in a brainstorming report on Chicago's ambitious retrofitting program are that the value of investing in retrofits is not reflected in market prices of homes or buildings and that there is no simple process for delivering services.[95] As Kent Peterson mentioned above, a uniform efficiency scoring system for buildings needs to be established. The real estate community will have to support this effort. Babylon, Cambridge, Chicago, Los Angeles, Milwaukee, and other cities are experimenting with different strategies to simplify the process of assessing efficiency, recommending retrofits, doing and financing the work, and following up on effectiveness. As federal money begins flowing into cities for energy efficiency, we will learn which strategies allow cities to go to scale the fastest.

As to new buildings, passing even the strictest LEED ordinances is not enough. Cities need to adopt much stricter energy and building codes to make significant inroads in becoming more energy-efficient. But changing the building code requires a number of interconnected systemic changes in how city departments work. Green building law expert Shari Shapiro identifies several problems that, if not corrected, will reduce the impact of new energy codes:[96]

- lack of integration among agencies and codes (plumbing, electrical codes, etc.)
- no clear process for obtaining variances to statewide building codes
- lack of enforcement of current codes
- lack of green building expertise or certification among code staff
- higher standards of proof for approvals of green buildings than standard buildings
- conflicts with other laws (fire code, historical preservation)
- lack of performance and financial data and cost/benefit analyses on green systems and technologies

Building expertise in city governments on energy codes also extends to knowledge of green building products. Boston architect Erin Hoffer gives this example: "Let's say a local manufacturing company is willing to produce an innovative roof membrane for use in my project. As the architect for the project, my firm might have done its own testing and reference-checking to satisfy us that the new product will deliver superior function. But because it lacks a track record, building code officials might not be comfortable with approving the selection, even if my engineers sign off on it."[97] She can't choose the green product if it's not likely to be approved. So cities implementing LEED requirements and stricter energy and building codes need to make sure that code enforcement officials and other city staff learn about what will likely be an ever faster introduction of new green building products and materials. As we saw with the Green Building Alliance, developers, contractors, and architects also need to update their knowledge of new building products, technologies, and systems.

Zoning is an important aspect of a green manufacturing agenda. One of the biggest barriers to groups like NYIRN is that New York, like many cities, has been rezoning industrial land in favor of other uses, having long given up on manufacturing expansion. Over the past five years, New York City has rezoned close to 20 million square feet of industrial space. New York City was late in focusing on brownfields relative to other cities, and in addition, the state's tax incentives rewarded high capital investment in new building on brownfield properties, which encouraged rezoning. In contrast, Chicago has developed several programs to maintain manufacturing land, including cleaning up brownfield sites, creating planned manufacturing districts, and establishing industrial corridors.[98] Each city must make zoning decisions based on the total industrial land available relative to trends in regional manufacturing activity and employment. It only makes sense for cities that have a manufacturing base to build on to target green building supply.

We also see that cities can plan for who gets the jobs—specifically, creating opportunities for disadvantaged groups to become part of the green economy. Many cities (and states) will be introducing energy efficiency initiatives. In Los Angeles, the mayor as well as LAANE and other community organizations made sure that GREEN LA created living-wage jobs for disadvantaged residents. Climate change and sustainability goals were integrated into a broader progressive agenda. In contrast, the Cambridge Energy Alliance was a response by key foundation thinkers about a narrower question: how to overcome a key hurdle to businesses and homeowners in investing in making their buildings more efficient, namely financing. Both initiatives will create jobs, but in Los Angeles, the mechanisms are in place to make sure that the initiative provides an entry point for the city's disadvantaged youth and other work-needy people to good jobs with career advancement potential. Los Angeles and Milwaukee are coordinating their initiatives with community colleges and unions to provide the education and training these groups need, linking sustainability, economic development, and social justice goals.

THE LINK TO WORKFORCE DEVELOPMENT

The American Recovery and Reinvestment Act provides $750 million for worker training and placement in high-growth and emerging-industry sectors. The majority of the funding, $500 million, is targeted for job training and related activities that prepare workers for careers in energy efficiency and renewable energy, as defined in the Green Jobs Act.[99] The occupations associated with energy efficiency are well known—energy auditors, plumbers, electricians, carpenters, heating, ventilation, and air-conditioning installers and so on. The education and training for these occupations are well established. Some new occupations such as energy management are emerging, and some occupations are changing dramatically as new building-efficiency systems become more commonplace. Community colleges and other education and training providers are just getting started on revising and adding curriculum in these areas. As more programs are developed, we need to be careful of two things: making the training too narrow and not providing trainees with recognized credentials.

Community colleges don't have to start from scratch in creating programs for new green jobs. Lane Community College in Eugene, Oregon, has been offering training and certifications in energy efficiency and related occupations longer than any other college in the country. Lane started its associate degree program in Energy Management in 1980 with a grant from the National Science Foundation. The program focuses on understanding energy systems in buildings and analyzing and quantifying energy efficiency efforts in residential and commercial buildings.[100] Related programs have been added over the years (table 4.2).

Program director Roger Ebbage started the program and periodically changes the offerings to meet new demand. Anticipating that the nation's new focus on efficiency would create demand for a new occupation, sustainability coordinator, Ebbage developed a program in Resource Conservation Management. Those hired as coordinators will be responsible for reducing and managing the throughput of the waste stream, including food waste, human solid waste, water waste, and virtually everything that we throw away.

Students come from throughout the western part of the country because of the college's track record in these programs. About 75 percent of the students in the certificate programs already have a college degree and are working. Displaced workers make up most of the rest of the students. While the availability of such high-demand programs is good news for practitioners and highly skilled displaced workers, these enrollment patterns suggest it will be difficult for low-skill workers to compete for a limited number of slots.

Graduates of many short-term programs that community organizations are developing to serve low-income disadvantaged groups will find that they are competing with much more highly skilled workers. That is why hiring agreements like those in Los Angeles are so important to achieving "green jobs for all" goals. Part of the answer is making sure these programs connect to recognized apprenticeships and certifications so participants can compete for jobs with good wages and advancement potential.[101] In many occupations, the credentials are just being established.

TABLE 4.2. Lane Technical College Energy and Environment Programs

Program	Program Emphasis	Occupations of Graduates
Two-year Degree Programs		
Water Conservation Technician	Graduates evaluate water use patterns; develop, implement, maintain, and market conservation strategies.	Water efficiency technicians, specialists, or managers.
Energy Management	Graduates apply basic principles of physics to analyze and evaluate building energy systems.	Energy auditors; energy program coordinators; control system specialists
Renewable Energy Management	Graduates design and install photovoltaic domestic hot water systems. Preparation for state licensing for solar PV installation	Energy system designer, manager; renewable energy systems installer
Certificate Programs		
Energy Management	Graduates study building energy use, glazing, insulation, building envelope, heating/cooling, secondary HVAC, controls, central plant equipment, energy auditing, operation, and maintenance.	For practicing engineers, architects, facility, maintenance and energy managers
Building Operations	Graduates are certified in energy- and resource-efficient operation of building systems at two levels: Level I - Building System Maintenance; Level II - Equipment Troubleshooting and Maintenance	For practicing building operations and maintenance staff
Energy Auditor and Inspector	Graduates learn principles of energy auditing and weatherization inspection, including the building shell, air leakage, insulation, windows and doors, heating and cooling systems, indoor air quality, lighting and appliances, and water heating.	Energy auditor or inspector
Sustainable Building Advisor	Graduates can apply energy conservation principles to building design, development, and construction.	For practicing architects, engineers and other building industry professionals

An interesting program developed by Los Angeles Community College District and specifically related to the city's and college's efficiency initiatives is the California Advanced Lighting Curriculum Training Program. The curriculum was developed through a partnership of investor-owned utilities, municipal utilities, the California Lighting Technology Center, the California Energy Commission, the California Community College system, the International Brotherhood of Electrical Workers, the National Electrical Contractors Association, and manufacturers of advanced, high-efficiency lighting and lighting controls systems. The goal is to make significant gains in conserving energy used for lighting in California through widespread deployment of advanced, high-efficiency lighting and control systems. The program will educate, train, and certify electrical contractors, electricians, and other interested parties in the best practices and the most effective techniques to market, sell, finance, commission, install, and maintain advanced lighting control systems. It will also stimulate demand for the systems, which are produced in the state. So far, the course has been offered to community college professors (to train the trainers of the future) and contractors in a series of tuition-free workshops.[102]

Professional organizations and states should lead in developing certifications for new jobs in energy efficiency. The New York State Energy Research and Development Authority (NYSERDA) has developed a certification for energy auditors and permits only certified auditors to work in the various statewide energy efficiency and alternative energy programs. Auditors are required to be certified as Building Analysts or Multifamily Building Analysts, certifications of the Building Performance Institute (BPI), a nationally recognized training, certification, accreditation, and quality-assurance program.[103] BPI certifies individuals and accredits organizations that do auditing, efficient building operation, and efficient heating system design. BPI has been working with the state's community colleges to develop curriculum and certification tests in these occupations. NYSERDA is also creating standards for new occupations such as certified auditor, weatherization specialist, and others. To increase access to these growing occupations, NYSERDA pays between 75 and 100 percent of the cost for students, depending on income.

While it is important for community college programs to focus on occupations, it is important to keep in mind that inner-city contractors are often sole-proprietor businesses, so they are really entrepreneurs as much as they are plumbers, electricians, etc. Some cities are experiencing a shortage of efficiency-related businesses (e.g., insulation suppliers and installers), so a comprehensive workforce strategy must go beyond placing employees with contractors to training contractors to become entrepreneurs.

Community colleges throughout the country are developing programs to meet the demand for the various energy efficiency occupations. The often-repeated pattern is for colleges to independently create their own curriculum when model curricula are available that can be adapted as needed to meet local needs. The other potential problem is creating too many programs. Lane Tech serves a national audience, mainly because few programs of their type have existed elsewhere. As other community colleges develop programs, state higher education boards and regional workforce investment boards should ensure that we don't oversupply training.

We know a lot about what it takes to make community college programs accessible to disadvantaged groups. The broader challenge is to make sure that new green jobs targeted to minorities and other disadvantaged populations are good jobs. There is a checkered history of some unions in the building trades welcoming additional public funding but resisting expanding their ranks in order to protect established members whose employment is often cyclical. The devil is in the details. Many community developers of affordable housing, whose broad social justice goals are consistent with those of the labor movement, have chosen to go nonunion because there are not sufficient funds to employ community people at union pay scales.

The blue-green-environmental justice alliances of recent years have begun to create some breakthroughs. In San Jose, the city government and the South Bay Labor Council have worked together to assure that all new green jobs are union jobs, and a healthy share of them have gone to people from disadvantaged groups. Los Angeles and other cities are showing us how unions can open their apprenticeships to groups previously left out. And we have seen programs in new areas jointly developed by unions and community colleges to meet demand in new areas of the green economy. As in other areas addressed in this book, there is potentially a powerful synergy between environmental, economic development, and social justice goals.

5

Is There Treasure in Our Trash?

A S A NATION, WE ARE NOT MAKING MUCH HEADWAY ON REDUCING the amount of waste we produce. And more than two-thirds of the materials we use are burned or dumped in landfills.[1] We generated 251 million tons of garbage in 2006, about 4.6 pounds per person per day, according to the Environmental Protection Agency. This is more than any other country—about twice as much as Japan and European Union countries.[2] About 55 percent of that garbage went to landfills.[3] The Container Recycling Institute estimates that 144 billion drink containers were sent to landfills or littered in 2005 alone. This astonishing total comprises approximately 54 billion aluminum cans, 52 billion plastic bottles and jugs, 30 billion glass bottles, and 10 billion pouches, cartons, and drink boxes.[4] Likewise, the majority of our fastest-growing waste stream—electronics waste, such as old computers, copiers, cell phones, televisions, VCRs, stereos, and fax machines—also ends up in landfills or in storage until we figure out what to do with them.

American industry generates another 7.6 billion tons of solid waste annually.[5] Love Canal and the large-scale pollution of Woburn, Massachusetts, recounted in the book and film *A Civil Action* remind us that it wasn't all that long ago that industrial waste, frequently hazardous, was most often stored in surface lagoons, discharged into our waterways, or was incinerated, polluting our water and air. Federal and state regulation starting in the mid-1970s addressed the hazardous waste problem,[6] but did nothing to reduce the volume going to landfills.

Among their other problems, landfills are the single largest man-made source of methane gas in the United States, accounting for almost 25 percent of U.S. methane emissions.[7] As a greenhouse gas, methane is 23 times more effective at trapping heat in the atmosphere than CO_2.[8] Although landfills are a relatively small source of CO_2, the Institute for Local Self-Reliance maintains that conventional greenhouse gas inventories underestimate how much greenhouse gas landfills generate, because they do not account for the amount of resource extraction that is needed to re-create goods that should have been either banned or recycled but end up in landfills. And waste disposal is becoming an increasingly large budget item for cities, because many are running out of landfill space. Almost half of California counties will exhaust their disposal capacity in the next 15 years. And it takes 10–15 years to design and permit a landfill, so other solutions are needed.

Some have suggested that we must not only reduce the waste going to landfills as a necessary environmental end in itself, we also need to view waste as economic opportunity. There are signs that the next generation of waste reduction and waste-processing technologies could be sources of economic development and jobs. There are some heartening technical innovations, most not yet taken to scale, but it remains to be demonstrated that most of the jobs are good jobs. However, this is a journey we need to take, whether for environmental or economic benefits, and in some cases for both.

We need to reduce the amount of waste we produce, and then make better use of the waste that we do generate. Waste can be recycled; it can also be turned into energy. Reducing waste can be achieved in a number of ways, from making producers more responsible for disposing of their products to banning certain types of waste. Japan and several European countries have laws that require manufacturers and importers to collect and recycle their own appliances and e-waste. In the United States we rely on cities and states to create such requirements. Nine states have producer responsibility laws that require free collection of e-waste, and another 13 states are considering such laws.[9] These laws put the responsibility of waste disposal on the producer and are designed to motivate producers to produce less packaging and to produce products that are more easily disassembled for recycling. Recently, cities have begun to act as well, by either banning products or providing financial disincentives for single-use products. San Francisco was the first city in the country to impose a 17-cent tax on disposable supermarket checkout bags to reduce its 50-million-bag-

The Fate of U.S. Recycled Material

While we may feel virtuous about separating materials for recycling, the unfortunate fate of too much of this material is that it is processed, often by children, in developing countries using unsafe, inhumane, and environmentally unsound recycling methods. Trash is in fact a global business, with transnational trade in secondary materials reaching 135 million tons in 2004.[a] Between 50 and 80 percent of electronic equipment collected for recycling in the United States is exported to China and other Southeast Asian countries.[b] China is also the largest importer of U.S. scrap metal and recycled paper and plastic.[c]

The 1989 Basel Convention on the Control of Transboundary Movements of Hazardous Wastes and their Disposal was a comprehensive attempt to address the issue of hazardous waste disposal internationally. The United States is not one of the 160 countries that has signed the agreement, which defines what substances are considered hazardous and sets the framework for their proper international shipment and handling procedures. Following a 2002 Basel Action Network (BAN) report on unsafe processing of waste in developing countries, the Chinese government issued regulations to control e-waste imports, including a ban on the import of toxic e-waste, and mandatory registration of all scrap importers. But loopholes mean that a considerable amount still makes it into China. In early 2007, the U.S. Environmental Protection Agency (EPA) banned export of electronics with cathode-ray tubes to other countries for recycling due to their high lead content. Other types of e-waste were not included, despite the fact that they contain equally dangerous materials. A 2008 U.S. Governmental Accountability Office (GAO) investigative report discovered that lax enforcement of the EPA regulations means that many American companies export e-waste to developing countries where it is disassembled by hand, often in backyards, without benefit of safety regulations, let alone safety equipment or training in handling highly toxic materials that can cause neurological damages, kidney disease, cancer, and other health problems. The GAO recommended that the EPA enforce its existing regulations and create new ones that prohibit the recycling of other hazardous e-waste in the Third World.[d]

Plastics are frequently processed overseas as well. Jim Puckett, the coordinator of BAN, visited several Chinese recycling factories where ordinary consumer plastics, such as plastic soda bottles, were broken down using plastic chippers and open-air plastic melters. He found

(*continued*)

workers, including children, standing over indoor melters breathing petroleum fumes without safety goggles or protective masks—for $1.50 a day. Further, much of the recycled plastic that ends up in China is contaminated and thus ends up being sent to landfills there. The reason is that recycling companies are required by law to buy plastic 3–7 even though there is no market for them. So they are often mixed in with plastic 1 and 2 and sold to overseas factories. Just a small amount of 3–7 plastic ruins an entire batch of number 1 plastic, so it is most likely just thrown out once it reaches its destination.[e]

[a]This waste is mostly metal (93 million tons), followed by paper and cardboard (35 million tons), plastics (4 million tons), textiles (1 million tons), and other miscellaneous materials (see Lacoste and Chalmin, 2007: 18).

[b]The U.S. government literally doesn't know how much e-waste is being exported, but the 2002 Basel Action Network (BAN) report estimated it to be between 50 and 80 percent, and, with no alternative official statistics, this figure has become the standard among researchers of the topic (see Pucket and Smith, 2002). India, Pakistan, Bangladesh, Malaysia, Russia, Croatia, and Nigeria also receive U.S. e-waste and other recycling for processing.

[c]Royte, 2005.

[d]GAO, 2008.

[e]Ibid.

a-year habit and other cities and states are following. Other cities are banning bottled water at some events and locations.

While reducing the waste stream is important, recycling has an even bigger impact in saving energy and reducing greenhouse gas emissions. But with a national recycling rate of 32.5 percent, we have lots of room for improvement. The EPA reports that 82 million tons of municipal solid waste were recycled in 2006, saving the energy equivalent of more than 10 billion gallons of gasoline. Californians Against Waste, a waste reduction and recycling advocacy organization, reports that in California alone the amount of recycling in 2007:

- reduced atmospheric CO_2 emissions by over 2 million tons;
- reduced other toxic air pollutants by over 1 million tons;
- reduced water pollution by almost 5,000 tons; and
- saved enough energy to power roughly 400,000 homes for one year.

A key question is whether recycling also creates jobs. The Institute for Self-Reliance and other advocates calculate that recycling creates about ten times more jobs for the same amount of trash as landfilling. But these numbers depend on including manufacturers that use recycled products as part of a "recycling and reuse" industry—a questionable claim, since an industry is not defined by the inputs it uses but by what it produces. In these estimates, industries such as paperboard, iron and steel, and plastic products count as part of the "industry" (and together account for more than half of recycling/remanufacturing economic activity).[10] Yet if we only use standard industry indicators, we underestimate employment. The most commonly used source for calculating employment in a given industry, the North American Industry Classification System (NAICS), only counts the collection aspect of the industry as the category Waste Management and Remediation Services.[11]

An equally important question is whether recycling creates good jobs. Scholar-activist David Pellow at the University of Minnesota finds a "vast disparity between the promise of recycling and the reality of recycling work."[12] He and his colleagues have examined recycling programs in several cities and found that even in community-based recycling facilities committed to the triple bottom-line goals of equity, ecology, and economy, the jobs are dirty, dangerous, and low-paying, and rarely provide health benefits. In most cities, community-based recyclers rely on dumpster divers ("alley entrepreneurs") to provide the feedstock that is sorted manually ("appropriate technology") in year-round outdoor lots. Such workers are self-described as otherwise unemployable, and they have little chance for advancement.[13] Is it possible that renewed efforts at recycling and reuse also offer possibilities for creating decent jobs? A few cities are now explicitly treating waste reduction, recycling, reuse, and reprocessing as economic development strategies. Perhaps the markets, technology, and approach to waste have changed enough to create real economic development and job creation opportunities.

CITIES SOLVING THE PROBLEM: FROM WASTE DISPOSAL TO WASTE RECOVERY

Several cities are undertaking strategies that represent a paradigm shift from waste disposal to waste recovery. These efforts, like most forms of urban development, create conflicts among different interests—cities trying to operate programs efficiently, the private sector pursuing profits, and social justice organizations seeking to link economic and environmental goals.[14] This chapter examines these conflicts as they play out in initiatives in three cities. We start with New York City, which has witnessed many conflicts over where and how garbage should be managed. Currently, several groups in the Bronx are promoting transformational strategies that recycle and reuse construction and demolition waste to create economic development opportunities for the urban poor. If history is our guide, their chances of success seem slim. In *Garbage Wars*, David Pellow chronicles the transformation of recycling from a community social justice and environmental movement to "a commodity-based, profit-driven competitive industry in which large private firms using public dollars are squeezing the life out of smaller nonprofit and family-owned recyclers."[15] And as mentioned above, Pellow's research finds that whether on a small or large scale, recycling typically does not create good jobs. But what if we could replace the dirty, dangerous recycling jobs with new technologies? A new wave of technologies offers the opportunity to transform garbage into compost and energy. Los Angeles, a city with one of the nation's highest recycling rates, is embarking on a leapfrogging strategy of using one or more of these new technologies to dispose of garbage, and explicitly links the strategy with job creation for poor urban residents. In this case, the new technologies are at the heart of a conflict. Some environmentalists argue that the technologies are untested at large scale and could be every bit as polluting as earlier technologies. And the job creation potential is limited. This case reveals that the best waste solutions may not have much job creation potential, but may have merits in their own right.

And what if we could find a way to transform how industry generates and uses waste? A waste reduction strategy that first received much attention in the 1990s is the eco-industrial park. The idea is to create an industrial ecosystem by colocating businesses that use each others' waste streams as inputs. Cities benefit from reduced industrial waste and job creation. The eco-industrial park that cities in Europe and the United States have tried to replicate is in Kalundborg, Denmark; it is home to a power plant, an oil refinery, a fish farm, a pharmaceutical company, a wallboard manufacturer, and others. Among the synergies is the steam from the power plant being used for heat by the city, the fish farm, and the wallboard manufacturer. The power plant's fly ash is used by a cement company, and its gypsum is an input for the wallboard manufacturer. These synergies developed over many years, and all were initiated by the companies themselves to reduce the costs of doing business.[16] Attempts to replicate this closed-loop system as a sustainable economic development strategy have met with little success in the United States or elsewhere.[17]

A virtual version that doesn't require colocation, the waste-to-profit network, may prove easier to implement. A leading example is Chicago's Waste to Profit Network, which is linking businesses profitability to waste reduction by helping businesses identify by-products and waste from one business that can be used as inputs by another. And the network has led to the creation of two new businesses in just one year of operation.

The cases presented in this chapter reveal that trash is very political. It's not simply a matter of finding the most technically and environmentally appropriate way of getting rid of it and counting up the jobs. The debate over what is technically and environmentally sustainable is itself political, and so is the decision-making process. Why? Because different technical paths produce different winners and losers.

Recycling: An Economic Development Strategy for the Bronx?

Omar Freilla, a 34-year-old Bronx-born environmental activist, received the first Rockefeller Foundation Jane Jacobs medal for New Ideas and Activism. He was listed as one of "the new school of activists most likely to change New York City" by *City Limits* magazine in 2000. He's featured in *The 11th Hour*, a documentary on global warming produced by Leonardo DiCaprio, as well as in the *New York Times*, several environmental magazines and Web sites, and even *Men's Vogue*.[18] Why all the attention? Because he sees trash as an economic development opportunity for low-income communities like the South Bronx. He created an organization called Green Worker Cooperatives to put the idea into action.

The main reason trash might be an economic development opportunity in the Bronx is that there's a lot of it. The Bronx receives about a third of the 12,000 tons of garbage New York City produces daily, all by truck. This includes half of the city's construction and demolition debris, about 2,035 tons a day. The waste comes into the Bronx by truck to 16 transfer stations and 26 recycling facilities, where it is sorted and processed before being shipped out, again by truck, to landfills or incinerators. It creates a lot of pollution—Bronx County is one of ten counties in the state that exceed current federal air quality standards for fine-particle pollution. And it's no coincidence that the Bronx has one of the highest rates of childhood asthma in the country.

A recent NYU study connected the borough's high incidence of asthma to truck traffic.[19] It's one of the poorest communities in the country, too; census data reveal that median estimated household income in the South Bronx was about $21,100 in 2006, compared with $31,494 for the Bronx overall, $46,500 for the rest of the city, and $48,500 nationally. The unemployment rate, at 14 percent, is twice as high as in the rest of the city.

Under the leadership of Organization of Waterfront Neighborhoods (OWN), several environmental justice organizations have been advocating for years to reduce the amount of trash that gets processed in the Bronx. They argue that a more just approach to waste handling would be for each New York's five boroughs to assume a fair share of the responsibility of waste handling, rather than concentrating it in poor minority neighborhoods. More recently, however, new organizations such as Freilla's Green Worker Cooperative see some treasure in the trash. The core idea of the cooperative is to help people start small recycling and reuse businesses. Part of the cooperative's mission is to build public awareness of the strategy, and part is to create more cooperatives. The first one, ReBuilders Source, opened in April 2008. Freilla donated his $100,000 Jane Jacobs prize money and raised $900,000 more from the state, foundations, and church groups to fund the first few years of operation. Run by four neighborhood residents recruited by Freilla, it sells discarded building and construction materials headed for the trash stream.

ReBuilders Source seemed like an ideal link between social justice, the environment, employment, and economic development, so I paid a visit. When I finally found it on a side street in an industrial area of the South Bronx close to the Bruckner Expressway, I didn't know quite what to expect "a worker-owned Home Depot for used stuff," Freilla's frequently used description of the venture, to look like. It's essentially an 18,000-square-foot garage with different areas designated for doors, kitchen cabinets, bags of mulch and paving stones, boxes of toilets, used paint, and even rows of theater seats. All of the merchandise would have become part of the waste stream. Each of the cooperative's four workers earns a salary of $35,000 with benefits. While I was impressed with this small-scale urban development success story, I had to ask: Where does it lead? To what extent can this type of business catalyze the green revitalization of inner-city neighborhoods? And how might it compete with other more capitalized businesses that may eventually see treasure in the same trash?

Freilla's isn't the first rebuild-and-reuse center in the country, or even in New York City. Tri-City Community Economic Development Corporation (Tri-CED) in Alameda County, California, is a minority-run nonprofit organization that operates a buyback recycling center. The center has contributed more than $3 million to the local economy since it started in 1986. Tri-CED employs 25–30 youths, mostly from the surrounding community. About 250 youths have benefited from training and employment at Tri-CED. And in New York's borough of Queens, Astoria Residents Reclaiming Our World (ARROW), a nonprofit environmental organization, opened the city's first building materials reuse center in 2003. The business was started with funding from Waste-Free NYC, a waste prevention program of the city council through the Department of Sanitation. It is modeled after successful reuse centers in Berkeley and Portland, Oregon, that have been around for decades.[20] And NY Wa$teMatch, an online brokerage initiative through which businesses can buy, sell, and trade recyclables and reusables online, has diverted over 25,000 tons of reusable materials from the waste stream since 1998 and has more than 6,000 registered users. Director MaryEllen Etienne reports that the most frequently handled materials are office furniture, building materials, fixtures and fittings, packaging, and containers.

While these successful operations are reusing waste, even Freilla agrees that cooperative reuse centers are only one small part of a broader economic development strategy for reducing and reusing waste. It would be hard to imagine enough of them developing to put much of a dent in the multimillion-ton piles of recyclable goods and materials produced in most big cities. Reuse centers also illustrate the nagging question of whether green jobs are necessarily good jobs. A proposal to take the idea to a much larger scale in the form of an "eco-industrial park"* is igniting serious debate in the Bronx over this question. Enter another Bronx-born superstar, Majora Carter.

Carter was honored with a MacArthur Foundation "genius" award in 2005 and has since become a green media phenomenon, with features on her and the organization she started, Sustainable South Bronx, in *Newsweek*, *New York*, *Ebony*, *Essence*, *USA Today*, the *New York Times*,

---

*Technically, an eco-industrial park is defined by colocated businesses that use each other's by-products as inputs to their production processes. A more accurate term for the Hunts Point proposal is an industrial recycling park.

and many more.[21] Carter left the Bronx in 1984 thinking she would never return. But she did return in the late 1990s, and when she saw the high unemployment, waste dumps, pollution from heavy truck traffic, lack of green space, and climbing asthma rates, she decided to take action. By 2001 she organized Sustainable South Bronx, determined to mobilize the community to connect greening the environment, improving the area's quality of life, and creating green jobs.

Sustainable South Bronx quickly built an impressive track record. Carter raised funds from city and other sources to develop Hunts Point Riverside Park, the first new Bronx park in 60 years. The organization created green job training opportunities by establishing the Bronx Environmental Stewardship Training program, which offers job training and certification in a dozen different types of ecological restoration jobs, targeting ex-offenders and people trying to get off public assistance. And Sustainable South Bronx became one of at least 20 groups participating in the Organization of Waterfront Neighborhoods (OWN), the umbrella group that opposes locating additional waste transfer stations to handle Manhattan's trash in low-income minority neighborhoods.[22]

When the city's Department of Corrections announced a plan to acquire a 28-acre parcel, Oak Point, in the Hunts Point neighborhood through eminent domain to build a jail, Sustainable South Bronx didn't waste any time responding.[23] Already mobilized by the city's efforts to locate additional waste transfer stations in the area, Sustainable South Bronx responded with a different vision for the parcel—an "eco-industrial park" that would use New York City's recyclables as inputs to products such as railroad ties and paper towels. The jail proposal presented an opportunity and an urgency to promote the eco-industrial park as an alternative that could help the city meet the recycling and waste diversion goals of its 2006 solid waste management plan.[24]

Sustainable South Bronx and the Green Worker Cooperative received funding from the federal Empowerment Zone for a feasibility study of relocating a scrap metal recycling facility owned by Hugo Neu, the city's recycling contractor, to the Oak Point site. The study estimated that if other businesses located there, the park could create about 335 jobs and generate at least $90 million in gross revenue annually.[25] The study estimated that the businesses in the park would use about 30 million pounds of the city's plastics per year and recycle approximately 1,900 tons of construction and demolition waste per day. Further, the study calculates that the park would eliminate 21,000 truck trips per year in hauling away the construction and demolition waste out of the city (the study did not estimate the amount of increased truck traffic that would result from bringing waste to the site). Although no firm commitments were made, the report suggests the park could attract:

- *a construction and demolition (C&D) debris recycling facility* that would generate $27 million in annual revenues from fees and material sales and would replace about 36,500 outgoing truck trips from the Bronx annually with shipments by barge and rail (material would still be trucked in, however). It would create 80 jobs.
- *a plastics product manufacturer* that would produce railroad ties, pallets, and marine timber using mixed plastic waste. The facility would create a market for the city's annual recycling stream of 31.5 million pounds of mixed plastics and also use some of the 245 million pounds of unrecycled plastics in the city's refuse stream. At full production the company projects annual revenues of $46 million and employment of 55 people.
- *a paper converting facility* that would convert large rolls of 100 percent recycled paper into toilet tissue and paper towels. The company anticipates $11 million in annual revenue based on its supply contracts with the federal government and major commercial and institutional buyers. It would create 50 jobs.
- *a wood salvage and remilling operation* that would use salvaged antique timber to sell to lumber mills and timber-framing companies. The salvaged wood would be used by highway construction and bridge-refurbishing contractors or be remilled for fine carpentry applications. Already a successful company located in Brooklyn, the company expects to produce $4.5 million in revenues operating at full capacity in the Bronx and create 20 jobs.
- *a glass powder manufacturing facility* that would use about 77,870 tons of glass from the city's recycling program to make a powder that replaces up to 40 percent of the Portland cement used in making concrete masonry blocks and ready-mix concrete. The company is prepared to invest and/or borrow $14 million to build its facility and estimates it will create $4.4 million in annual revenue. The green building material would help reduce a shortage in the supply of Portland cement and create 30 jobs.

The city's Department of Corrections ruled out the Oak Point site for the jail in March 2008,[26] but questions about the desirability of the Sustainable South Bronx proposal have emerged from within the environmental justice community. After 15 years of advocating and even taking the city to court over the siting of transfer stations in poor neighborhoods, the environmental justice groups finally won a key concession when Mayor Bloomberg sponsored, and the city council approved, a waste management plan that would hold each borough responsible for processing its own garbage and would rely more on barge than truck transfer.[27] Representatives of several OWN-affiliated organizations were stunned that Sustainable South Bronx was advocating for an "eco-industrial park" that they saw as a glorified transfer station right after this victory, arguing that it would double the amount of construction and demolition debris trucked into the Bronx (since the proposed C & D facility would not replace others already located there). Sustainable South Bronx policy director Rob Crauderueff argues that the trash would be trucked into the Bronx anyway and now will not go through residential streets, and that it would be shipped out by barge or rail.[28] Freilla suggests that critics are more bothered by the type of jobs that would be created, noting that the critics, like the public in general, are biased against manufacturing and blue-collar jobs. He notes that in the course of conducting the feasibility study, he and others talked to potential occupants of the park about pay, benefits, and working conditions and were satisfied that they would create good jobs. "Everyone wants to do solar—solar is sexy. But recycling is looked at with disdain," Freilla told me.[29]

The debate has raised the issue of what constitutes a green job. In voicing opposition to the plan, 16th Congressional District Representative José Serrano (D-NY), a longtime supporter of cleaning up pollution and of Sustainable South Bronx, focused on job quality: "I can't support the idea of putting a lot of fanfare behind a project where some people will be sorting other people's garbage." He continued, "It's for all intents and purposes a waste transfer station. It's not okay because it's being called a recycling plant, rather than what it is, a waste transfer station."[30] Others point out that pulling steel rods out of concrete for $10 an hour with no union to advocate for better working conditions is not exactly their vision of a green job. Marian Feinberg, environmental health coordinator at For a Better Bronx, asked, "Is this the best we can do in terms of jobs?" Her concern is over the amount of truck traffic that the facility would generate. Feinberg has been a critic of recycling jobs, noting the poor working conditions and pay and the lack of regulatory enforcement.[31]

Representative Serrano and others argue they would be more supportive of recycling jobs if they were unionized to offer workers decent pay and working conditions. He is initiating a project to build a commercial pier and new refrigeration facility at the bulkhead of the Fulton Fish Market in Hunts Point, which would generate close to 200 union unloading and processing jobs with a starting wage of $17 per hour. Further, Serrano and others have an alternative vision of green jobs that involves electric vehicles. One hope was that the Bronx or nearby city would be chosen as the location for an assembly plant by British Smith Electric Vehicles. Although Kansas City, Missouri, was selected as the location in March 2009, some are positioning the Bronx for economic activities related to electric vehicles such as installing charging stations and maintenance facilities. This conflict over recyling in the South Bronx reveals important questions about what constitutes a green job.

The Sustainable South Bronx model was criticized as too low-tech—a glorified transfer station. However, there are other strategies for reducing waste and pollution that rely on new advanced technologies. These strategies produce better jobs, but it seems not many of them. And in some cases, their environmental sustainability is in question. Los Angeles is testing an approach that uses high-tech solutions that involve transforming waste into energy to solve the landfill pollution problem and maybe create better jobs.

LOS ANGELES: RENEW LA

Los Angeles has one of the highest rates of recycling in the country, 62 percent, though several other California cities, such as San Francisco have even higher rates.[32] The city's goal is to reuse or recycle more than 90 percent of all solid waste by 2025. A plan is in motion to go beyond recycling to turning waste into usable products such as biofuels, compost, and fertilizer. This plan is linked to an economic development strategy to expand the waste recovery industry named RENEW LA (Recovering Energy, Natural Resources and Economic Benefit from Waste for Los Angeles), which calls for seven new waste processing and conversion facilities to be built in the city. These facilities will convert trash into energy, fertilizer, and other reusable by-products. Los

Angeles plans on building seven facilities in the city that will employ anaerobic digestion and other technologies to reprocess waste. As the plan's architect, council member Greig Smith, sees it, reprocessing waste is a source of economic development and social justice as well as an environmental initiative. Each of the seven facilities will be located in the city and will employ work-needy residents. But RENEW LA has to be understood in the broader context of recycling in LA.

Recycling and Jobs

Los Angeles achieved its high rate of recycling thanks to the 1989 California Integrated Waste Management Act (AB939), which required all cities and towns to reduce the amount of solid waste they sent to landfills by 25 percent by 1995 and by 50 percent by 2000. The legislation was motivated by the high cost of landfilling waste and difficulty in siting new facilities. It seems to have worked; with recycling rates in the 50 percent range, California cities lead the nation. AB939 also created jobs—waste disposal creates about 2.5 total jobs for every additional 1,000 tons of waste disposed, while the same amount of waste diverted creates about 4.7 jobs.[33] California's recycling industry employs about 85,000 and generates close to $4 billion in wages, salaries, and benefits (plus another 179,000 indirect jobs). The state's 5,300 recycling and reuse establishments generate more than $10 billion in sales and contribute more than $21 billion in total output impacts (value added in manufacturing using recycled inputs). These figures are more than double what they would have been if the legislation had not been passed.[34] Other states are following California's lead in exploring the economic development potential of recycling and reuse.[35]

To stimulate more sales and job growth, the California Integrated Waste Management Board created the Recycling Market Development Zones program, which provides below-market loans, streamlined issuing of permits, and technical and marketing assistance to new or existing businesses that use recycled inputs. All of Los Angeles was designated a zone in 1993, and the program was renewed for another ten years in 2003. Since 1993, $11.5 million has been distributed to 15 manufacturing or recycling companies, which have diverted more than 140,000 tons of material from landfills.[36]

Enrique C. Zaldivar, director of the Los Angeles Bureau of Sanitation, tells me that his department is entrepreneurial in finding markets for more recycled materials. The Department of Sanitation pushed for recycling plastic bags as a way to create a market for them. Despite state legislation that requires grocery stores to provide on-site recycling of plastic bags, most people don't take their bags back for recycling or reuse. Less than 5 percent of the 19 billion single-use plastic bags distributed annually in the state are recycled. The result is that there is not a sufficient supply to create much of a market for their reuse. In 2006, the department decided the only way to create a market for plastic bags was to ensure a steady supply by adding them to the recyclable items that are picked up at curbside. The idea was that residents would be more likely to recycle bags if they could put them in blue bins rather than returning them to a grocery store. Zaldivar relates that when he presented the idea to waste pickup subcontractors they balked because they would have to purchase new baling and sorting equipment to recycle bags, including an optical sorting machine that reads the density of an object.[37] Ongoing pressure from the city finally convinced them to purchase the equipment. At first, the subcontractors were left with bales of plastic bags with no buyers. But once end users realized that they had a steady supply available, markets started opening up. In the course of two years, the city has found a market for all of its plastic bags from producers of plastic lumber, grocery buckets, and similar products.

Zaldivar used the same strategy in leading Los Angeles to be the first large city in the country to recycle polystyrene (e.g., foam beverage cups and plates). As with the plastic bags, he had to find recyclers willing to take it. He contacted Timbron in Stockton, California, a company that makes interior crown and base moldings from recycled polystyrene. Timbron, as it happened, was looking for suppliers. "We were seeking each other out at the same time," Zaldivar notes. Once this end user was identified, the city's collection of polystyrene began in the summer of 2007. The department began a public education campaign to let people know that they could recycle additional items and printed new stickers for bins (coat hangers were added at the same time).

Some environmental groups oppose adding both plastic bags and polystyrene to the recycling stream, arguing that both products should be banned instead. Another problem with relying on recycling rather than eliminating the waste product is that recyclables often get contaminated and cannot be recycled. In Los Angeles, 30 percent or more of the polystyrene from blue bins is too contaminated to use and ends up in landfills. Department of Sanitation staff work with the material recovery facilities to evaluate the recovery rates for plastic bags and polystyrene food packaging in the curbside blue bin program. More data are needed before the city can assess whether these programs will increase diversion and reduce litter.[38] In July 2008, the Los Angeles City Council, led by three Council Committees (Ad Hoc River, Energy and Environment, and RENEW LA), unanimously approved a new city policy banning all polystyrene food packaging from city facilities (e.g., parks, airports, community centers, street events, convention centers, libraries) by July 2009. The policy also addressed the issue of plastic-bag litter by adopting a citywide policy to ban the use of plastic bags at all supermarkets and retail establishments by January 1, 2010, if a (state) fee has not been established by that date. Along with the ban, the city would impose a point of sale fee on all other single-use bags.

Lupe Vela, policy director for the Ad Hoc Committee on the Los Angeles River, has been involved in getting this motion on the city council agenda. She notes that many "drivers" converged for this historic vote: the growing zero-waste movement, the Clean Water Act mandates for the local waterways, the city's 70 percent diversion by 2015 goal, and the city's many sustainable initiatives. As a side note, the ban on city facilities will allow the city to test alternative products that complement its recycling program and to flex its purchasing power to increase the demand for these products.

While Los Angeles continues to promote recycling and source reduction, it is also moving ahead by increasing its diversion rate through conversion technologies. The city's goal is to divert 70 percent of waste from landfills by 2020. Councilman Smith argues that California cities will not be able to achieve the 70 percent diversion rate without using conversion technologies and developed RENEW LA to achieve this goal.

RENEW LA and the Debate over Conversion Technologies

The ideas behind RENEW LA began to take shape in 2005. Councilman Greig Smith, the architect of the strategy and longtime recycling advocate, started investigating technologies for reprocessing waste as a way to reach the city's diversion targets. Based on this analysis, he developed RENEW LA's strategy for building seven conversion technology (CT) facilities for turning trash into heat, energy, or compost. The strategy calls for building one CT facility in each of the city's six refuse collection districts. In addition, RENEW LA aims to promote social justice and expand the economy by creating jobs in reprocessing and remanufacturing recycled goods into new products.

RENEW LA marks a paradigm shift from waste disposal to waste recovery. It will also require significant investment; depending on the technology, a facility could cost between $50 million and half a billion dollars to build. But with landfill tipping fees (the price per ton for receiving waste) at $40–$60 per ton and rising fast as facilities close, the tipping fees for the new conversion technologies, which range from $50 to $100 per ton, begin to make sense—particularly if they generate energy.[39] The city's Internal Technology Development Fund, which generates about $3.5 million per year, will pay for part of the new facilities. The fund's income comes from a tax imposed on all trash dumped at the city's Sunshine Canyon landfill. The fee is $1.50 per ton and will soon increase to $3.00. The city will have to issue bonds once a conversion facility is selected and approved.

RENEW LA does not yet specify which conversion technology will be built. The Sanitation District and Smith's office are conducting an in-depth study to determine which technologies to employ. To collect information, Councilman Smith led a group comprised of elected officials and environmental advocates critical of some of the technologies on a world tour to see them in practice in July 2008. The group toured gasification, plasma arc, anaerobic digestion, and ArrowBio facilities in Europe, Japan, and Canada. They also met with officials from green parties in several European countries that have embraced high-heat incineration technology.[40] The decision of which technology to be used will be based on meeting state requirements of AB939 as diversion, environmental acceptance and worthiness of the technology, potential for energy production (Smith notes that the energy value is a critical factor, as it can drive the processing cost down by $10–$20 per ton),[41] whether an investment in a technology requiring a long-term waste input stream will stall efforts to reduce waste at the point of generation, cost, and community acceptance on where it would be located.

Conversion technologies group into thermal or biological processes. Anaerobic digestion is a biological process—it breaks down organic material into liquid, methane (diluted natural gas), and solids. The liquid is treated and piped into the sewer system. Methane can be cleaned, transferred to an on-site cogeneration plant, and converted into electricity and heat.[42] The solid is a product called digestate, which can be made into compost.[43] Anaerobic digestion is commonly used in Europe, and a few facilities are cropping up in Canada and the United States.[44] Another biological process is ArrowBio, which uses water to separate inorganic and organic waste, recovering the recyclable component of the stream and producing a synthetic diesel fuel. There have been several demonstration plants over the past 15 years, and a full-scale plant is operating in Israel (included on the Los Angeles group's tour). Biological processes are generally considered environmentally sound. The California Integrated Waste Management Board is inclined to consider anaerobic digestion as acceptable diversion under AB939, but this is not explicitly stated in the statute. Proponents argue that anaerobic digestion facilities are cheaper to build and that the diluted natural gas they produce comes from organic feedstock, making it less toxic than that produced in thermal technologies and thus requiring less cleaning. A bill to increase the diversion requirement and explicitly qualify anaerobic digestion is ready, but not yet introduced.

Plasma arc is a thermal technology. Currently, thermal technologies are not considered diversion under AB939, because they are classified as incineration. This point is at the core of the controversy surrounding them. Thermal technologies extract heat value and turn it into energy. In incineration, this happens directly. Plasma arc is a type of thermal technology that creates an intermediary process in which the waste stream is heated to such a high point that it melts, producing syngas as a by-product that is cleaned and converted to electrical/steam and/or liquid fuels/chemicals. The inorganic materials in the waste stream produce a rocklike by-product that can be used to produce other materials such as floor and roof tiles, insulation, and landscaping blocks, or used in road aggregate material.[45] Supporters define the end of the process as the production of the gas, which would certainly make plasma arc cleaner than incineration.

Many environmentalists argue that the combustion of the gas has to be counted as part of the process, making plasma arc and other thermal technologies as polluting as incineration. In response, Louis Circeo, director of plasma research at Georgia Tech's Institute for Research, points to his research showing that syngas from plasma arc produces 1,419 tons of CO_2 per MW, compared to 1,672 for oil and 2,249 for coal. Only electricity from natural gas, at 1,135 tons of CO_2 per MW, is cleaner. Circeo's research suggests plasma arc gas could be the nation's largest single source of renewable energy.[46] Plasma arc plants supply their own energy and sell the rest back to the grid.

For example, the syngas produced in a plasma arc facility scheduled to break ground in early 2009 in Port Lucie County, Florida, would have operated on about a third of the power it generated, and the rest will have been sold to a nearby Tropicana juice processing plant as steam to power its turbines.[47] But plans to sell the steam to Tropicana fell through and local protests organized by the Palm Beach County Environmental Coalition and technical problems have put the project on hold.

As Smith learned from the tour, and protesters in Florida have realized, all of the technical problems of plasma arc have not been worked out. And there have been no cost evaluations, which the city would want to have before committing to a very expensive way to convert trash into fuel. In fact, Los Angeles County rejected a pitch by GeoPlasma, the company seeking to locate a plasma arc facility in Port Lucie County, due to insufficient performance data and financial details.

Another concern is that thermal technologies could hinder efforts to reduce waste. The argument is that once a city has invested a half-billion dollars in a plasma arc facility that requires a steady stream of garbage, elected officials may not be motivated to adopt policies to dramatically reduce the waste stream. Scott Smithline, director of Legal and Regulatory Affairs at Californians Against Waste, argues that cities have to pass ordinances on reducing the waste stream at the same time they adopt conversion technologies rather than seeing them as incompatible strategies.[48] That may be happening already. As much as RENEW LA is criticized for its "end of the pipeline" focus, Smith supports the motions to ban plastic bags and polystyrene.

Both anaerobic digestion and thermal technologies produce energy, and either would count in terms of helping the city meet its renewable portfolio standard (explained in chapter 3). Los Angeles is one of a few cities with an RPS, which is usually a national or state policy. It requires the city to purchase 20 percent of its electricity from renewable sources by 2017, and the Department of Water and Power (LADWP) is trying to accelerate that goal to 2010.[49] Smith suggests that the city could meet one-third of the RPS requirement through gasification.

Even if the technical problems and cost concerns could be resolved for a particular technology, the question of community acceptance is likely to make siting a facility difficult. Vela points out that in the 1990s there was considerable opposition to siting recycling buyback centers in neighborhoods, let alone a waste-processing facility. Although she notes that the proposals being considered have very attractive buildings and grounds, many residents are still concerned about pollution, truck traffic, and odors. Los Angeles has a history of placing polluting land uses in low-income communities, so there is a lot of justified apprehension about accepting any kind of waste treatment facility. Smithline points out that the history of poor siting choices extends to the entire state, which has mobilized considerable opposition to any waste-processing facility. He notes that California has not sited a composting facility in almost 20 years, despite their qualifying as a priority recycling practice in the legislation. Smith is aware of the siting problem and says it is a factor being considered in the selection process.

Finally, it is not clear that the job claims of RENEW LA will be realized. The plan predicts that conversion technologies will create thousands of jobs for Los Angeles residents. This is only true if temporary construction employment is factored in. Plasma arc facilities typically employ about 40 people, and anaerobic digesters even fewer. There are some additional jobs for sorters, but probably no more than six to ten per facility.

CHICAGO: WASTE TO PROFIT NETWORK

Although Chicago's recycling program has not been one of the nation's most successful, the city government is attempting to reduce the amount of garbage it sends to landfills as a way of reducing CO_2 emissions and pollution.[50] An interesting waste reduction strategy the city recently launched is the Chicago Waste to Profit Network, which helps companies figure out how to transform the waste of one company into a production input for another. The double benefit here is that the city meets its waste reduction goals while helping businesses become more profitable by reducing their waste collection costs and/or reducing the costs of inputs.[51] The economic development link is strengthening the city's large manufacturing sector of 13,000 firms. And the potential extends beyond manufacturing; already the city of Chicago is saving money through the network.

The idea for starting such a network in Chicago was percolating on several fronts. Staff at the city's Department of Environment were looking for looking for a proven strategy for developing eco-industrial activities in the Chicago region. Coincidentally, the Chicago

Manufacturing Center (CMC) had begun collaborating with the U.S. Business Council for Sustainable Development to create a business by-product synergy network on the order of the National Industrial Symbiosis Programme (NISP) in the U.K., a network of more than 10,000 companies (discussed later in this chapter).

Through city leadership, investment to start a network was provided through the regional Environmental Protection Agency, Illinois Department of Commerce and Economic Opportunity Recycling Expansion and Modernization Program, and the National Institute of Standards and Technology's Manufacturing Extension Partnership. In October 2006, Mayor Richard M. Daley officially launched the Waste to Profit Network.[52] It started with 26 companies and seven City of Chicago departments, and in just 12 months expanded to over 100 businesses that were exploring possible by-product synergies. In its first year, the network exceeded its goal of diverting 20,000 tons of waste destined for landfills. In addition to tons of waste being diverted, the network realized $4.5 million in cost savings and new revenue creation and reduced CO_2 emissions by almost 50,000 tons.[53]

At the first meetings, members sign a confidentiality agreement and agree to share their inputs and outputs in order to identify possible synergies. Once the network is under way, participants form working groups based on particular by-product streams. An organics group, for example, explores how to use food and biodegradable wastes to make alternative fuels and compost, while a chemicals group examines uses for hazardous waste. As the network facilitators, CMC staff collect data on firm inputs and outputs, analyze the profitability of potential synergies, chronicle stories of successful exchanges, calculate cost savings, and record job creation and/or retention so that companies understand the value of the network.[54]

To date, 45 synergies are under way. Most exchanges are not released publicly in order to maintain confidentiality. One company that has benefited from the network is Curb Appeal Materials. Co-owner Michael Hill is enthusiastic about what the network has done for his business. Hill started out in Dupont's carpet reclamation program searching for technologies that could use carpet as a raw material. Despite Dupont's investment in several promising technologies, Hill concluded that "the recycling industry is broken." He describes an industry that is very fragmented, with many layers of brokers, and in which most companies have only been in business for a few years. As a result, many businesses that could use recycled products as inputs have concerns about a steady stream of inputs being available. Hill estimates that only 10 percent of the plastic that makes its way to a recycling bin actually gets recycled into new products. Most of it ends up in landfills or is incinerated. The most likely destination for recycled plastic is China. A U.S. recycling broker pays about 10 cents a pound for it and sells it to another broker, who typically is in China or Taiwan. This broker pays children 25 cents a day to sort the plastic so that it can be reused in the production of toys and other plastic consumer goods.[55] U.S. labor is too expensive to make sorting recycled plastic competitive with virgin plastic.

So most of the plastic juice or milk jugs we recycle, if they aren't incinerated, travel to China and end up back in the United States in some form of plastic product (see text box on pp. 118–19). In a sense, it's a closed-loop system, but not a very efficient one. And most people don't think of supporting child labor when they recycle.

Rather than being part of this value chain, Hill decided to focus on creating markets for recycled products in the United States. He found a partner and started Curb Appeal Materials—a company that produces car stops for parking lots, highway sound walls, picnic tables, outdoor furniture, and rubber playground mulch out of recycled materials.[56] By participating in the Chicago Waste to Profit Network, Curb Appeal Materials found local suppliers of waste plastic. City government is using its purchasing power to help this new business establish itself. The Chicago Department of Transportation signed a purchase agreement for the car stops. This locally supplied product costs the same and will outlast the cement car stops the department had been using. Hill provides a benefit to the city by using the plastics collected from residents at its Household Chemicals and Computer Recycling Facility in the form of nonsalvageable keyboards, monitors, printers, and cell phones as inputs.

But breaking into new markets is not easy. It took Hill two years to get the highway sound walls approved by the Illinois Department of Transportation. The plastic walls would replace a concrete product. But because the state had never tested the new product, they had to establish testing procedures first. Once the product was approved, Network staff helped Hill get recognized as a legitimate bidder. Hill signed the company's first contract with the Illinois Tollway in March 2008 for sound walls that used 150,000 pounds of recycled plastic. Like the car stops, the plastic sound walls will outlast the concrete walls typically used. Hill estimates that if Illinois switched entirely to plastic sound walls, it would use one million pounds of plastic per mile. In 2008 alone, Illinois will add 12 to 14 miles of sound wall—that's 12–14 million pounds of the state's waste reused. And the recycled plastic will replace cement, the manufacturing of which is one of the largest industrial emitters of greenhouse gases.

Another Waste to Profit member has found a local supplier for the company's products through the network. Like Hill, the company's founder, Garrett Obluck, started the business out of frustration with not being able to find green products. In 2002, he started InnerGlow Surfaces to make countertops and tiles (Gilasi) from recycled glass.[57] Obluck met a representative from Manufactured Glass Products at his first Waste to Profit Network meeting and learned that his company had been landfilling most of its glass scraps due to the heat coating, which prevents them from being recycled. Now the company sends the glass to InnerGlow Surfaces as an input for its countertops and no longer has to pay to get rid of it. InnerGlow Surfaces employs eleven people.

Start-up costs for waste-to-profit networks are low. It cost about $500,000 to start Chicago's network, which was provided by the city, the State of Illinois Recycling Expansion Modernization (REM) program, the U.S. EPA, and the Manufacturing Extension Partnership.[58] Participating companies pay a fee of $5,000 to join, which covers about 30 percent of the annual budget. A free community network membership is available for small companies, which allows them to participate in one meeting a year.

In just one year the city has met its waste diversion goals, created cost savings and new revenue for local businesses, and reduced CO_2 emissions. The low start-up costs and visible results suggest waste-to-profit networks can work in many cities.

The U.S. Business Council for Sustainable Development is the primary driver of by-product synergy networks in the United States. The Council provides technical assistance to networks for the first year, which means that cities and states do not have to re-create the program on their own. Andy Mangan, executive director of the Council, has been facilitating waste-to-profit networks since the mid-1990s.[59] He finds that companies are increasingly motivated to participate in networks to reduce carbon emissions but above all to cut costs. Still, he notes: "One of the biggest difficulties is getting people to consider doing something different. But once they see the possibilities for reducing costs, they get on board very quickly." Mangan says the first meeting starts out a bit awkwardly but typically ends up with participants discovering at least a dozen by-product exchanges.[60] As more networks develop, more is learned about which types of exchanges will lead to success.[61]

Waste-to-profit networks have broad replicability and are being established by a few other U.S. cities and one state. Like Chicago, many of them receive technical assistance from the U.S. Business Council for Sustainable Development. Ohio is about to become the first state with a by-product synergy network.[62] A key partner is the Center for Resilience at Ohio State University, where researchers developed Eco-Flow, a tool that calculates the environmental and economic impacts of possible by-product synergies so companies can determine which synergies to pursue. Joseph Fiksel, codirector of the center, notes that the problem the software addresses is the difficulty companies have in forming networks and figuring out synergies that cut across different industries.[63] The program's analysis of synergies among 15 companies in a Kansas City network determined that their collective waste disposal costs of $55 million could plausibly be reduced to less than $40 million. The program will become available to other networks as they form.

A BRITISH MODEL

In the U.K., 10,000 companies are participating in networks through the National Industrial Symbiosis Programme (NISP). Peter Laybourn, director of NISP, started the network at a regional level in 2002 after hearing a presentation on industrial symbiosis given by Andy Mangan. Rather than using the corporate business model of the United States, Laybourn was able to obtain additional government funding available from an £8 per ton tax, increasing annually by £8 per ton, on waste sent to landfills that Britain imposed on municipalities and businesses to meet the goals of the European Union's landfill directive. The directive sets targets for member states to reduce biodegradable waste sent to landfills).[64]

The 2008 funding for NISP is £5.025 million, which is supplemented with funds from regional development authorities.[65] Documented benefits from the nine English regions of the U.K., with a total of £17.75 million in funding, include:[66]

- Diverting 3.4 million tons of business waste from landfills
- Generating £123 million in sales revenues for member businesses

- Reducing carbon emissions by 4.4 million tons
- Saving companies more than £104 million
- Creating and saving 1,710 jobs
- Attracting more than £110 million in private investment in reprocessing and recycling facilities
- Eliminating 342,000 tons of hazardous waste
- Eliminating need for use of 5.9 million tons of virgin material
- Saving more than 9.2 million tons of potable water

From April 2005 to December 2007, network firms reported creating 706 jobs and saving 1,004 jobs as a result of by-product synergies. Dave Berrill, director of the Birmingham NISP, notes that once businesses find synergies they start looking for other ways to reduce the environmental impact of their operations.[67] Among the synergies established through the U.K. program is John Braada Limited, which supplies a national supermarket chain with all of its tomatoes by using the waste heat of a nitrogen producer. The company is now pursuing other opportunities to source waste heat from NISP members in several U.K. locations to produce other vegetables. Another participant, British Coal, discovered that 40 percent of its waste was reusable, and reusing it allowed the company to divert 10,000 tons of waste from landfills annually.

Two layers of policy directives underpin the National Industrial Symbiosis Programme, allowing it to have a much broader impact in a very short time frame (see figure 5.1).

In contrast to this publicly funded model, all of the by-product networks in the United States are public-private partnerships. The U.S. Business Council for Sustainable Development helps cities identify city, state, and federal funding for starting up, but the networks rely on membership fees for ongoing support. Mangan notes that businesses take it quite seriously when they are paying to participate. Under this model, he notes, businesses view the network as a business proposition rather than a government program. Further, Mangan points out that the NISP model leaves programs vulnerable to changes in government funding priorities, noting that there is ongoing discussion on redistributing the landfill tax funds to other programs, which would leave NISP no choice but to pay membership fees. The evidence is clear: the policy-driven model builds business participation much faster. There is no reason to believe that businesses wouldn't pay to continue participating in a program that saves them money should public funding be reduced.

European Union

EU Landfill Directive (1999)

sets targets for member states to reduce biodegradable waste sent to landfill to 75% of the

1995 level by 2010, 50% of the 1995 level by 2013, and 35% of the 1995 level by 2020.

↓

Great Britain

responded with *Waste Strategy 2000*

which set recycling or composting requirements for local authorities: 25% by 2005, 30%

by 2010, and 33% by 2015, with fines for noncompliance. Also established a

Landfill Tax

(administered by national Department for Environment, Food and Rural Affairs)

Tax increases by £8.00 per year and is currently £28.00 per ton.

↓

Department for Environment, Food and Rural Affairs

created the

Business Resource Efficiency and Waste (BREW) Programme

using landfill tax revenues.

↓

National Industrial Symbiosis Programme

uses BREW and regional funding to establish industrial symbiosis networks in all

nine regions of the country.

FIGURE 5.1 Policy Chain for Waste Product Synergy in Great Britain.

ASSESSING THE IMPACT

The cities discussed in this chapter illustrate very different types of economic development activity emerging from waste reduction. Chicago's Waste to Profit Network achieves three goals: reducing the waste stream that goes to landfills, increasing business profitability, and spurring the development of new businesses. It has great expansion and replication potential. The network illustrates an aspect of profitability that is often ignored. We often talk about labor productivity, but little about materials efficiency—the amount of energy and materials it takes to produce a given output. As waste disposal becomes more expensive, businesses will find that industrial symbiosis is increasingly important to profitability. However, even though some replication initiatives are moving forward, the United States is moving too slowly on this important strategy for waste reduction and business profitability.

In the Bronx, a small reuse sector is emerging and is linked to a broader environmental and economic justice agenda. RENEW LA clearly links reducing solid waste and increasing recycling with a job creation agenda that targets work-needy people in poor neighborhoods. The actual job numbers, however, are small in reuse centers, and it seems doubtful that Los Angeles or the Bronx will generate many jobs through waste reprocessing. Regardless of its job creation potential, waste diversion is an important goal for cities seeking to reduce landfill pollution and reduce greenhouse gas emissions and may be profitable for businesses in other ways.

Even with volatility in the markets for particular recycled goods, recycling needs to be part of every city's sustainability agenda. Another goal should be to linking sustainability to economic justice. I contrast Boston and San Francisco to illustrate a low-road and a high-road approach to sustainability and economic justice through recycling.

With a recycling rate of about 15 percent, Boston lags many cities. Boston's recycling is picked up by KTI Recycling, a $686 million company that is the nation's 32nd-largest waste handler (top two in the Northeast where the company is concentrated). KTI's drivers are represented by the Teamsters union and paid decent wages with benefits, but its sorters—those who process the recycled material—are nonunion. Sorters are currently paid $8.00 an hour to undertake this dirty and dangerous work, despite the fact that Boston has a living-wage ordinance that requires vendors contracting with the city to pay a wage sufficient to support a family of four above the poverty level, currently $12.79 an hour. The reason for the gap is that in 2003, Mayor Thomas Menino approved a waiver from paying the living wage on the grounds that doing so would create a hardship for the company. When granted in 2003, the waiver allowed KTI to pay sorters $6.75 per hour instead of the then living wage of $10.54 per hour (neighboring Cambridge and Somerville also have living-wage ordinances and also granted waivers). Workers describe conditions such as unheated buildings, inadequate safety equipment, violations of overtime pay requirements, inability to use sick days without a doctor's note, short breaks, and an overpriced health care plan.[68] At the time, KTI's parent company, Casella Waste, Inc., had strong earnings and the total compensation packages of its COO and CEO were between $1 and $1.7 million. Yet they argued that the company could not afford the $116,000 annually it would have cost to pay sorters the prevailing wage.[69]

A unionization drive by the United Food and Commercial Workers failed, but the public scrutiny of working conditions it created forced the company to increase sorter wages to $8.00 per hour and to provide protective gear for grinding glass. Pay is therefore still below the prevailing wages and working conditions have only improved modestly. Despite the fact that Boston has a fairly strong labor movement and one that supported Mayor Menino, at this writing the mayor has refused to reconsider the waiver. The Teamsters are said to be mounting a renewed effort to change his mind.

San Francisco has a recycling rate of 72 percent, partly the result of a public education campaign by the local recycling company Recology. When Recology (then Norcal) needed to open a new processing center in 2002, company officials wanted a waterfront location to facilitate shipping. In response, the city donated land at Candlestick Point and in exchange Norcal agreed to the city's request that it recognize a union and give preference (called first-source hiring) to hiring workers from poor neighborhoods close to the facility. The agreement worked for all involved. About 80 percent of the 2,100 workers at Recology's worker-owned facility are covered by Teamsters Local 350. Sorters start at $20.00 and hour with vacation and full benefits and can earn up to $28.50 per hour and more if they move into other positions. All workers are provided with gloves, goggles, and other protective wear. The company is profitable—Recology is the 13th largest waste management firm in the United States, with annual revenues of about half a billion dollars. Recology walks the talk on its commitment both to workers and the environment.[70] The $38 million state-of-the-art facility processes 750 tons of recyclable material daily. A connected facility processes 350 tons of organic waste, which is sent to one of California's composting facilities.[71] The company's fleet of 400 trucks run on biodiesel fuel produced locally from vegetable oils.

Can all recycling companies afford to take the high road? The Teamsters union, which represents 300,000 sanitation workers nationwide, says yes and is leading a national campaign to organize recycling workers. A recent Teamsters' report, *Trash and the Public Interest*, documents the privatization and concentration of the sanitation industry since the 1970s and the dangerous low-paying jobs that exist in most facilities.[72] A key point of the report is that sanitation companies such as the top three (Waste Management, Allied/BFI, and Republic Services), which control 40 percent of the industry's revenues and realize between $225,000 and $260,000 in revenue per employee per year, can certainly afford to pay union wages and benefits. Meanwhile, much smaller Recovery is expanding to other California cities and just purchased two Oregon-based composting firms and fully expects these facilities to be unionized. And other cities, such as Seattle and Los Angeles, are supportive of unionization campaigns for recycling workers. These and other cities are demonstrating that recycling and good jobs are highly compatible.

6

Creating a Green
Transportation Economy

TRANSPORTATION PRODUCES ONE-THIRD OF THE NATION'S carbon dioxide emissions and is the fastest-growing source of greenhouse gas emissions. Next to improving the energy efficiency of buildings, the biggest impact larger cities can have in reducing their carbon footprint is to increase public transportation options and make walking and biking feasible means of getting around. Many cities are adding public transportation and taking other measures to get people out of their cars. In addition to their environmental aspects, these initiatives save consumers time and money and may have economic development spin-offs. Every $1 million of public transportation spending produces on average 36 jobs. The United States spends about $47 billion per year on public transportation, supporting almost 1.7 million jobs. The jobs are relatively good jobs in a range of skilled and semiskilled blue- and white-collar occupations.

In this chapter we examine four distinct strategies for linking sustainable transportation to economic development. The first two are linking strategies. Denver is linking its transit strategy to an economic development strategy to develop areas of the city around new transit stations; it is also marketing the convenience of its extensive transit system to attract companies and lure skilled workers. The transit strategy also has an economic justice component evident in measures to ensure that the new housing and jobs created are accessible to working families. Los Angeles is linking transportation to economic development in a completely different way. In Los Angeles, efforts to clean up one of the city's key economic development engines, the port, link to an economic and environmental justice agenda to make trucks less polluting and trucking jobs better paying. Portland's leadership in developing new public transportation options such as light rail, streetcars, and biking to work has created opportunities to transform an existing manufacturer into streetcar production and to create a new niche industry in bicycles. Seattle has attempted to leapfrog the development of a biodiesel industry in the state. Also a leader in adding public transportation, Seattle has added light-rail and increased bus service as part of its broader climate change strategy, as well as purchasing hundreds of hybrid electric buses; it has attempted to promote the development of an integrated biodiesel industry in which the city's solid waste is used to fertilize crops for local biodiesel production.

TRANSPORTATION AND CITIES: CARS, CARBON, AND SPRAWL

Cities have much to gain by reducing driving. Getting away from cars reduces pollution and has economic development and job potential. Vehicles in the United States create 1.3 billion tons of carbon dioxide per year.[1] Reducing car use would both increase national energy security by decreasing reliance on foreign oil and put a big dent into the nation's massive contribution to greenhouse gas production. Increasing fuel efficiency and moving to hybrid and all-electric cars is one part of the solution. Without electric cars and trucks, Los Angeles and other large cities will not be able to come into compliance with federal clean air laws. Since cities are not players in the development of electric cars, that worthy strategy is beyond the scope of this book. Where cities do have a unique role to play is in reducing vehicle miles traveled by increasing public transportation and other nonautomobile options. With only 4.7 percent of U.S. workers commuting by public transportation, there is a lot of room for improvement (figure 6.1). Public transit produces 95 percent less carbon monoxide and 90 percent fewer volatile organic compounds than private vehicles, and about half as much carbon dioxide and nitrogen oxide per passenger mile.[2] The American Public Transportation Association provides a vivid description of the impact of moving more people out of their cars and into public transportation: "Communities that invest in public transit reduce the nation's carbon emissions by 37 million

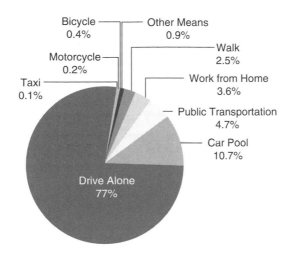

FIGURE 6.1 How Americans Get to Work. *Source:* U.S. Census Bureau, 2005 American Community Survey.

metric tons annually:– equivalent to New York City; Washington, DC; Atlanta; Denver; and Los Angeles combined stopping using electricity." Individuals would benefit too—public transportation saves the United States 1.4 billion gallons of gasoline annually, which amounts to $6,200 in savings per year for the average two-worker family using public transportation.[3]

Increasing public transit ridership reduces greenhouse gas emissions and contributes to the nation's energy security. And it creates good, green jobs. The job creation potential, however, is not just in transportation systems. A recent study by the Economic Development Research Group for the American Public Transit Association estimates that the $8.4 billion investment in mass transit from the stimulus package will create 252,000 jobs, about two-thirds of which are semi-skilled and skilled jobs in manufacturing, service and repair, drivers, crew, ticket agents, and construction. The remaining third are white-collar clerical, managerial, and engineering jobs. Public transit creates about 20 percent more jobs than the same amount of expenditure on highways.[4]

The feasibility of increasing use of public transit for commuting depends on the size of the city and the density of its built environment. Some cities can use transit-oriented development to increase density, reduce car use, and create a sense of neighborhood. Transit-oriented development—compact development that mixes commercial, residential, and office uses close to transit stops—has been around since mass transit was introduced in the late 1800s, but has been rediscovered lately as part of the "smart growth" movement in urban planning to counter sprawled development.[5] Urban density matters; the transportation-related emissions of people living in cities and compact neighborhoods is up to 70 percent less than for those living in suburbs.[6] But the connection between transit and density is complex. We know from numerous planning studies that highways influence where development occurs and the density of the growth they catalyze.[7] It is difficult to drastically alter the density of sprawled metro areas like Columbus, Miami, or Dallas by adding mass transit options after the fact. However, that effect is partly a function of whether planners seize the opportunity and concentrate new development around transit nodes. UC Davis transportation planner Susan Handy points out that light rail does not cause a metropolitan area to grow faster, but rather redistributes growth. She concludes that new transit systems are most likely to have an impact in rapidly growing regions with demand for dense development.[8] Denver is such a region.

Denver: T-REX and Economic Development

Denver illustrates a linking strategy that uses transit-oriented development to create denser neighborhoods in its downtown core and to bring economic development to those neighborhoods. Elected officials and the business community have seen transit as a way to continue the city's growth rather than having growth sprawl into Denver's exurbs.

Denver has grown by more than 10 percent since 2000. In 1992 the Denver Regional Council of Governments (DRCOG) released a study that warned that traffic was reaching gridlock levels and that the situation would only worsen given expected growth in the region's two largest employment centers, downtown Denver and the Denver Tech Center 15 miles to the south. This study laid the groundwork for Denver's expanding light-rail, commuter train, and bus rapid transit systems. A multiagency planning process started, and in 1999 DRCOG produced Metro Vision 2020, which prioritized the development of a light-rail line, a transportation expansion that came to be known as T-REX (which stands for "transportation expansion").[9] And in 1999, Denver area residents approved a ballot measure to impose two property tax increases to raise some of the funding for the $1.67 billion

T-REX project. The T-REX initiative is widely acclaimed both for introducing public transportation to a sprawling region and for the efficiency of its implementation—it came in under budget and ahead of schedule.[10]

Buoyed by this success, the Metro Denver Economic Development Corporation spearheaded a campaign for a sizable expansion of the system that would include six new rail lines and three extensions, plus a bus rapid transit system. The FasTracks YES! campaign had considerable financial support from the business community, including the Denver Chamber of Commerce. The business community saw light and commuter rail as essential to continued economic growth, and city officials also saw it as a way to develop several nodes of development around transit stops. To top off the $563,000 donation from the Metro Denver Economic Development Corporation to start the campaign, various businesses provided $3.6 million in donations and loans.

The $4.7 billion, 12-year expansion would be the largest urban mass transit expansion in the country, including 122 miles of new track and a new bus rapid transit service. The 18-mile bus service would have six stations. The project got the green light in 2004, when voters approved a 0.4 percent sales tax increase to partially support it.

There is no doubt the transit system is popular; in 2007, the Denver Regional Transportation District reported an average of about 61,000 rider-trips every weekday, 7,000 more than it had estimated.[11] But rising costs have raised some concerns about the expansion. Since the measure passed, costs have escalated, meaning that the project will end up costing close to $6.9 billion. The Denver Regional Transportation District is considering whether to reduce the scale of the project, extend construction over a longer time period, or find $2.2 billion to meet the gap that will not be covered by the sales tax. The Metro Mayors Caucus has asked for another ballot initiative in 2010 that would approve another 0.4 percent tax increase to keep the project on schedule. The new tax would be repealed once the extra money is raised. A new coalition to support the measure is being formed, but it is a difficult economic environment in which to pass a tax increase.[12]

Transit has also delivered on its economic development goals of attracting people, employers, and commercial development that will produce tax revenue for the city. Several new high-density, mixed-use developments have emerged around the system's stations, including the area around Denver's historic train station, Union Station. The site of Stapleton International Airport (replaced by Denver International in 1995) now houses a $5 billion development. This 4,700-acre mixed-use development is trying to incorporate economic development by creating an environmental technology incubator that sponsors hope will spin off new businesses over time. Further, a workforce housing program requires that 30 percent of housing be affordable to low-income renters and purchasers.[13]

Other neighborhoods along the light-rail line are now prospering. City planners are expecting the FasTracks expansion to stimulate 50 transit-oriented developments.[14] So far, about 3,704 residential units, 460,000 square feet of retail, and 300,000 square feet of office space have either been built or are currently under construction in 15 projects near transit stations, and an equal number of new residential units and retail space have been proposed, plus an additional 860,000 square feet of office space. According to the Denver Regional Transportation District, these projects represent about $1.7 billion of investment.

No development is perfect in its implementation. Denver mayor John Hickenlooper and Colorado governor Bill Owens have been engaged in "beggar thy neighbor" economic development practices, traveling to California and other places to convince companies to relocate in Denver, promoting their public transportation as an asset.[15] Although this is common economic development practice, Denver has many assets on which to develop new green industries, such as the incubator at the old Stapleton site. Some goals are seemingly incompatible. Part of what Denver hopes to achieve through its transit city is attracting a large "creative class," to spur further economic development.[16]

The very success of this goal is increasing demand for housing in the central city, making it prohibitively expensive for working families, who are also part of the city's growth. The Center for Housing Policy estimates that Denver families earning between $20,000 and $50,000 spend 59 percent of their income on housing and transportation.[17] To help Denver achieve its goal of not displacing working families, the John D. and Catherine T. MacArthur Foundation provided grants to help Denver expand the amount of affordable housing near the rail lines. In February 2009, the foundation gave $250,000 to Denver and $2 million in low-interest loans to Enterprise Community Partners, a national nonprofit developer of affordable housing, to start a fund to finance 1,200 units of affordable housing within a half-mile of light rail and within a quarter-mile of bus routes. The fund already has $15 million in commitments. The foundation is looking to Denver's Office of Economic Development to create a model for how other cities can use public-private partnerships to link transit development to housing development. A new nonprofit organization, the Urban Land Conservancy, was created to acquire properties (federally subsidized and unsubsidized rental properties rented to low-income households, as well as vacant residential and commercial property) to develop.

Transit-oriented development is spurring local economic growth in the Denver area. As we will see in later cases in this chapter, it could achieve even higher growth if national policy were in place to promote the development of a domestic railcar industry.

THE COALITION FOR CLEAN AND SAFE PORTS: TURNING BAD JOBS INTO GREEN JOBS IN LOS ANGELES

The ports of Los Angeles and Long Beach are huge, in terms of both land (7,500 acres) and activity; they are the country's busiest container ports, with more than half a billion dollars in goods loaded onto trucks for delivery daily. About 40 percent of the country's imported goods enter through these ports. They are a significant source of employment, facilitating about 919,000 jobs.[18] The *Los Angeles Times* reports that the value of containerized trade grew from $74 billion in 1994 to $305 billion in 2006, and despite a downturn in the current recession, port business is expected to continue to grow at a fast pace.[19] The ports, however, are also a significant source of pollution, producing more than one-fourth of the toxic pollution in the Los Angeles region. The California Air Resources Board estimates that Southern Californians pay between $100 million and $590 million each year in health costs caused by freight-related truck pollution, and will pay up to $10.1 billion between now and the year 2025.[20]

Neighborhood organizations in the surrounding communities and the Natural Resources Defense Council (NRDC) began to oppose dirty port development in 2001, and eventually formed part of the Coalition for Clean and Safe Ports, which has been instrumental not only in cleaning the ports but in improving the quality of jobs for port workers. Although framed by some stakeholders as a jobs-versus-environment struggle, the movement has made clear that the choice is between dirty growth and clean growth and between bad jobs and good jobs. Both sides recognize the importance of the ports as an engine of economic development. The Coalition works to assure that this growth is clean and that workers are paid a decent wage. It is the ultimate linking strategy.

The origin of the problem goes back to 1980, when Congress passed legislation to deregulate the trucking industry. It didn't take long for low-cost competitors to enter the market and for unionized trucking companies that couldn't compete to simply sell the trucks to the drivers. No longer employees, these independent contractors have no union protection and have little power to negotiate wages or working conditions. Those who could got out of trucking, leaving the field wide open for immigrants, often with fake social security cards and driver's licenses, willing to work for low wages. The average driver nets $30,000 or less annually, due to all the costs of doing business—truck leases, fuel, maintenance and repair, licenses, taxes, etc.[21] The result is that drivers often don't maintain their vehicles, leading one analyst to refer to their trucks as sweatshops on wheels.[22]

For the Los Angeles region, deregulation, combined with massive growth in shipping, means hundreds of trucks idling at the port daily as they wait to load or unload, spewing diesel exhaust into the environment. The largely Latino working-class neighborhoods near the ports were disproportionately affected by the pollution. A survey completed by the Los Angeles County Department of Health found that 20 percent of Long Beach children under 17 were diagnosed with asthma, a rate dramatically higher than the 3 to 4 percent rate nationally. And a review of studies by the California Office of Environmental Health Hazard Assessment found that people exposed to diesel emissions—truck drivers, railroad workers, and equipment operators—were more likely to develop lung cancer and experience other more immediate health problems than workers who were not exposed to diesel emissions.[23]

Opposition intensified in 2001 when the city approved plans by the Port of Los Angeles to build a new terminal for shipments from China. Neighborhood organizations and the Natural Resources Defense Council (NRDC) filed lawsuits in both state and federal courts, arguing that the environmental impacts of the decision were not evaluated, as required by the California Environmental Quality Act. The construction was stopped until an environmental impact statement could be completed, and a settlement of $50 million was granted to be used toward mitigating the pollution from the ports.[24] Stunned by the decision, port officials knew that they had to get serious about environmental pollution if they were going to expand.

Then-mayor Jim Hahn initiated a "no net increase in pollution" policy for the port and established an air-quality task force to develop a plan. State law was on the Coalition's side. In September 2000, the California Air Resources Board adopted the Diesel Risk Reduction Plan, which recommended measures to reduce diesel particulate matter by 75 percent from 2000 levels by 2010 and 85 percent by 2020.[25] Among the measures are using cleaner-burning diesel fuel, retrofitting existing engines to trap more particulate matter, and adopting new diesel engines with the latest technologies for trapping particle emissions.

In 2005, the Los Angeles Alliance for a New Economy (LAANE)[26] and the NRDC organized a coalition of environmental justice organizations, social and economic justice organizations, the American Lung Association, unions affiliated with Change to Win and the AFL-CIO, and the Teamsters and others into the Coalition for Clean and Safe Ports to pursue a campaign to decrease the toxic emissions produced by the ports while still allowing growth.[27] The concerns of these organizations converged around the ports. The power of the Coalition for Clean and Safe Ports is described by Occidental College professor Martha Matsuoka:[28]

> The formation of the coalition and the campaign came as a natural extension of the organizing of community residents, many of whom were truckers. EJ [environmental justice] organizers were able to engage with truckers on issues of home, family, and children and to rely on social networks rather than on labor unions and worker solidarity alone. It was a welcome new approach to many truckers soured by the unsuccessful organizing efforts of the past 27 years.

When Antonio Villaraigosa became mayor in 2005, he appointed harbor commissioners who would support a plan that both reduced emissions and would help organize truckers to improve job quality. By late 2006, a Clean Air Action Plan was adopted by the Port of Los Angeles and the Port of Long Beach (collectively referred to as the San Pedro Bay Ports). The plan calls for reducing the ports' emissions (including those from ship, trains, trucks, harbor craft, cargo handling, and terminal equipment) by close to 50 percent in five years.[29] All stakeholders realized that the ports would have to address the public health problems created by their pollution in order to stop opposition to needed expansion and modernization projects.

The plan emphasizes the largest sources of pollution—ships entering the port, harbor craft that help guide the ships into port, cargo-handling equipment that unloads goods from the ships, and the trucks and trains that take the goods to their final destination. To reduce ship emissions, ships docked at the port for loading or unloading are now required to be plugged into a ship-to-shore electrical power source (a process known as cold ironing) rather than running their engines.[30] The ports are investing $180 million in upgrading to these power systems, which will take between five and ten years.[31] To further reduce emissions, the ports are requiring ships entering the harbor to reduce speeds and use low-emissions fuel. The ports are subsidizing the additional cost, but will phase out the subsidy when regulatory programs by the state are in place. The ports' own vehicles will become more efficient and move to electric power supplies as well, with the goal of eventually obtaining electricity from solar sources.

In October 2008, the ports implemented the Clean Trucks Program component of the plan. Trucks produce about 10 percent of the port's diesel particulate matter emissions and a quarter of its smog-related emissions.[32] This initiative will reduce truck-related air pollution by more than 80 percent. The plan institutes a series of truck bans, starting with a ban on those built before 1989 (the first year of federal diesel pollution control), and eventually requires that all trucks at a minimum meet federal EPA 2007 heavy-duty vehicle emissions standards by 2012.[33] It also imposes a clean truck fee of $35 per 20-foot equivalent unit (TEU) on the owners of cargo loaded onto trucks that do not meet the 2007 emissions standards. Cargo loaded onto trucks that meet the 2007 emissions standards are exempted from the fee.

Further, the plan requires that all trucks entering the port must operate under the authority of a trucking company (a licensed motor carrier) that has received a concession from the port (a concession is a kind of permit to do business at port terminals). Prior to implementation of the Clean Truck Program, the port had no ability to manage the roughly 16,800 frequent and semifrequent truck visitors coming in and out of San Pedro Bay Port terminals each week.[34] The five-year concession agreements require trucking companies to document their compliance with license, insurance, maintenance, and safety requirements and to provide adequate off-street parking (to prevent idling and its resulting pollution in nearby neighborhoods). Trucking companies pay a one-time concession fee of $2,500 and a $100 per truck annual fee. The revenue from the clean truck fee funds grants and subsidies to help trucking concessionaires purchase EPA-compliant trucks.[35]

The most controversial element of the program requires that all truck operators entering the port be employees of a concessionaire trucking company by 2013, which will place the responsibility of maintaining trucks and documenting that workers meet federal standards back on the companies (this requirement is only for the Port of Los Angeles).[36] Although the program is union-neutral, the first step of unionization, having an employer of record, will be satisfied with the employer requirement. Companies must also agree to use the First Source Hiring Program, which gives preference to local drivers and those with previous port experience.

Not surprisingly, the plan met with considerable opposition from the shipping and trucking industry. The California and Los Angeles chambers of commerce lobbied against the fee, arguing that California would lose jobs as shippers looked to other ports.[37] The Federal Maritime Commission also filed a lawsuit against the ports of Los Angeles and Long Beach in the U.S. District Court for the District of Columbia, arguing that the Clean Trucks Programs reduced competition and caused irreparable economic harm. In April 2009, the U.S. District Court for the District of Columbia ruled against the Federal Maritime Commission.[38]

In July 2008, the American Trucking Association (ATA) filed a suit against Los Angeles and Long Beach in the U.S. Federal District Court for the Central District of California and asked for a preliminary injunction to hold implementation of all elements of the plan. The motion was denied, and the ATA appealed to the Ninth Circuit Court of Appeals, which reversed the decision and sent the case back to the district court. In April 2009, District Court Judge Christina Snyder issued a tentative ruling until the case is tried in December 2009, suspending implementation of the phase-in of employee drivers, concession fees, and off-street parking requirements.[39]

While the ATA lawsuit moves through the courts, the TEU fees, which were not under question, have gone forward. As of June 2009, approximately 4,700 of the San Pedro Bay Ports' frequent and semifrequent truck visitors meet the 2007 emission standards. About 2,500 of these trucks were purchased with subsidies from the ports' various grant and incentive programs. Because the number of frequent and semifrequent trucks needed to serve the San Pedro Bay Ports since the recession has dropped from over 16,000 to about 10,000, this means that almost 50 percent of trucks are EPA-compliant. Port of Los Angeles Executive Director Geraldine Knatz notes that what port officials expected would take five years has been achieved within the nine months following implementation of the fee. Chris Cannon, who manages the Clean Trucks Program, explains that the motivation for cargo owners is high: "a company that moves 50,000 containers a year would pay $3.5 million a year in fees." So they're telling the trucking companies to either get compliant trucks or lose their business.[40] With the stick of having to pay the fee and the carrot of port incentives, the trucking companies are catching on fast. Cannon estimates that at the current pace, 10,000 of the frequent and semifrequent truck visitors will be 2007-compliant by the end of 2009.

The environmental benefits of greening the ports will also produce economic benefits; the Southern California Air Quality Management District estimates that the Clean Trucks Program could produce a cumulative economic benefit of $5.9 billion from reductions in premature deaths, lost work time, and medical problems.[41] LAANE estimates that the clean trucks program will provide $4.2 billion in financial benefits to the area from more money being injected into nearby communities due to truckers receiving employee status and fewer public dollars being spent on health care because the truckers would have employer-provided benefits.

As other port cities follow Los Angeles's lead, the nation's dirty truck fleet will gradually be replaced, which has both a climate change and an economic development impact. To the extent that the new trucks are being produced in the United States, the economic development benefit will occur somewhere, although not in the cities that are mandating the changes that are creating demand for new trucks and parts to retrofit trucks already on the road. That is not a negative—the point is that cities seeking to reduce carbon emissions will create economic development opportunities somewhere.

PORTLAND: STREETCARS AND BICYCLES

Portland is among the top three cities on all the major green city ratings. It is known for its leadership in increasing public transportation and bicycling, energy efficiency, and recycling. Although it is idyllic from a sustainability perspective, Portland's economy struggles. The city's unemployment rate in mid-2009 was 12.9 percent, far above the

nation's 8.5 percent average. Even when the region's economy is growing, the city has lagged in job growth. As in many cities, most job
growth is occurring in the suburban fringe. In 2009, Portland released
a new economic development strategy that hopes to link the city's success in sustainability with job growth.[42] Among the goals are to target
key niche sectors such as bicycle production and parts and to build on
the city's strength in advanced manufacturing. One promising area of
development on this front is streetcar production.

Portland has taken public transportation and transit-oriented
development seriously since the 1970s. TriMet, the regional rail system, manages the area's bus, light-rail, commuter rail, and streetcar
systems. Residents have voted three times to expand the systems. The
result is that Portland is the first city in the country to reduce vehicle
miles traveled.[43]

In addition to the light-rail and commuter system that connects
downtown Portland to its suburbs, Portland started building a streetcar line in 2001, and has been expanding it ever since.[44] It links neighborhoods and frequently visited institutions (Legacy Good Samaritan
Hospital is at one end and Portland State University at the other) in
the city, with the goal of reducing short inner-city trips and encouraging new residential development in the inner city. The streetcars
run on an eight-mile continuous loop, making 46 stops—about every
three to four blocks. The system carries 12,000 riders per day. Portland Streetcar estimates that it reduces vehicle miles traveled per year
by 70 million.

Compared to a subway, streetcars are easy to add, as the cars and
track are relatively narrow and they can fit the scale and traffic patterns of existing neighborhoods. And while development is stimulated
at light-rail stops, streetcars tend to stimulate development along a
broader swath. The two areas that Portland hoped to revitalize with
the streetcar system, the River and South Waterfront Districts, were
large brownfield sites occupied by abandoned rail lines and industrial
buildings.[45] In addition, the city hoped to stimulate new development
along the entire line and create new businesses and jobs.

The sustainability and economic development dividends to the city
have been realized. Since the streetcar's emergence, 55 percent of all
central business district development has occurred within one block of
the streetcar line. Prior to the streetcar, most developments were built
at less than half of the density allowable under zoning codes. Since
the streetcar, most developments are close to the maximum allowable

density.[46] The Portland Streetcar has helped stimulate $3.5 billion in new downtown development and has contributed to the revitalization of the two target neighborhoods as well as the Pearl District, according to Portland Streetcar, which operates the system. The streetcar has stimulated the addition of 10,000 housing units and 400 new businesses, 90 percent of which are locally owned, accounting for more than 5 million square feet of new construction. These successes are why the owner of the renowned Powell's Bookstore in the Pearl District says the term of art should be "development-oriented transit." He notes that the affected neighborhoods needed a development tool, which turned out to be a streetcar.[47]

Further, Portland has achieved social justice goals that were part of the transit plan. The Pearl District is one of the few transit-oriented development projects in the nation that has achieved a significant mix of low-to-moderate income housing—about 25 percent.[48] In terms of long-term employment, a significant economic development spinoff of the system has been a move to local manufacturing of the streetcars. Because there were no longer streetcar manufacturers in the United States, the cars were originally purchased from Skoda-Inekon in the Czech Republic.[49] They are now being manufactured in the Portland area by United Streetcar, a subsidiary of Oregon Iron Works (OIW).

OIW has been in Oregon since 1944, with its headquarters in Clackamas since the 1970s, fabricating large metal products such as bridges, barges, boats, and nuclear casks. The company also specializes in prototype fabrication and design, such as buoys used to produce electricity from ocean waves. Chandra Brown, a vice president of the company, told me how OIW got into streetcar production. At a meeting with Clackamas County economic development officials in 2004, someone mentioned that there were no streetcar producers in the United States. A fan of the Portland system, she immediately thought that a streetcar was something OIW could produce, but knew the company would need assistance with the investment required for developing a new product. So she and a team of elected officials from Portland and Clackamas sought assistance from their congressional delegation, congressmen Peter DeFazio, chair of the Subcommittee on Highways and Transit, and Earl Blumenauer. They, with the City of Portland, put in a successful request for an appropriation for $4 million to build a prototype streetcar, $3.2 million of which went to OIW for product development.[50]

Since OIW specializes in production more than design, the company obtained an exclusive license to manufacture Skoda streetcars in the United States. From there it was a matter of obtaining all the parts and figuring out the production process. Brown estimates that the company has invested at least another $4 million to build the prototype, which has just passed an initial test period with flying colors. The hope is that the company will earn back its investment with more orders from cities developing or adding on to streetcar systems. Already, OIW is building six more cars for Portland's Eastside streetcar expansion, and it recently won a contract to build seven streetcars for Tucson, Arizona. United Streetcar hired 20 additional workers in streetcar design and production and will hire additional employees as new orders are secured. The company has the capacity to build 20 to 50 streetcars annually, which could create approximately 300 additional jobs. In addition, OIW has contracted with more than 100 vendors to supply parts for its streetcars. Brown doesn't know if the orders are big enough for the vendors to hire new workers, but notes that OIW is giving many of them a new product line.

Streetcars have not been a major component of the public transportation solution. Except in Portland, San Francisco, and New Orleans, streetcar systems have been small and focused mostly on tourists. But dozens of cities, including Charlotte, Cincinnati, Columbus, Kenosha, Little Rock, Memphis, New Haven, New York City, Tampa, and Washington, are planning or building streetcar systems. As Alex Marshall, a senior fellow at the Regional Plan Association in New York City, reminds us, "When combined with good land use policy and good urban design, streetcars could once again be a vital part of an urban transportation system."[51] And that could mean jobs if we build the cars in the United States.

Bicycling to Economic Development

Portland was an early mover in incorporating bicycles into its transportation mix—the city's first bicycle master plan was completed in 1996. Mia Burke, then the city's bicycle program manager, toured 18 European cities to see firsthand how to create safe and user-friendly bicycle lanes. With a staff of five and a $1.5 million budget, the Department of Transportation was charged with planning and building a network of bike lanes and trails that has expanded to more than 300 miles. Bike commuting has grown along with it. The Portland

Office of Transportation reports that daily bike traffic over Portland's four bridges has tripled since 2000 and is now at about 16,000 bike crossings. At 8 percent, Portland has a higher percentage of workers commuting by bike than any other city in the country. In addition to being the nation's top city in terms of using bikes as transportation, Portlanders participate in close to 4,000 annual rides, races, events, and tours in the area.

An unanticipated side effect is that biking has become a niche industry in Portland. *Oregon Business* magazine estimates that about 50 bike-related businesses have started in Portland in the past two years alone, with about $90 million in sales. Alta Planning & Design, an international bicycle industry consulting firm based in Portland, estimates that the value of the bicycle industry grew by 38 percent between 2006 and 2008, from 95 to 143 businesses, accounting for between 850 and 1,150 jobs (figure 6.2).[52] About 20 percent of Portland's bike industry is in manufacturing, including bicycles and precision components, although many of the custom bicycle producers think of themselves more as artists than manufacturers. However they're classified, they're successful—several customized bike makers have backlogs of more than a year. And some of the small companies have penetrated international markets. Nutcase Helmets was launched in 2005 to meet what owner Michael Morrow hoped was demand for helmets with unique graphics by bikers, skateboarders, and in-line skaters. Sales have been growing ever since. Nutcase helmets are sold throughout the United States, and in 2008 the company sold 20,000 helmets in Denmark alone. Morrow told *Oregonian Business* magazine that he is on schedule to sell 100,000 helmets in 2009.[53] And most produce in an environmentally sustainable manner—making them green businesses in every respect.[54] While most are small start-ups, a few large bicycle-related companies are located in the Portland area. Swedish Sapa Profiles, one of the largest aluminum extrusion companies in the world, produces bike frames that are sold internationally and is one of the leading suppliers of high-end bike frames in the country.

There are several other aspects to Portland's bicycle sector. Mia Burke left city government to start Alta Planning & Design, a consulting firm that works with cities throughout the United States and in other countries on designing bike and pedestrian pathways, urban landscapes, and greenways. The 40-person firm has offices in Portland and six other cities. And what started out as a one-person blog, Bike-Portland.org, on all aspects of bicycle culture and business, now has

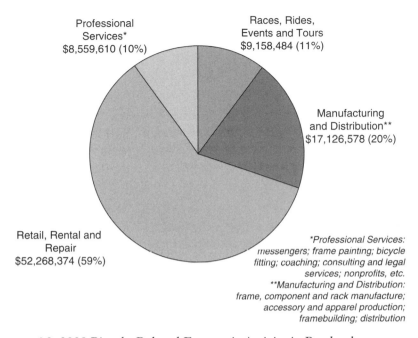

Professional
Services*
$8,559,610 (10%)

Races, Rides,
Events and Tours
$9,158,484 (11%)

Manufacturing
and Distribution**
$17,126,578 (20%)

Retail, Rental and
Repair
$52,268,374 (59%)

*Professional Services:
messengers; frame painting; bicycle
fitting; coaching; consulting and legal
services; nonprofits, etc.
**Manufacturing and Distribution:
frame, component and rack manufacture;
accessory and apparel production;
framebuilding; distribution

FIGURE 6.2 2008 Bicycle-Related Economic Activity in Portland.
Source: Alta Planning (http://www.altaplanning.com/App_Content/files/fp_docs/2008%20Portland%20Bicycle-Related%20Economy%20Report.pdf).

a reporting staff and numerous advertisers. Furthermore, the United Bicycle Institute, a licensed private technical school that offers certifications in bike repair, bike maintenance, and frame building in southern Oregon, opened a branch in North Portland.

Portland will face tough competition in advancing bicycles from a niche to a bigger sector of its economy, from both international and domestic competitors. For at least 20 years, most bicycles sold in the United States have been made in China. *Bicycle Retailer & Industry News* reports that the United States imported 13 million bicycles in 2008—200 times more than it exported.[55] Taiwan is fast becoming an even more efficient producer, beating out many Chinese companies. Further, Oregon has domestic rivals. Oregon's $150 million in revenue from the bicycle industry is only one-fourth that of Wisconsin-based Trek Bicycle Corporation alone (which employs 1,200 people). Some analysts are optimistic that more bicycle production can return to the United States. An article on a Portland biking blog cites bicycle industry analyst Jay Townley, who predicts that declining labor costs due to automation, rising oil and shipping costs, and the need for faster turnaround could bring the industry back to the United States.[56] But even if economic factors could bring some of the industry back, coastal Portland is not well positioned as a national distribution center in the same way that many U.S. cities are.

Jennifer Nolfi, a manager of the business and industry team in Portland's Department of Urban Development, emphasizes strengthening what already exists.[57] The city has offered several workshops to business owners on accounting and other business operations and is helping the Bicycle Transportation Alliance identify what Portland can do to support the industry. The city's visibility as a bicycling town is increased by events such as Oregon Manifest, an industry-supported two-day frame builders' exhibit that has been expanded to a five-week event that includes a national design competition for bicycles custom built to excel on a designated route.

Nolfi sees bicycles as one part of the city's broader outdoor industry, which is gaining in importance nationwide.[58] Jerry Norquist, a former executive at Trek who now heads Cycle Oregon, notes that the number of people who bicycle to work in Portland, regardless of the weather, is closer to northern European cities such as Copenhagen or Amsterdam than any other U.S. city.[59] This and the niche bicycle industry that has grown around it are part of Portland's cachet as a green city. Nolfi does not expect any large manufacturers to relocate to Portland. Even so, as a niche industry, bicycle producers are an important part of the city's vitality and green image.

KING COUNTY/SEATTLE

Seattle, which calls itself the Emerald City, is also on every top-ten list of sustainable cities. Mayor Greg Nichols, a national leader on climate protection, has started numerous initiatives to green every aspect of the city's development.[60] In September 2006, Seattle passed a Climate Action Plan that outlines specific strategies for reducing dependence on cars, increasing use of biofuels, and achieving higher efficiency in residential and commercial buildings and other areas. Increasing public transit options was a goal before the plan. In 1996, voters in the three counties of the Seattle metro area approved a measure creating Sound Transit, a regional transit agency including commuter trains, express buses, and light rail.[61] The light rail's Central Link is expected to be completed in 2009; it is estimated that more than 42,000 will use it daily by 2020.[62] In 2008, Seattle-area voters approved another $17.9 billion to expand the light-rail, bus, and commuter train service.[63] A 1.3-mile streetcar line connecting the South Lake Union area to the central city and to other public transportation systems has been operating since 2007. These alternatives are getting people out of their cars: in the past five years, transit ridership increased 23 percent in the Seattle region, compared to 10 percent nationally.[64]

For the most part, these initiatives haven't had explicit links to economic development. Perhaps the most instructive policy—a hopeful model and also a cautionary tale—was the decision of local government to combine a purchase of 234 hybrid diesel buses with an economic development strategy to promote local production of the biodiesel used to run them. The county even worked out a plan to use the city's sewage, politely termed biosolids, as fertilizer for the canola crops used to make the biodiesel. A local startup venture, Imperium Renewables, opened a larger facility in Grays Harbor, two and a half hours southwest of Seattle, with a capacity of a hundred million gallons a year, creating well-paying jobs and hope for economic renewal. Seattle and King County planners proudly viewed the whole project as a closed loop of economic development connected to smart environmental policy—the buses providing the demand for the biodiesel, which provided the market for local canola crops, and new production facilities to turn the canola into biodiesel.

However, unforeseen price increases in canola oil made the market price for biodiesel uncompetitive for Seattle's bus fleet. In 2008, the county did not renew Imperium's contract. The company has other customers and will likely survive, but the story suggests that city governments, as price-takers, are too small to influence the larger market conditions in which they find themselves. Nonetheless, the decision to shift to hybrid diesel buses made great sense in its own terms, and a new local enterprise was born. Here is the story of what occurred, in detail.

In June 2004, King County Metro Transit (the agency that operates the region's bus system) began replacing traditional buses with hybrids that run on diesel and electricity that is generated by the vehicle and stored in batteries on the roof. King County Metro now boasts the largest hybrid bus fleet in the world—235 hybrid buses out of a 1,400-bus fleet.[65] As part of the county's climate change agenda, King County Executive Ron Sims (now deputy secretary of the U.S.

Department of Housing and Urban Development) issued an executive order in 2006 that called for powering all the county's diesel vehicles on a blend of 80 percent diesel and 20 percent biodiesel (referred to as B-20). At about the same time, Seattle City Light, the city-run utility, began a pilot program to reduce greenhouse gases by subsidizing the city's garbage trucks and three Washington State ferries to run on biodiesel blends. The program paid the cost difference for the more expensive biodiesel.

A year later, in June 2007, King County Metro Transit signed a one-year contract to purchase two million gallons of biodiesel from a local start-up producer, Imperium Renewables. In fact, this agreement helped put Imperium in business. Nancy Floyd, founder and director of Nth Power, the first venture capital firm to invest in the company, said it was the purchase agreement that King County signed with Imperium that convinced her to invest in it.[66] Eleven other investors followed, providing a total of $113 million in private equity capital.[67]

State policy was also important to Imperium's location. Washington's renewable portfolio standard (RPS), passed in 2006, requires that at least 2 percent of diesel sales be biodiesel. The eventual goal is to replace about 10 percent of the state's diesel supply with a locally produced fuel—a significant shift of income to in-state producers, since the state of Washington spends $3 billion a year on diesel fuel. To reach this goal, cities, counties, and businesses with large fleets would have to switch to biodiesel blends.

Imperium started as Seattle Biodiesel in 2004 with a pilot facility to test its processing technology. Once the technology was perfected, founder and president John Plaza began looking for a site to build a large-capacity production facility. He chose Grays Harbor County because it had both the rail and port access needed for bringing in feedstock from the Midwest, Canada, and Asia and for exporting to California, Europe, and Asia. Construction of the $60 million, 100-million-gallon-per-year plant began in November 2006, and it opened in August 2007. The company hired 60 people, with the lowest-paying job in the plant starting at $19 per hour plus benefits.

The company offered a unique economic development opportunity to a town that lost its timber industry when the federal courts ruled that the habitat of the spotted owl was being destroyed. The Port of Grays Harbor estimated that the company would create another 350 indirect jobs and provide increased revenue to local firms through sales to local distributors and retailers.

The final link in the closed loop is that Seattle's sewage is an input to the biodiesel. Seattle has been turning biosolids from its sewage treatment plants into compost—now a relatively common practice—for almost 30 years. Starting in 2003, the biosolids have been used to fertilize canola (rapeseed) crops on farms in nearby Yakima County. Peggy Leonard, King County's supervisor of waste recovery, got the idea of creating a closed-loop system in which biosolids would come back to the city as biodiesel produced from local crops. With a grant from the USDA, she and two University of Washington professors tested 30 types of canola and different applications of biosolids to see which yielded the most oil. The state provided assistance to open a seed-crushing facility in Sunnyside, which would ship the feedstock to Imperium for processing into biodiesel. In April 2007, King County Metro signed a contract to purchase two million gallons of biodiesel from Imperium using the local canola at $2.30 per gallon. Processing biosolids results in a net CO_2 savings toward meeting the city's climate protection agreement.[68] So the loop closes with the city's sludge becoming the biodiesel that runs the hybrid buses.

If the story ended in 2007, it would be an ideal illustration of a sustainable economic development loop and a leapfrogging strategy that created a new industry statewide. But the economic landscape for biofuels changed considerably in 2008. Demand for canola and soybean oil, key feedstocks for biodiesel, increased dramatically, particularly in China, more than doubling prices.[69] And rising oil prices increased transportation costs for feedstock. Although Imperium has been committed to purchasing as much feedstock locally as possible (most of the nation's canola oil is produced in the Pacific Northwest and Canada), that goal has been difficult to reach. Imperium's researchers are exploring next-generation feedstocks, but for now it is using palm oil from Malaysia, soybean oil from the Midwest, and Canadian canola oil.[70]

As the price of feedstock spiraled, by mid-2007 biodiesel was selling at about $6.00 per gallon (compared to $4.80 for diesel). Washington's monthly sales of biodiesel fell by almost two-thirds from July 2007 to March 2008.[71] By January 2008, Imperium had to cancel a $345 million initial public offering filed for in May due to poor market conditions. Three additional plants planned in Hawaii, Pennsylvania, and Argentina were put on hold. Later in the year, King County Metro and other bulk buyers chose not to renew their contracts. Carnival Cruise Lines not only cancelled its annual 18-million-gallon contract, but also sold a 7 percent stake it had in the facility.[72] Imperium's employment has gone from 85 to 20, and almost all of its production is exported to Europe, where renewable fuel standards are at least twice as high as those in the United States.[73] In 2009, exports to Europe will decline as a result of the European Commission's imposing stiff duties on U.S. biofuel to offset heavy government subsidy of the industry.[74]

The story is by no means over. It does reveal, however, that cities, even when working in coordination with an entire metropolitan area (e.g., King County Transit), do not have sufficient purchasing power to create enough demand to support some new green industries. State policy to create steady demand is also needed. But we see from Washington's experience that passing an RPS is just the beginning. Washington's Renewable Fuel Standard has several provisions to target biofuels. The standard requires that at least 2 percent of the diesel sold in Washington be biodiesel, beginning November 30, 2008, and the minimum will increase to 5 percent as capacity develops (2 percent is about 20 million gallons a year). State government planners figured they would need to develop capacity in growing the canola and in the next step in the production process, crushing the seed to release the oil in preparation for refining. Unfortunately, the state's efforts are not succeeding in either area, for a variety of reasons.

Kathleen Painter, an agricultural economist at Washington State University, estimates that it would take between 133,000 and 400,000 acres to produce enough canola to reach the 2 percent RPS. Although canola production expanded from 7,500 to 13,675 acres in 2007, the amount is not likely to expand significantly beyond this, because even with today's current high prices (up from 9 cents a pound in 2006 to 27 cents a pound in 2008), the crop can be risky for farmers, particularly in the eastern part of the state where hotter temperatures can reduce the crop's productivity substantially. Washington State University researchers are exploring alternative oilseeds that would pose less risk to farmers than canola.

Another component of the economic development strategy was to create a crushing industry. At the time the standard was passed, Washington had no in-state crushers. So the Energy Freedom Act passed in conjunction with the RPS, a $100 million low-interest loan program for supporting renewable energy start-ups, earmarked $10.25 million for five crushing projects in 2006.[75] Only one facility is operating in conjunction with a biodiesel producer. One was cancelled, and the others are awaiting construction of a biodiesel plant, which is not likely to occur until prices come down.

The final link in the chain is getting the biofuel to the consumer. Here, too, there are hurdles to overcome in adopting new technologies. Rob Elam, founder and president of Propel Fuel, a company that establishes biofuel kiosks at existing gas stations, explains the reticence of station owners. One stumbling block in getting more people to adopt biofuels is availability. Station owners hesitate to add a $100,000 pump without knowing whether they can recoup the cost in sales. So Propel leases a space about the size of two parking spaces from stations to set up its biodiesel stations. The owners earn $1,000 a month through the lease, and Propel builds, owns, and operates the pumps. Elam believes that the fastest way to get biofuel to scale is to open it up to consumers, but at current prices, there is not enough demand for Propel to expand in the Seattle area beyond the three stations that have been built. So Elam is moving the company's base of operations to Sacramento: "That is where the strong policy is, where the markets are, and where the investment money is. Capital and entrepreneurs will take path of least resistance. Green rhetoric isn't enough—the money knows and will go to the place that provides the best opportunity to succeed."[76]

The efforts of King County Metro and Seattle to increase public transportation with buses and light rail are essential components of the city and county's climate change strategy. But local government has no control over the market trends that would make using local biodiesel (or any biodiesel) a feasible strategy for reducing the area's carbon footprint. Nor is there enough consumer demand for a fuel that is priced considerably higher than regular diesel. Even though state policy—the RPS—was in place to create demand for biodiesel, state officials did not fully grasp how difficult it would be to ramp up local canola production.

ELEMENTS OF A GREEN TRANSPORTATION ECONOMY

There are immense benefits for cities that pursue clean-energy strategies in improving quality of life and reducing the city's carbon footprint. These are desirable for their own sake, even when they do not lead directly to economic development in the sense of incubating or attracting new industries. Cities that are attractive places to live tend to attract employers and workers. As we have seen, green building and public transportation produce jobs both directly and indirectly. But the development of new industries that create substantial numbers of jobs is trickier, in two key respects.

First, even if demand is created locally, the jobs are not necessarily created locally. This is normal in a national (and global) economy. Another producer in another city may have first-mover advantage or be the low-cost producer. It would be absurd to think that Portland would emerge as a bicycle production capital simply because a lot of its residents use bicycles. Second, there is only so much cities can do in promoting manufacturing. If the goal is to use transportation strategies to create a new generation of domestic manufacturing industry, federal policy is more important than what individual cities can do.

All of this presumes that significant investment will occur in mass transit and that cities will pursue transit-oriented development. Yet few cities have and fewer yet have linked transit-oriented development with an equitable development agenda. A considerable amount of policy, investment, and planning will have to take place to realize a vision that links transportation, sustainability, economic development, and social justice.

Organizing and Planning for a Good Green Jobs Agenda

Investment in transportation creates jobs in construction, engineering, and manufacturing. Federal investment will increase the job creation potential, as will a more explicit manufacturing policy. But these cases illustrate that a considerable amount of organizing work at the local level is necessary to move transit projects forward.

In Denver, the first ballot initiative to fund FasTracks failed. Voters didn't understand how public transit would benefit them personally or the region economically, and the transit agenda was seen as complex and expert-driven. The stakeholders learned from this failure, and elected officials, environmentalists, and the business community organized as the Transit Alliance to take the message to the people. The FasTracks Yes! Campaign clearly identified the economic development, quality of life, and environmental benefits of public transit. With the Metro Mayors Caucus (an alliance that seeks consensus among mayors in the metro area for mutually beneficial projects) and the Denver Chamber of Commerce on board and clear benefits, the measure passed with 58 percent of the vote the second time around.[77] Once it was approved, the Denver Transit Authority and the Metro Denver Economic Development Corporation took over in determining which transit stops to develop into mixed-use communities. While such changes are often associated with gentrification, the planning and development process in this case ensured that lower-income working families were not displaced or excluded from the dense urban communities being created.

The Coalition for Clean and Safe Ports, an alliance of environmental justice, economic justice, and community development organizations, pressured the Port of Los Angeles to develop a growth strategy that dramatically reduced emissions that were causing health problems in surrounding neighborhoods as well as for the port's truck drivers and other workers. With support from Mayor Antonio Villaraigosa, the Coalition's campaign resulted in turning bad jobs into good, green jobs. As we have seen in chapter 4, the mayor has made climate change and green jobs a priority and works with various organizations and elected officials throughout the city to ensure that green job opportunities are created for low-income residents.

In Portland, the green jobs agenda emerges from a long-standing commitment to sustainable planning that has been stepped up even more as part of a climate change agenda. Portland elected officials and planners saw early on that a commitment to sustainable development would require developing a public transit infrastructure. Portland has used new transit lines to stimulate the development of new areas of the city and to clean up brownfield sites in the process. Cities seeking to follow Portland's example should know that the planning process for the streetcar system started 15 years ago. The planning process included mapping the route, working with a citizen advisory board, planning with utilities, and seeking the support of the business community, which was asked to raise 20 percent of the cost of building the system. Bookstore owner Michael Powell chaired the Local Improvement District created to seek business support and addressed concerns and was able to obtain backing from all the businesses along the route, even though it wasn't clear to them that it would necessarily benefit them directly.[78] By luck of having Oregon Iron Works in its backyard, Portland also linked transit to manufacturing.

A transit-oriented jobs agenda requires a transit-oriented development agenda. Yet worldwide, an analysis by University of California, Berkeley planner Robert Cervero found that few cities outside of Stockholm, Copenhagen, Singapore, and Tokyo have been able to coordinate high density development and transit successfully.[79] Major factors in their success is public ownership of land and strong metropolitan-wide planning. Over the years Toronto has attempted similar coordination with its suburban growth, which was coordinated by a regional planning agency, but success has been limited by changes in political regimes and priorities, neighborhood opposition, and creation of smaller regional agencies with competing visions of how growth should proceed.[80] We learn from Toronto that achieving the dense, mixed-use and mixed-income growth of transit-oriented development requires significant changes in how most cities plan, with changes in zoning ordinances being just a starting point.

In a recent Ford Foundation convening on achieving equitable and sustainable transit-oriented development, supporters identified the lack of coordination between land-use and transit decisions, the expense of land assembly, competing real estate interests (residential, commercial, and retail), and a local rather than regional focus in decision making as factors limiting implementation.[81] Achieving equitable development is complicated by land speculation, developer reluctance, the cost of brownfield remediation, and adding new streets, parks, and other amenities.[82] Given all the barriers, it is not surprising that so few cities have been successful at transit-oriented development. Portland's success in achieving transit-oriented development with equity can be attributed to a "perfect storm" of land availability, political will, and planning expertise.

A FEDERAL COMMITMENT TO PUBLIC TRANSPORTATION

At least 30 U.S. cities are building streetcar systems. Approximately 400 light-rail projects have been proposed for 78 metropolitan areas in 37 states. But Shelley Poticha, CEO of Reconnecting America, estimates it would take 77 years to build the $248 billion worth of proposed projects at the current rate of federal transit investment, and that's not counting needed repairs to existing systems.[83] In the last two federal transportation bills, the United States spent about $19 billion for mass transit, compared to $300 billion on highways.[84] The Obama stimulus commits $8.4 billion for mass transit and $27 billion for highway projects.[85] Of the $8.4 billion provided for public transit, $6.9 billion will be distributed to public transit systems through the Federal Transit Administration's existing formula program. The remaining $1.5 billion is part of a new discretionary program that cities can use for new projects and modernizing existing transportation infrastructure. The American Recovery and Reinvestment Act of 2009 (ARRA, the stimulus act) also includes $9.3 billion for intercity passenger rail, including $8 billion for high-speed rail corridors and $1.3 billion for Amtrak. While this seems like a lot, China is dedicating $88 billion for the construction of 1,062 miles of urban rail in 15 cities from 2001 through 2015.[86]

In addition to the $8.4 billion in ARRA funds for high-speed rail, the Obama administration's high-speed rail strategic plan recommends spending an additional $1 billion annually on high-speed rail in ten corridors over the next five years.[87] These funds are built into the FY2010 budget proposal. What will be critical is increasing the ratio of public transportation to highway spending in the federal surface transportation legislation, which expires at the end of September 2009. An advocacy campaign by the American Public Transportation Association, *Public Transportation Takes Us There*, is building congressional support for several items in the legislation, including more than doubling federal investment in public transportation and strengthening the funding guarantees needed for long-term capital investment projects.

Industrial Policy for Creating a Transit Manufacturing Industry

The United States once produced subway, light and heavy rail, and streetcars. The nation's last subway car producer, Budd Company, stopped production in 1987. The nation's last three streetcar builders closed down by 1970. France's Alstom, Canada's Bombardier, and Japan's Kawasaki are the key suppliers of subway cars to United States and Europe.[88] The Czech Republic, England, Australia, Japan, France, and Italy have also become suppliers to the world. The reason for the decline of the U.S. industry was not high labor costs; most of the countries that have taken over have wages comparable to the United States. Nor was it simply a matter of U.S. companies getting out of a business that was no longer profitable. Economic historian Jonathan Feldman explains that U.S. companies didn't keep up with state-of-the art technology as subway and other railcars became more sophisticated. Companies such as Pullman began subcontracting out more complex electronics systems, but were not able to manage suppliers, leading to quality problems. The other domestic subway car producers simply moved into more lucrative markets.[89]

As the domestic transit manufacturing industry crumbled, Congress passed a Buy American provision requiring that 60 percent of the value of the subcomponents of transit vehicles and equipment be produced in the United States and that final assembly be in the United States.[90] The provision has led to a number of foreign-owned assembly operations in the United States, but as Feldman points out, assembly only captures about 10 percent of the value-added in subway-car production.[91] So the rail transit industry in the United States, like renewable energy, is dominated by transplants from Europe, Asia, and Canada.

These transplants provide modest employment opportunities. Germany's Siemens Transportation Systems has a light-rail assembly plant in Sacramento, California, and expects to double its current production of 72 trains a year after an ongoing $26 million expansion.[92] Siemens plans on expanding employment, currently at 550, by hiring 200 people over the next few years.[93] Siemens assembles the cars used in the Denver transit system as well as several other western cities. Canadian-owned Bombardier, the leading supplier of passenger railcars in North America, opened its third U.S. rail transportation equipment manufacturing facility in 1995 in Plattsburgh, New York. The plant employs 150 now, but could expand to up to 500 workers.[94] Pittsburg, California, lured Italian-based AnsaldoBreda in 2004, which assembles cars for San Francisco's MUNI system and recently signed a $185 million contract to produce light-rail cars for Los Angeles. The company plans on expanding from 50 to 200 workers by 2011. The cars will be manufactured in Italy and assembled at the Pittsburg facility. Japan's Kinki Sharyo has been leasing production buildings in the United States to assemble cars close to its customers.

A better policy would be to support the redevelopment of a domestic industry. Collectively, U.S. cities can create enough demand for U.S. companies to get back into manufacturing train, subway, trolley, and light-rail cars in the United States. In 2004—before many of the streetcar and light-rail expansions discussed above had started, and before the stimulus plan to invest in high-speed rail—Rutgers transportation engineer Thomas Boucher estimated the nation would need more than 6,000 railcars between 2002 and 2007 and that at an average unit cost of approximately $1.2 million, we could support a domestic industry with sales of about $1 billion per year.[95] Robert Paaswell, distinguished professor of civil engineering and head of the CCNY University Transit Research Center, argues that New York City alone should be able to dictate markets for transportation supplies and could support a broad spectrum of transportation-based industries. With 7,849 railcars in the Metropolitan Transportation Authority system, regional and local manufacturers could provide new and replacement vehicles. Yet in 2001, when the New York Transit Authority requested bidders for an order of several thousand new subway cars, not one American firm responded. The contract, valued at $3–4 billion, went to Alstom (60 percent) and Kawasaki (40 percent). In contrast, Paaswell notes that "Parisian subway cars are made in France, London subway cars are made in England, and Tokyo subway cars are made entirely in Japan."[96]

The reason other countries can support railcar industries is that demand is stabilized through a policy of planned replacement by domestic producers. Boucher demonstrates that unstable demand was a key factor in the demise of the U.S. railcar industry: "During the period of the 1970s, annual domestic demand for and production of railcars bounced between a low of 268 units to a high of 1,067 units. Instead of a series of steady orders for cars every year, the pattern of demand absorbed capacity for one or two years and left the industry with little work in other years. At the same time foreign suppliers entered the market to supplement a stable internal demand for equipment in their own countries."[97] Stable demand is essential if engineering firms and manufacturers are to invest the time and resources needed to enter into the railcar market. Boucher estimates that a U.S. railcar industry could employ up to 16,000 people.[98] That number could be much higher if the United States were to export railcars and other components of transportation systems. Asia will soon have more than 300 cities with populations of more than 1 million, many of which will develop subway or light-rail systems. Feldman estimates that of the 115 cities worldwide that already have rail transit systems, one-third will expand in the next decade, creating another source of demand.

Even more production could be captured as more cities invest in bus rapid transit (BRT). Made famous in Curitiba, Brazil, BRT systems run on dedicated roadways using vehicles that resemble railcars more than buses. A few U.S. cities have limited BRT lines, including Berkeley, Boston, Cleveland, Eugene, Kansas City, Las Vegas, Los Angeles, Miami, Oakland, and Orlando, and a few other cities are considering them.[99] Paaswell points out that there are overlapping design features between BRT buses and light-rail cars—in many cases the buses are, in effect, a railcar body on a bus chassis. With this design, buses could be adapted and built by railcar manufacturers.

There is an expanding market for hybrid buses as well. New Flyer Industries, the Canadian company that produces hybrid buses for

Seattle and several other U.S. cities, has a long backlog of new bus orders. Seattle ordered 22 more buses in July 2008 and will be purchasing about 150 more over the next four years, according to fleet manager Jim Boone. Portland, Oregon, ordered 40 clean diesel buses and has options for another 160. Vancouver, British Columbia, ordered 24 electric trolley buses with options for an additional ten. The list goes on—Phoenix, Cleveland, and Washington, D.C., have placed orders. The company had orders for 3,332 buses in 2008, representing $1.78 billion in sales from U.S. cities.[100] New Flyer is the largest manufacturer of transit vehicles in Canada and the United States producing diesel and liquid and compressed natural gas buses, electric trolleys, and gasoline-electric and diesel-electric hybrid vehicles. The company employs 2,300 in three facilities in Winnipeg, Manitoba, and St. Cloud and Crookston, Minnesota.

Beyond railcars and buses are transportation systems and manufacturing the various subcomponents of the rail and BRT systems. Transportation engineers argue that a systems engineering approach to designing and managing transit systems could result in even more economic development benefit. The possibilities could include subsystems such as energy-efficient lighting in the railcars, stations, parking lots, etc., that a transit agency manages. These subsystems are completely independent of the transit vehicle, but quite important to the overall transit system and its contribution to a city's sustainability or climate change plan.[101]

Building a domestic transportation system industry will require considerable public and private investment. Oregon Iron Works invested $4 million in prototype development, but couldn't have succeeded without federal investment. Portland used Oregon Lottery funds to pay for the seven new streetcars that Oregon Iron Works produced. The funding bill required that the streetcars be manufactured at an Oregon-based and Oregon-owned company. But building a transit systems industry will require more than a few companies willing to be risk takers and a few cities creating demand. Experts in the field such as Boucher, Feldman, and Paaswell suggest that the United States needs to create a National Infrastructure Bank to finance a transit-manufacturing industry. An additional funding mechanism could be a national triple-exempt bond for mass transit. And a research and production consortium would need to be established. Transit agencies would have to change their procurement and contracting policies to create a more consistent demand for cars. These solutions suggest that building a transportation industry is more of a political than a technical challenge. To that end, Paaswell's Urban Transportation Research Center, the D.C.-based Institute for Policy Studies, and several unions organized meetings in June and September, 2009, to move the agenda forward.

A manufacturing strategy should be thought of as a state and national strategy as much as a local one. Not all cities will be able to follow Portland's path of local production of streetcars. Seattle has purchased more hybrid buses than just about any other city, but it will not be able to create a bus manufacturing industry.

This discussion takes us back to an issue that has almost been a forbidden concept—the need for explicit industrial policies on a national scale. Since World War II, the United States has had a tacit industrial policy, under the aegis of the Pentagon.[102] It has also had implicit industrial policies for a few industries that benefit from spillovers of government investment in basic science, such as biotech.[103] But efforts to promote explicit industrial policies for other commercial industries have run into broad ideological opposition based on the premise that government is not competent to "pick winners and losers." The fact, of course, is that government does this all the time, through its tax policies, R&D policies, trade policies, highway subsidies, labor-market policies, and defense and homeland security policies, not to mention the recent banking and auto bailouts. And sometimes, as in the demise of the light-rail industry, it practices industrial policy by neglect. The real question is whether government will practice industrial policy deliberately and discerningly, something that all of America's global competitors do. Industrial policy is intrinsically linked to the urban sustainability and climate change agenda.

7

Only Connect

I N THIS BOOK, WE HAVE SEEN SOME HEARTENING EXAMPLES OF leadership by American cities in creating more sustainable development through energy efficiency, recycling, public transit, and renewable energy. We have seen cities link sustainability and climate change initiatives to green job creation and even the development of whole new industries. We've also seen how cities have inspired national policy, after a long period of federal government inaction. From this tour of emerald cities, three interrelated conclusions are inescapable.

First, the American aversion to comprehensive planning, whether at the national or local level, gives the United States and its great cities a distinct disadvantage compared to other nations. In the United States, the default premise is that markets will sort things out. And when policy intervention is allowed, policies tend to operate in silos, disconnected from other policy areas that could create synergies that multiply impact.

Second, linkage is everything. The supply of lower-cost solar and wind energy, for example, connects to the demand for renewable power and policies to expand that demand, and to the need for accepting some environmental impacts in building the transmission lines to connect the power to urban centers. The development of new industries connects to the demand for their products. The creation of good green jobs, in turn, requires policies to promote efficiency and industrial development, which in turn requires standards and subsidies. And connecting green economic development to social justice requires policy that explicitly directs job training and jobs to the disadvantaged. Here, too, policies at the state and federal level will determine the extent to which climate change drives economic development and job creation.

And third, even though cities and states are the main actors in economic development in the United States, it is ultimately a national challenge. Although economic development is practiced by cities and states to enhance tax bases and to create jobs, it doesn't count only when it stimulates local activity. By definition, particular cities won't capture all the jobs their sustainability efforts generate, but adding to nationwide demand promotes a sustainable development path that produces jobs and industry in other locations. Still, there are many options for cities seeking to create green economic development.

THE DIFFERENCE GOOD PLANNING MAKES

The conclusions are interrelated because planning does not occur in isolation. For the United States to become a leader in reversing climate change and in developing and producing the necessary clean technology requires planning at all three levels of government. It will not happen otherwise. How would this look in practice?

We began our tour of U.S. cities with a brief detour to a pioneering European city, Freiburg, Germany, which offers an example of what can be done when a city—and nation—are serious about linking environmental goals to the incubation of new technologies and industries. I'll close with another European detour.

Sweden is famous for planning—actually infamous, in some circles. When my Northeastern University colleague and former Massachusetts governor, Michael Dukakis, a serious student of comparative public policy, was running for president, a popular put-down was that Dukakis's idea of light summer reading was a book on Swedish land-use planning.

But thanks to Sweden's consensual view of comprehensive planning as a policy imperative rather than a slanderous accusation, Swedish cities are able to achieve synergies that elude their American counterparts. As the result of sustainability planning that began in the 1970s, Sweden is ranked first in efforts to reduce its greenhouse gas emissions among 56 countries that comprise 90 percent of the world's greenhouse gas emissions.[1]

Sweden's commitment to clean technology goes back to the oil crisis of the 1970s. Hit hard by high oil prices, the Swedish government decided to reduce dependence on oil, which is now down to about one-third of Swedish energy consumption, mostly for transportation purposes. Maud Olofsson, minister for Enterprise and Energy and deputy prime minister of Sweden, points out that since Sweden introduced the world's first carbon tax, equivalent to $100 a ton (since raised to $150), in 1991, renewable energy has increased to 40 percent of energy consumption and CO_2 emissions have fallen 9 percent, while GNP increased by 44 percent. In 2003, a market-based green electricity certificate system was introduced. Certificate sellers are producers of electricity from renewable sources, who are issued certificates based on the amount of electricity they feed into the grid. Buyers are consumers or utilities that are required to use a certain percentage of renewable energy certificates. The goal is to increase the amount and cost-effectiveness of electricity produced from renewable sources such as bioenergy, wind power, hydropower, and geothermal.[2] In 2005, Sweden announced a goal of becoming oil-independent by 2020.

Complementary planning is taking place at the local level. City planners in most Swedish cities have taken to heart every principle that defines sustainable and "smart growth" in urban planning. Take Stockholm's Hammarby Sjöstad area, where planners decided to create a new residential ecocommunity in what had been a decaying factory district. Despite Sweden's planning, Stockholm witnessed suburban sprawl during the 1970s and '80s. Although there was not as much sprawl as in most U.S. cities, Stockholm city planners decided to counter the trend with dense infill development in the city. One of these areas was Hammarby Sjöstad, an area just south of the center city.

The original plan was to develop the 494-acre area into an environmentally sustainable Olympic Village in the city's bid for the 2004 Olympics, and later use the new infrastructure for a planned community. Stockholm wasn't chosen for the Olympics, but proceeded to develop Hammarby Sjöstad as an ecocommunity anyway. The project is about three-quarters of the way toward completion of 9,000 apartments housing 25,000 people, and 200,000 square meters of commercial floor space that will employ 10,000 people by 2015.

The planning team, comprised of representatives from several city planning departments, architects, and developers, created an integrated ecological model to guide the development. Its features include high density, mixed land uses, and easily available public transportation (a new tram line with four stops connects to the city's subway, and a free ferry connects to central Stockholm). The buildings feature green roofs, eco-friendly construction products, passive solar design, and solar panels and are heated and cooled through Stockholm's extensive district heating and cooling system (more on that below). The area is dotted with accessible green spaces that double as a natural drainage system that doesn't tax the sewage system with rainwater.

The single most impressive innovation, in my view—perhaps because it drew upon childhood memories of *The Jetsons*, "the modern space age family"—is the trash collection system, which is also an energy and compost system. There is no curbside trash pickup. Rather, trash is dropped by residents in their buildings or outside directly into one of three cylinders—for recyclables, organic waste, or burnable waste—from which it moves underground through a vacuum system of pipes to a central processing facility. The burnable waste is used to provide electricity and heat for the district. The organic waste is turned to compost, which is used to fertilize city parks. The rest is recycled.

As an urban planner, I was impressed by the degree to which planners from every department worked together to create the synergies that define an ecocommunity. More impressive is that Hammarby Sjöstad is not an isolated pilot project in an otherwise unsustainable city.

Stockholm embraced sustainability in the early 1970s and has received several awards for its efforts, including being the European Green Capital of 2010.[3] Stockholm excels in every aspect of sustainable development, but particularly the two areas where cities have the most impact—public transportation and building efficiency.

In transportation, all modes are planned synergistically. The result has been to reduce not only Stockholm's greenhouse gas emissions, but also the need for costly street and highway expansion. The city's extensive subway system, which opened in 1950, was converted from an underground light-rail system. The system is widely used, but to increase ridership even more, a low-cost, unlimited-use monthly pass was introduced in 1995.[4] A popular bus system supplements the subway, with about one-fourth of city buses running on biogas or ethanol. In 2008, the city began adding electric hybrid buses.

Like many northern European cities, Stockholm relies on bikes as a means of transportation. In 1975, the city began implementing a plan to introduce 300 kilometers of separate public bike lanes.[5] Stockholm implemented a ridership and safety plan in 1998 to better separate bike lanes from traffic, making cycling safer and encouraging greater bicycle use. While most cities simply paint a demarcation for the bike lane on the street surface, Stockholm used historic-looking brick and cobblestone to create a highly visible divide between auto traffic and bicyclists along many of its streets. The change in pavement signals drivers that they are encroaching on the bike lane. City transportation planners re-engineered some of the city's busiest intersections so that bikers could cross more safely. The 1998 plan, which already went beyond what any city in the United States is currently doing, was updated in 2006. One change was to make almost all transit stations bike-accessible. It is not surprising that Stockholm has one of the highest bicycle ridership rates in Europe.

To get more people out of their cars and reduce greenhouse gas emissions, congestion pricing was introduced on a trial basis in 2006.[6] The results were impressive: the expectation was that traffic would be reduced by 10 to 15 percent, but the actual figure was between 22 and 25 percent. Carbon dioxide emissions were reduced 2 to 3 percent overall in Stockholm County, and 14 percent in the inner city.[7] Public transport use increased by about 6 percent (though about 1.5 percent of that is credited to higher fuel prices during this period). At the start of the trial, 55 percent of Stockholmers were against the system, but resistance declined and acceptance took over to the point that the system was made permanent a year after its introduction. The system uses an automatic license plate recognition system to charge drivers. Entering or exiting vehicles pay the equivalent of $1.49 to $2.98, depending on the time of day. The maximum daily charge is $9.00.

Like many Swedish and other European cities, Stockholm has long employed district heating and cooling. We're not talking new technology here—it's more than 100 years old. In district heating, hot water is typically obtained from a cogeneration plant and is the by-product of electricity generation. The hot water is distributed through pipes for space heating and industrial purposes. It is one of the most effective ways to reduce the amount of energy it takes to heat and cool buildings. The energy efficiency of a cogeneration plant (also referred to as combined heat and power) is impressive—a rate of 90 percent versus 47 percent for a steam-electric power plant. Most Swedish cities use district heating, and much of Stockholm uses district cooling as well.

In 1995 the city assigned three committees (departments) to work together to establish criteria for ecological building: Real Estate, Streets, and Traffic; Environmental Health Protection; and City Planning. The goals they established would further reduce energy usage, promote renewable energy, and create demand for green products:

- Construction should cause minimal environmental impact and be resource-efficient, minimally polluting, and recyclable.
- Nonrenewable energy should account for no more than 30 percent of a building's total energy need.

What is every bit as significant as the ecological goals is how they are incorporated into an integrated planning process, as we saw in Hammarby Sjöstad.

Curiously, Stockholm's planners have not made an explicit effort to connect these carefully linked systems of renewable energy, green buildings, waste collection, and transport to economic development opportunities. But Stockholm does have an emerging clean-tech business sector, supported by a Cleantech Business Network that works like many of the public-private partnerships in the United States that pair university researchers and small-firm development. The city has large information and communication technology (ICT) and biotechnology clusters, and is the financial capital of northern Europe.[8] Stockholm was home to more than 2,700 companies in the clean technology sector in 2006, specializing in renewable energy, new fuels, waste-to-energy, and underground waste systems. Venture capital investment in these areas is growing rapidly.[9]

It is the national government that has taken the lead in promoting the development of the clean-tech industries that are now a key component of the economies of Stockholm and other Swedish cities. In 2009, the Swedish government committed $590 million to environmental projects to be spent over the next two years, $180 million of which will be used to commercialize new green technologies.[10] Stephan Edman, who was involved in the efforts that made Växjö,[11] Sweden, one of Europe's greenest cities, told the *Sydney Morning Herald*, "Clean technology and energy solutions are the biggest emerging global sectors. We can earn a lot of money and create a lot of jobs by being at the frontier. We are a small country, but we're exporting management, ideas and technical solutions to China and elsewhere. And China is sending technicians here to work for free just to learn. That's our chance to make a difference."[12]

Like Germany, Sweden is targeting investment to revitalize declining areas. Two industrial cities an hour and a half south of Stockholm, Norrköping and Linköping, have been transformed into clean-tech centers. In just five years, the area has spawned 230 technology companies employing 5,800 people. Several of the businesses got their start at Linköping University's Mjärdevi Science Park.[13] In many ways we see the same economic development policies at the local and state level in the United States. What is different is the level of linkage and support at the national level.

The closest to this level of interplay between local and higher levels of government in the United States is California, which has, in turn, become the model for national policy on energy efficiency, renewable energy, emissions, and waste. In each of the book's chapters we see how strong state policy in California paved the way for local action and how the state policy makers learned from what cities were doing. The state motivated development of renewable energy first by introducing net metering (1996), then by establishing a renewable portfolio standard (1996, updated 2006) and the country's first feed-in tariff (2008). To increase investment in renewable energy and other clean technologies, California's Green Wave Initiative called for using $1.5 billion from the state's pension funds for investment in clean technologies and providing incentives for residents and businesses to go solar (the Million Solar Roofs). California developed efficiency standards for buildings and appliances in the 1970s. The 1989 mandate that all cities and towns reduce the amount of trash sent to landfills by specified amounts resulted in California's cities having the highest recycling rates in the country. The state's Global Warming Solutions Act, passed in 2006, requires a 25 percent reduction in carbon emissions by 2020, and is stronger than the federal energy bill passed in 2009. California has adopted effective programs from its cities, such as the $10 million California Green Jobs Corps, a statewide replication of Oakland's Green Jobs Corps Act.

Building on the state's policies, Los Angeles is becoming quite entrepreneurial in its pursuit of green economic development, and in some ways is acting like its own country in pursuing its climate change agenda. The city's clean energy plan requires that it produce 40 percent of its electricity from renewable sources in more than ten years, and requires that 1,280 megawatts be supplied by solar energy. In July 2009, Los Angeles entered into a memorandum of understanding with China's Jiangsu Province to cooperate on solar energy through exchanging expertise and accessing each other's markets. Jiangsu Province has become a hub of solar energy production in China, exporting $6.5 billion of solar energy products annually from 500 manufacturers. The province is unique in China in having a clean energy stimulus plan.[14]

State-city environmental/energy policy synergies are also emerging in Oregon and Washington, motivated by environmental priorities. Other states and cities by necessity are starting with an economic development agenda (Michigan, Ohio, Pennsylvania), and hopefully will back into a sustainability/climate change focus.

THE NEED FOR INDUSTRIAL POLICY

Climate change is real, and our window of opportunity is narrow. The clean technologies that are being developed to address climate change will be the growth industries of the future. As China, India, and others try to leapfrog development past the dirty development of Western countries, the United States should seek to become a leading exporter of clean technologies. Yet the American Clean Energy and Security Act passed by the House in 2009 does not go as far as Germany, Sweden, and other countries in catalyzing clean technologies. If the United States is to become a leader, we need a national industrial policy to drive demand.

Just as the United States has been averse to planning, it has also been resistant to explicit industrial policies. Although government has had technology policies—as we saw in chapter 2, the National Institutes of Health consciously promoted biotech, and government grants and contracts helped research universities develop advanced computer technologies—the idea that government should promote particular industries is generally frowned upon in the prevailing U.S. ideology. Government, it is said, is not competent to pick winners and losers; that is the function of market forces.

Of course, the reality is that the U.S. government, as well as cities and states, has helped create industrial winners for more than two hundred years, beginning with Alexander Hamilton's Report on Manufactures and extending through the government subsidy of the railroads and the development of land grant agricultural and mechanical universities during the Lincoln administration. Government also promotes technology in its tax and R&D policies, though these tend to be scattershot rather than focused. American leadership in agriculture was the fruit of government policies. And during the Cold War, the Pentagon functioned as a vast, if tacit, set of industrial policies.[15] Lately, the huge expenditures on homeland security have created subsidies for surveillance technologies.

With the challenge of reversing climate change, and the opportunity to use an environmental imperative to create new environment-friendly technologies, industries, and jobs, the question is whether our government at all levels will recognize the ubiquity of market failures when it comes to the environment and acknowledge the need for planned industrial policies. If we hold on to the idea that manufacturing is not essential to the nation's economy, we will miss the opportunity to have environmental goals serve economic goals, and leadership will pass to other nations.

The larger conclusion is one that should be familiar to students of ecology: the parts are linked to the whole, and to each other. We must only connect them. Renewable energy, energy efficiency, green building, recycling, waste reduction, fewer cars, more trains, walking, and biking are not individual policies but parts of the whole of how cities must be transformed. As impressive are the efforts of many American cities, they will realize their full potential only when the exercise is understood to be comprehensive and only when federal and state policy is working to support them.

Notes

1. Benchmark Study: European Sustainable Urban Development Projects. Available at http://www.secureproject.org/download/18.360a0d56117c51a2d3080007 8420/Vauban_Germany.pdf (accessed May 4, 2009).

2. Badenova, the area's utility, offers energy audits for households on efficiency and advice on installing renewable systems and spends about €2.4 million annually on promoting renewable energy.

3. "Projekt '10% Strom aus erneuerbaren Energiequellen,'" February 4, 2004. Available at http://www.solarregion.freiburg.de/downloads/g03222.pdf (accessed May 5, 2009).

4. The feed-in tariff was proposed by the German Association for the Promotion of Solar Power in 1989 and first adopted by the cities of Aachen, Hammelburg, and Freising, shortly followed by 40 more cities. The feed-in tariff helps defray the average €4,500 cost of installing a residential system. About 40 percent of Germany's PV market is residential, 50 percent is commercial, and the remaining 10 percent consists of large-scale ground-mounted systems (see Stryi-Hipp, 2009, 2004).

5. Karin Schneider, head of public relations for the Fraunhofer-Institut für Solare Energiesysteme ISE. E-mail correspondence, May 4, 2009.

6. Freiburg's solar activity and the Fraunhofer Institute attracted the International Solar Energy Society to move its headquarters from Australia to an existing building that was retrofitted with transparent insulation and solar cells—technology developed at Fraunhofer. In 2006, the German Federal Ministry of the Environment financed the creation of the Photovoltaic Technology Evaluation Center in Freiburg to conduct research and development to accelerate technology transfer to industry. It is located close to the Fraunhofer Institute in a solar-powered center. See "Freiburg Green City: Approaches to Sustainability," available at http://www.freiburg.de/servlet/PB/show/1199617_12/GreenCity.pdf (accessed May 5, 2009).

7. The purchases included Global Expertise Wafer Division (GEWD), a Malaysian wafer trader in 2005, a majority share of cell manufacturer Solar Energy Power of Singapore, and an 80 percent share of Poseidon Solar Services, an Indian wafer recycler.

8. Data provided in e-mail correspondence from Thomas Dresel, director of SolarRegion Freiburg, January 28, 2009.

9. Fell, 2009; Solarenergie-Förderverein, 1994.

10. Cited in German Federal Ministry for Environment press release, "Erneuerbare Energien geben 235.000 Menschen Arbeit," September 17, 2007, available at http://www.erneuerbare-energien.de/inhalt/39983/4592/ (accessed August 8, 2009).

11. International Energy Agency, 2008.

12. European Renewable Energy Council, 2004.

13. Yoon and Yoon, 2007.

14. Joint Global Change Research Institute, 2006.

15. Stryi-Hipp, 2004.

16. Sawin, 2004.

17. According to BSW, a German solar industry trade group.

18. See http://www.wind-energie.de/en/wind-energy-in-germany/ (accessed January 9, 2009).

19. Government estimates cited in Burgermeister, 2008; Dürrschmidt and van Mark, 2006.

20. Germany Trade and Invest, "The Photovoltaic Industry in Germany—The World's Strongest PV Cluster," Spring 2009 Industry Overview.

21. For example, International Council for Local Environmental Initiatives (ICLEI), Energy Cités, U.S. Council of Mayors Climate Change Group.

CHAPTER 2

1. Gavron, 2007.

2. For a discussion of how various advocates of the practice define smart growth, see Ye, Mandpe, and Meyer, 2005; Gillham, 2002. Among the numerous organizations identifying smart growth practices are the American Planning Association, Smart Growth America, Smart Growth Network, Urban Land Institute, and the U.S. Environmental Protection Agency.

3. Conway et al. (2007: 13) note that a sector is an employment strategy that has economic development ramifications, while a cluster is an economic development concept that has employment ramifications.

4. Porter, 1997.

5. Fitzgerald, 2006.

6. See Conway et al., 2007; Fitzgerald, 2006; Giloth, 2004.

7. Pollin, Wicks-Lim, and Garrett-Peltier, 2009: 7. The city mayors' poverty figures are derived from a National League of Cities survey conducted in 2008.

8. Pollin, Wicks-Lim, and Garrett-Peltier, 2009.

9. See Fitzgerald and Leigh, 2003, ch. 2, for an extended discussion of sectoral strategies, including critiques.

10. See Kuttner, 1997: 209–218 for a historical analysis of U.S. government involvement in economic development. This theme is elaborated in chapter 7.

11. See Fitzgerald and Leigh, 2003; Theodore and Carlson, 1998; Siegel and Kwass, 1995.

12. See Portney, 2003; Devuyst, 2001.

13. This definition is from the 1987 Brundtland Report. In 1983 the UN created the World Commission on Environment and Development to address dilemmas created by world population growth. The 1987 report of the Commission, the Brundtland Report (named after Gro Harlem Brundtland, then prime minister of Norway, who chaired the Commission), is considered the beginning of the sustainable development movement. The 1992 UN Earth Summit in Rio de Janeiro resulted in the Rio Declaration, which was signed by 179 countries. The declaration's action plan, Agenda 21, stresses the importance of both national and local action to solve environmental problems and promote sustainable development practices. Over 2,000 cities have signed on to Local Agenda 21. Since then, several organizations have defined sustainable cities, including Local Governments for Sustainability USA and the Sierra Club. See also the Urban Accords Institute, organizer of an accord signed by cities around the globe in 2005. The cities committed to practices in the areas of energy, waste reduction, urban design, urban nature, transportation, environmental health, and water.

14. Adapted from http://www.rec.org/REC/Programs/SustainableCities/What.html (accessed November 13, 2008).

15. As Newman and Kenworthy (1999) point out, Agenda 21 has an environmental and economic agenda that includes eliminating poverty, reducing resources and waste in first-world countries, global cooperation on environmental issues, and citizen participation in policy making. Scott Campbell's seminal article in the *Journal of the American Planning Association* discusses the inherent conflicts of attempting to achieve all three in detail (Campbell, 1996).

16. See White, 2001.

17. American Planning Association, 2000.

18. Portney, 2003: 224.

19. See Krueger and Gibbs (2007) for a discussion of this literature. See also Gunder (2006), who reached similar conclusions in case studies of Toronto, South East England, Melbourne, and Sydney.

20. See Warner, 2002. A recent survey of 40 cities by Living Cities found that few climate change or sustainability plans incorporated working families or poor people into the agenda (Hecht, 2009).

21. See Fitzgerald, 2006; Mier, 1993; Krumholz, 1991; Krumholz and Forester, 1991; Giloth and Betancur, 1988.

22. Dreier, 2009.

23. Gould, Pellow, and Schnaiberg, 2009; Bullard, 2005; Lake, 2000.

24. Agyeman, Bullard, and Evans, 2003: 5.

25. Agyeman, 2005: 43.

26. Formerly the International Council for Local Environmental Initiatives.

27. For the most part, we do not see the terms "social equity" or "environmental justice" much in writings on urban climate change. For example, the U.S. Mayors Climate Protection Agreement unanimously endorsed in 2005 by the U.S. Conference of Mayors has 825 participating cities agreeing to work toward meeting the suggested 7 percent reduction in greenhouse gas emissions from 1990 levels by 2012 in the Kyoto Protocol and to urge their state and the federal government to enact policies and start programs to achieve this goal and to support a carbon tax. In addition, cities are asked to inventory their greenhouse gas emissions and create an action plan to achieve emissions reductions through land use policies that reduce sprawl and create compact, walkable urban neighborhoods; to promote transportation alternatives to the car; to increase use of renewable energy; to promote energy efficiency through building code improvements and retrofitting city facilities and all buildings; and other related activities. While acting in each of these areas is essential, none of the recommended actions mention social or environmental justice (or economic development).

28. Apollo Alliance, 2004. A later report estimates that about 5 million jobs could be created over ten years with $500 billion in investment in green technologies (Apollo Alliance, 2008).

29. See http://www.oaklandnet.com/Oil/default.html (accessed July 29, 2009).

30. See http://www.oaklandcityattorney.org/PDFS/Council%20Reports/Annual Report02–03.pdf for details of the class action law suit and settlement (accessed April 15, 2009).

31. Personal interview with Ian Kim, April 13–14, 2009.

32. See http://californiagreenstimulus.org/ for list of organizations (accessed April 14, 2009).

33. See Fitzgerald and Leigh, 2003.

34. See LeRoy, 2005; Peters and Fisher, 2004.

CHAPTER 3

1. Kutscher, 2007.

2. Apollo Alliance, 2004.

3. Martinot, 2007.

4. Zweibel, Mason, and Fthenakis, 2008.

5. The comparison to coal is not the installed cost per kilowatt, but rather the levelized cost of electricity, a calculation of the cost over the lifetime of the technologies being compared. The levelized cost includes the installed cost, efficiency of production, and financial parameters (cost of debt, percent equity, depreciation, and incentives).

6. Maycock, 2007.

7. Grama and Bradford, 2008.

8. American Wind Energy Association, http://www.awea.org/newsroom/releases/ AWEA_Market_Release_Q4_011708.html. (accessed September 1, 2009).

9. Galbraith, 2009.

10. Harvey, Bryant, and Hille, 2009.

11. Makower, Pernick, and Wilder, 2009.

12. Furnas, 2009: 4.

13. About 90 percent of China's solar production is for export. China's share of the world market has expanded from 1 percent in 2003 to over 18 percent in 2007 and is still growing. Domestic demand is just beginning. China's national renewable energy policy is investing $3.5 billion to develop 500 megawatts of annual capacity by 2010, moving to 3 gigawatts by 2020 and 60 gigawatts by 2050. The plan focuses on increasing production of all components of the supply chain. A planned 100-megawatt solar PV farm in Dunhuang City will have five times the capacity of the current largest PV power plant in the world (see Dorn, 2007; LaPedus, 2006).

14. Other European countries have realized the same results with feed-in tariffs. Europe now produces 40 GW of wind power, about 75 percent of world capacity (Pernick and Wilder, 2007).

15. New Energy Finance, 2009.

16. Kammen, Kapadia, and Fripp, 2004; Sissine, 2006. Innovation is measured by patents.

17. The bill extends a 30 percent tax credit for residential and commercial solar installations for eight years and extends it to utilities and alternative minimum tax filers. It also authorizes $800 million for clean energy bonds for renewable energy generating facilities.

18. Farber et al., 2008.

19. McMahon, 2008.

20. American Wind Energy Association. Available at http://www.awea.org/newsroom/releases/AWEA_Market_Release_Q108.html (accessed December 15, 2008).

21. Aeppel, 2008. Aeppel cites economist Jeff Rubin, who estimates that every 10 percent increase in distance adds 4.5 percent in energy costs for shipping.

22. Bezdek, 2007.

23. Frantzis et al., 2008 and http://www.seia.org/cs/solar_jobs_map (accessed September 30, 2009).

24. If 25 percent of property owners participate, Berkeley can expect to reduce greenhouse gas emissions by 2,000 tons a year, accounting for about 10 percent of Measure G's goal.

25. Jones, 2009.

26. See http://www.cityofberkeley.info/ContentDisplay.aspx?id=27076 (accessed February 9, 2009).

27. DeVries is right—despite a comprehensive array of policies to promote renewable energy, California is not capturing the production jobs. As discussed earlier in the chapter, the big players in the highly concentrated solar PV industry are

following a corporate strategy of integrating across the value chain. Take SunPower, the Silicon Valley parent company of Richmond's SunPower Systems. The company has regional offices throughout the United States and in Germany, Italy, Spain, Switzerland, Australia, Korea, Australia, and the Philippines, where most of its production occurs. SunPower has followed the path of other leading solar companies by acquiring its suppliers. In 2007 SunPower acquired PowerLight Corporation, a leading global provider of large-scale solar systems. The company's goal is to reduce the cost of solar systems by 50 percent by 2012, and to do this it needs to control as much of the value chain as possible to ensure a steady supply of parts at a stable price. While this is the pathway to firm growth, it doesn't necessarily maximize job creation in California or the United States.

28. Personal interview, Gary Gerber, December 3, 2008.

29. See http://www.ci.richmond.ca.us/archives/66/ord.%2052–06%20%20LEO% 207%2018%2006%20final.pdf

30. See http://urbanhabitat.org/node/2307 for a full description of the agreement (accessed April 30, 2009).

31. Personal interview, January 27, 2009.

32. See http://www.workdayminnesota.org/index.php?news_6_4007

33. See http://www.ibew.org/articles/09daily/0904/090416_TrainingCenter.htm

34. See http://www.workdayminnesota.org/index.php?news_6_4007

35. Cited in press release on the plan. Available at http://www.ci.austin.tx.us/ council/mw_acpp_release.htm (accessed October 1, 2008).

36. GreenChoice has been ranked first among 600 of the nation's utility-sponsored green-power programs by the Department of Energy's National Renewable Energy Laboratory for the last five years. In a recent agreement, the rate, 5.5 cents per kilowatt, is about 2 cents more per kilowatt than the utility charges other customers (the average residential customer ends up paying a premium of about $18.50 per month for green power). The utility agrees to purchase all of the provider's power (a wind farm) at a guaranteed price over a 10–15-year contract. Demand from ecologically minded residents was so high in 2006 that Austin Energy had to hold a raffle to select new participants in the program. In addition to residents, Austin City Hall, the Austin School District, and about 500 businesses participate.

37. Personal interview, August 19, 2008.

38. Austin Chamber of Commerce report cited in Krueger and Gibbs, 2007.

39. The plan also included several solar projects, including 60 schools and other public buildings, and a zero-net-energy housing subdivision.

40. Personal interview, January 26, 2009.

41. AE commissioned a study to estimate the cost of adopting solar energy soon after the announcement was made. When the study was released in mid-2006, critics argued that it undervalued the air quality, climate change, and energy security benefits of developing solar and feared that AE would use the study to justify not investing in solar. The RMC then passed a resolution requiring that all energy acquisitions be subjected to the same type of cost analysis as solar so that citizens could compare the

costs of development. Another resolution asked the city council to include the environmental and energy security benefits of solar that were not evaluated in the original study (see Mottola, 2005; Clark-Madison, 2003).

42. Thin-film solar technologies use non-silicon semiconductor materials to create photovoltaic cells that convert sunlight into electricity. They are cheaper than silicon-based cells, but currently less efficient. In addition to price, their advantage is that they can be printed on flexible substances such as roofing material. Helio Volt's cells are made from copper indium gallium selenide, referred to as CIGS. They are 100 times thinner than solar cells made from silicon. Because of its thinness, the CIGS coating can be imbedded in roofing material, windows and skylights, and shades.

43. Austin's aggressive 2007 Climate Protection Plan will create more demand for renewable energy, but a state RPS is needed to drive large-scale demand. The Austin Climate Protection Plan calls for eliminating all CO_2 emissions from municipal activities by the year 2020. To achieve this goal, the city will power all city facilities with 100 percent renewable energy, convert the city's vehicle fleet to alternative fuels and electric power, and implement greenhouse gas reduction plans in every city department. The plan increases the renewable goal for Austin Energy to 700 megawatts and increases the RPS to 30 percent by 2020. It also calls for requiring new single-family houses to be zero-net-energy-capable by 2015 and increasing efficiency in all new commercial buildings by 75 percent in the same period.

44. Mayor Wynn relates that Austin Energy's conservation programs have led to business development, netting a few thousand jobs. When the programs began in the 1980s, several "mom and pop" weatherization companies sprang up. Several of them were certified by Austin Energy and are now successful companies in plumbing and HVAC. If new companies and jobs can be created through even larger-scale energy efficiency programs funded by the stimulus package, Wynn projects that a couple thousand more jobs could be created (personal interview, January 24, 2009).

45. Personal interview, John Merritt, VP of Marketing, Solar Array Ventures, November 6, 2008.

46. See http://www.statesman.com/business/content/business/stories/other/0411/0411solar.html (accessed May 15, 2009).

47. Rowan, 2008.

48. See http://greeninc.blogs.nytimes.com/2009/06/01/solar-push-in-texas-fails/?hp (accessed 13 August, 2009).

49. Personal interview, January 24, 2009.

50. Carlton, 2007.

51. Friedman, 2008: 387.

52. First Solar's 2008 third-quarter profits were $99.3 million ($1.20 a share), showing signficant growth from 2007's $46 million (58 cents a share) (Chavez, 2008).

53. Interview with Xunming Deng, January 14, 2009.

54. Personal interview with Solargystics CEO Jeff Culver (January 6, 2009).

55. Personal interview, December 3, 2008.

56. Dykes et al., 2008.

57. See Environmental Law and Policy Center of the Midwest, 2002; Sterzinger and Svrcek, 2004, 2005.

58. Critics such as the Sierra Club say that the plan should place more emphasis on energy efficiency and less on unproven "clean coal" technologies.

59. The RPS also requires electric utilities to implement energy efficiency programs to achieve energy savings of 22.5 percent by the end of 2025 and to reduce peak energy demand by 1 percent in 2009 and by an additional 0.75 percent per year through 2018.

60. Great Lakes Wind Network. http://www.wire-net.org/wind_newsletter.htm (accessed November 12, 2008).

61. Sterzinger, 2009.

62. Breckenridge, 2009.

63. Personal communication, May 18, 2009.

64. Personal interview, November 18, 2008.

65. See http://www.awea.org/windletter/wl_08mar.html

66. Caldwell, 2007.

67. See http://seattle.bizjournals.com/seattle/stories/2008/03/10/story8.html

68. See http://www.portoflongview.com/page.asp?view=4322; http://www.all-business.com/north-america/united-states-oregon/4084473-1.html

69. See http://www.oregonlive.com/news/index.ssf/2009/02/port_of_vancouver_announces_wi.html; http://columbian.com/article/20090206/BIZ01/702069984

70. See http://www.startribune.com/local/34968914.html

71. See http://www.corpuschristi-mpo.org/Newsletter.html

72. Personal interview, 8 June, 2009.

73. Burgermeister, 2009. German economy ministry information from http://www.platts.com/Nuclear/News/8338150.xml

74. Browning, 2008.

75. Asmus, 2008.

76. Cited in Galbraith and Wald, 2008.

77. World Business Council for Sustainable Development. 2009.

78. Bradsher, 2009.

79. See http://cleantech.com/news/node/554 and http://www.democraticunderground.com/discuss/duboard.php?az=view_all&address=115x132045 (accessed 13 August, 2009).

80. U.S. Department of Energy, 2008.

81. Furnas, 2009: 2.

82. For the most part, Europe's electricity grid is already interconnected, allowing energy to be stored and transported over large distances. And soon the grid will be extended to desert regions of North Africa, where energy from solar-thermal farms can be transported to Europe. The continent's vast grid also acts as a storage facility for renewable energy, so overcoming difficulties that arise from the intermittent nature of green energy production (Burgermeister, 2009).

83. See http://blogs.wsj.com/environmentalcapital/2008/04/28/green-line-california-transmission-battle-divides-environmentalists/?mod=WSJBlog; http://www.nytimes.com/2009/02/12/science/earth/12solar.html?scp=1&sq=mojave&st=cse

84. Revkin, 2009.

85. Barringer, 2009.

86. http://online.wsj.com/article/BT-CO-20090320-706706.html

87. Talbot, 2009.

88. Cited in Ling, 2009.

89. See Feist, Schlesinger, and Frye, 2008, for a more detailed discussion of how smart grids work.

90. Sterzinger, 2009.

91. U.S. Department of Commerce, 2008.

92. Sterzinger, 2009.

93. Sterzinger, 2009; unpublished document of the Renewable Energy Policy Project and personal communication, February 11, 2009.

94. U.S. Department of Commerce, 2008.

95. Cited in Klein, 2007.

96. Mattera, 2009.

97. See http://www.nytimes.com/2008/12/05/business/05power.html (accessed February 8, 2009).

98. Joint Global Change Research Institute, 2006.

99. In 2007 EU Commissioner Stavros Dimas noted that as a world leader in renewable energy Germany needed to intensify its efforts to reduce greenhouse gases by implementing stronger policies to promote fuel-efficient vehicles. See http://www.dw-world.de/dw/article/0,2144,2436091,00.html (accessed September 23, 2008).

100. Personal communication, February 2, 2009.

CHAPTER 4

1. U.S. Environmental Protection Agency, 2004. See also source data in the 2002 Annual Energy Review from the U.S. Energy Information Administration, available at http://tonto.eia.doe.gov/FTPROOT/multifuel/038402.pdf (accessed August 3, 2009).

2. This estimate includes residential, commercial, and industrial space. The makeup will vary significantly by region and use. Less than half of the new construction will be in the Northeast, while 87 percent will be in the rapidly growing West and Southwest. Most of the new construction will be residential, but that varies too—70 percent of the new space in the Midwest will be industrial (Nelson, 2004).

3. Working with the Powell Center for Construction and Environment at the University of Florida, Eric Sundquist, a researcher at the Center on Wisconsin Strategy at the University of Wisconsin, Madison, estimates that every $1 million invested in

energy efficiency retrofitting creates 10–11 jobs for the duration of the project (report in progress; information obtained by personal communication September 8, 2008). Pollin et al. (2008) estimate that 15 direct and indirect jobs are created per $1 million of energy efficiency investment. The experience of European residential energy efficiency programs is that every million euros invested creates 11.3 to 13.5 full-time equivalent jobs, mostly in installation of more efficient residential heating systems, windows, and other energy-saving systems or appliances (see Dupressoir et al., 2007).

4. McGraw-Hill, 2006. McGraw-Hill is a global information services provider working in the financial services, education, and business information markets.

5. Hildt, 2001. Goldstein (2007) provides a striking example of regulation producing innovation in the refrigerator industry. Many manufacturers resisted regulation thinking that it would raise costs, but actually found that their production costs decreased. As refrigerator manufacturers began adding new features beginning in the late 1940s, energy efficiency actually decreased over time. Forced to act after California initiated energy performance standards in 1975, Congress passed the National Energy Conservation and Policy Act of 1978, partly by request of the industry, which wanted uniform standards. The national legislation required the Department of Energy to develop mandatory standards. Two years later, DOE did not issue standards. But manufacturers built according to California standards and actually exceeded them, and at the same time reduced their per-unit cost of production.

6. Roland-Holst, 2008.

7. Cited in Palmer, 2007.

8. Rogers, 2007.

9. McKinsey Global Institute, 2008.

10. Farrell et al., 2008.

11. Schneider, 2006.

12. Renner, Sweeney, and Kubit, 2008: 70; Dupressoir et al., 2007.

13. German Ministry of the Environment, Nature Conservation and Nuclear Safety. "Kurzinfo Energieeffizienz (Energy Efficiency Brief)." Accessed May 6, 2009, from: http://www.bmu.de/energieeffizienz/kurzinfo/doc/37891.php

14. Ibid.

15. German Ministry of the Environment, Nature Conservation and Nuclear Safety. "Nationaler Energieeffizienzplan: Strategie des Bundesumweltministeriums." October 16, 2008. Accessed May 6, 2009, from: http://www.bmu.de/files/pdfs/allgemein/application/pdf/energieeffizienzplan.pdf

16. Gabriel, Sigmar. "Umweltschutz als Wirtschaftsfaktor [Environment Protection as Factor of the Economy]." BMU-Magazin. Accessed May 6, 2009, from http://www.bmu.de/dossier_arbeit_und_umwelt/doc/43540.php

17. The only federal efficiency-oriented program in the United States is the U.S. Department of Energy and the Environmental Protection Agency's ENERGY STAR program, which helps low-income families weatherize to reduce energy costs. At a cost of $2.5 billion per year, the ENERGY STAR programs yield $600 million per year in energy savings. Energy efficiency businessman and advocate Stephen Cowell estimates

that over ten years, this $2.5 billion investment produces more than $5 billion in consumer savings. Figures cited in Cowell, 2008.

18. Rogers, 2007.

19. Other allowable activities include transportation programs that conserve energy, reducing methane and other greenhouse gas emissions from landfills, renewable energy installations on government buildings, energy-efficient traffic signals and streetlights, deployment of combined heat and power and district heating and cooling systems, and others; see http://www.eecbg.energy.gov/ and http://www.energy.gov/news2009/7101.htm (accessed May 17, 2009).

20. Of the $3.2 billion DOE Energy Efficiency and Conservation Block Grant program, $1.9 billion will be distributed to cities and counties and $456 million will be available competitively for local energy efficiency projects. To ensure accountability, the Department of Energy will provide guidance to and require grant recipients to report on the number of jobs created or retained, energy saved, renewable energy capacity installed, greenhouse gas emissions reduced, and funds leveraged. See http://www.energy.gov/news2009/7101.htm (accessed May 17, 2009).

21. The legislation requires state governors to assure the Secretary of Energy that their states are moving toward adoption of energy codes that meet or exceed 2009 IECC for residential buildings and ASHRAE standard 90.1–2007 for commercial buildings (ARRA—H.R. 1 Sec 410, p. 60). The program structure for the block grants is based on that established in the Energy Independence and Security Act (EISA, P.L. 110–140). Based on this structure, states must also pay prevailing wages "as determined by the Secretary of Labor, in accordance with sections 3141 through 3144, 3146, and 3147 of title 40, United States Code."

22. Other rating systems exist, such as the Green Building Initiative's Green Globes, but LEED is a trademarked guidance and assessment system for new construction and renovation and the most commonly used. See http://www.thegbi.org/green-globes-tools/ (accessed August 14, 2008).

23. See American Institute of Architects, 2008, for a discussion of these and other incentives.

24. Statistics from http://www.usgbc.org/LEED/Project/CertifiedProjectList.aspx (accessed September 17, 2009). The World Green Building Council promotes LEED certification programs in other countries as well, with particular success in India, Mexico, and Brazil. Other well-established green building certification systems include the BRE Environmental Assessment Method (BREEAM) in the U.K; Australia's GreenStar, which is being adopted by South Africa; Comprehensive Assessment System for Building Environmental Efficiency (CASBEE) in Japan; and Canada's GreenGlobes. Germany has created its own standards, the Deutsche Gesellschaft für Nachhaltiges Bauen. Many of these systems are related, as they draw from BREEAM, which was created in 1990. Unlike LEED, the BREEAM system relies on a network of independent assessors who validate compliance with the system. This differs from LEED's internal system of validation.

25. See Energy Information Administration, 2005, 2003, 1999.

26. See Turner and Frankel, 2008 and Gifford, 2008.

27. One line of LEED criticism targets the paperwork, time, and expense of the certification process (the cost of the actual construction of a green building is typically only 2 percent more than a traditional building). Many more buildings are eligible for LEED certification than actually apply, because the certification process is onerous and costly. James W. Hunt III, chief of Environmental and Energy Services for the City of Boston, notes that this is why the city's LEED ordinance requires all construction projects to meet LEED certification requirements, but not to go through the official certification process. Instead, developers submit explanations to the city on which LEED credits they have achieved. The USGBC points out that having official certification has benefits that cannot be realized without it, such as better loan-to-value ratios, lower insurance premiums, and even higher building value. Another line of criticism is that points don't reflect the importance of different design elements, the most commonly cited example being earning the same point for a bicycle rack as for an efficient heating and cooling system. Further, LEED does not take into account regional differences (e.g., in some places water efficiency is more of a priority). Finally, LEED does not take into account the location of buildings with respect to public transportation, with many studies finding that the energy used by employees or customers in driving to them exceeds the energy realized in the green building (see Wilson, 2007).

28. Among the ways to earn these points are decreasing lighting power density, installing automated lighting or HVAC controls, improving general HVAC efficiency, and using EPA Energy Star–eligible equipment.

29. See http://www.architecture2030.0rg/about.php (accessed August 18, 2008).

30. Kent Peterson, former president of ASHRAE, notes that although the European Union is far ahead of the United States in building regulation, there is very little enforcement. He suggests that building energy consumption in most European countries is far below that of California (personal interview, August 4, 2008).

31. During the energy crisis of the 1970s, the federal government asked ASHRAE to develop building energy standards, resulting in Standard 90.1 becoming the national reference for state building codes. Standard 90.1 is updated every three years.

32. A draft of the standard was available for public comment in early 2007. A disbanding of the committee in October 2008 caused some to question whether the standard would be released. There has been speculation that the disbandment was in response to objections from the steel and wood industries and utilities. ASHRAE reports that the committee is being reconstituted and will produce the standard on time.

33. Personal interview with Edward Mazria, founder of Architecture 2030, August 15, 2008.

34. Personal interview, August 4, 2008.

35. The U.S. Department of Energy rating system designates Energy Star status to commercial buildings that use 35 percent less energy and emit 35 percent

less carbon than projects of similar size and type. The ratings are based on building performance data in the Environmental Protection Agency Target Finder and the Commercial Buildings Energy Consumption Survey data on national averages for building energy use.

36. For details on AB 1103 see http://info.sen.ca.gov/pub/07–08/bill/asm/ab_1101–1150/ab_1103_bill_20071012_chaptered.pdf (accessed March 7, 2009).

37. See https://mail4.neu.edu/mailp22/jofitzgerald.nsf/0/C6DA134D444CE54585 25757C005AC01A/$File/LIGH%20brochure_6-30%20version.pdf?Open Element&FileName=LIGH%20brochure_6-30%20version.pdf (accessed 15 May, 2009).

38. ESCOs are businesses that develop, install, and arrange financing for projects designed to improve the energy efficiency and maintenance costs for facilities. They typically monitor and maintain the project over a defined time period, sometimes as long as 20 years. The value of ESCOs is that they assume the risk that energy savings will occur to the building or facility owner. See http://www.naesco.org/resources/esco .htm (accessed 28 May, 2009).

39. Personal interview, 26 May, 2009.

40. See Lee and Ito, 2008 and the collaborative Web site, http://www.lattc.edu/dept/lattc/redi/utility.html (accessed May 22, 2009).

41. See http://www.laccdbuildsgreen.org/building_green_laccd_is_building_gre-en.php (accessed March 15, 2009).

42. See http://www.propositiona.org/green_room.html (accessed March 12, 2009).

43. See http://www.laccd.edu/news/PropAStatus.htm (accessed March 12, 2009); personal communication, Stuart Silverstein, May 27, 2009.

44. Personal interview, Stuart Silverstein, Public Affairs Director, /BuildLACCD.

45. Gordon and Hays, 2008; White and Walsh, 2008.

46. Personal interview, 28 May, 2009.

47. Employment figures from COWS, http://www.cows.org/pdf/rp-Greening-Wisconsin.pdf (accessed 20 June, 2009).

48. At the time of writing, the city was soliciting public input on the draft plan. See http://www.portlandonline.com/osd/index.cfm?c=41896 (accessed 26 May, 2009).

49. Summary based on interviews with Susan Anderson, director, Bureau of Planning and Sustainability and Erin Flynn, Urban Development director, Portland Development Commission, City of Portland (7 May, and 15 May, respectively), and a presentation by Andria Jabob available at http://www.solaramericacities.energy. gov/PDFs/2009_Annual_Meeting/Financing_Solar_Local_Government_Facilitator_Residential_and_Community_Purchases/Portland_Utility_Bill_Financing_Model_Development.pdf (accessed 26 May, 2009).

50. The Pittsburgh Urban Redevelopment Authority (URA) just began offering lower interest rates for green building projects on its urban development loan programs. These include the Urban Development Fund, Technology Zone/Enterprise Zone, and the Pittsburgh Business Growth Fund. For more details on the programs

see http://www.ura.org/bdcFinancingPrograms.html and http://www.ura.org/technol-ogyZoneBackground.html. In November 2007, the city council approved changes in the city's building code to offer sustainable development density bonuses. Developers of nonresidential projects that are green-certified can add 20 percent more floor area and 20 percent more height to their projects.

51. The LEED green building rating system is a nationally accepted bench-mark for the design, construction, and operation of high-performance green build-ings. LEED's whole-building approach to sustainability recognizes performance in five key areas: sustainable site development, water savings, energy efficiency, materials selection, and indoor environmental quality. See http://www.usgbc.org/DisplayPage .aspx?CategoryID=19 (accessed March 20, 2007).

52. O'Toole, 2009.

53. Flora, 2006.

54. Personal interview, December 18, 2006.

55. The Ben Franklin gave another $1 million to Philadelphia University to lead the same activities in the eastern part of the state.

56. See http://www.paggp.org/

57. See http://www.earthtimes.org/articles/show/green-building-alliance-announ ces-240000,688677.shtml (accessed March 1, 2009).

58. LEED for New Construction or LEED for Core & Shell certification.

59. The New York legislature has funded eight Strategically Targeted Academic Research (STAR) centers. The Centers of Excellence were created by then Governor Pataki to revitalize the rust belt cities of upstate New York. The other centers focus on bioinformatics and life sciences, nanoelectronics, photonics and microsystems, small-scale systems integration and packaging (microelectronics), and wireless and information technology; see New York State Foundation for Science, Technology and Innovation, "Centers of Excellence," available at http://www.nystar.state.ny.us/coes .htm (accessed August 19, 2008).

60. The other centers are: Buffalo, Center of Excellence in Bioinformatics & Life Sciences; Albany, Center of Excellence in Nanoelectronics; Rochester, Center of Excellence in Photonics and Microsystems; Binghamton, Center of Excellence in Small Scale Systems Integration and Packaging; and Stony Brook, Center of Excellence in Wireless & Information Technology.

61. In addition to indoor environmental quality, the CoE focuses on clean and renewable energy and water resources.

62. Luo and Polgreen, 2003.

63. Battelle Technology Partnership Practice, 2007.

64. The company's first commercial product is not a green one. It's skateboards. When a California skateboard company, Comet, discovered the material, company officials tried to lure e2e Materials to relocate. When company president Pat Govang turned him down, the company moved to New York and is now the first subsidiary of e2e Materials.

65. Patel-Predd, 2007.

66. The attraction effort was led by the Central New York office of Empire State Development in partnership with Syracuse CoE, CoE partner National Grid, and Syracuse University. Other partners of the recruitment team included the New York State Energy Research and Development Authority (NYSERDA), New York State Foundation for Science, Technology and Innovation (NYSTAR), Onondaga County Industrial Development Agency, and the Central New York Technology Development Organization.

67. Syracuse received $135 million from state and federal sources for this project.

68. The West Street Initiative is a part of a larger Syracuse Arts Initiative project, sponsored by Syracuse University, the City of Syracuse, and Onondaga County.

69. The university relocated its School of Architecture and College of Visual and Performing Arts in an old furniture warehouse in Armory Square, the entrance to the Near West Side, and plans on investing an additional $13.8 million in the area as a result of a debt restructuring agreement with the state. The debt restructuring requires the university to invest money owed on a state loan in an operating fund for the redevelopment. The University will be repaying approximately $8 million of the $13.8 million debt by creating the Syracuse Arts, Technology & Design Quarter. The university will purchase and renovate warehouses in a three-block area into artist live-and-work space.

70. In addition to private development, the city received a $10 million state economic development grant for the $56 million revitalization.

71. WCNY radio. See http://www.wcny.org/content/view/103/206/ (accessed September 15, 2008).

72. A proposal that has not yet been added to the project is a $750 million monorail that would link Destiny to the airport and downtown.

73. The study, conducted by *Environmental Building News*, estimates that commuting by office workers accounts for 30 percent more energy than the building itself uses (Wilson, 2007).

74. McKnight, 2007.

75. Quoted in Senville, 2007.

76. In addition to his own $69,084 in contributions to the 2004 Bush campaign and to congressmen promoting the energy bill, Congel's political action committee, the Green Worlds Coalition Fund, raised $82,897, which mostly went to the same campaigns. Other project advocates spent $200,000 over two years lobbying Congress to approve the green bonds proposal (Milligan, 2004).

77. The other projects are in Georgia, Louisiana, and Colorado (Milligan, 2004). Eligible projects must be at least 1 million square feet or on 20 acres of brownfield land. Projects must create at least 1,000 construction jobs in most states and at least 1,500 full-time permanent jobs. At least 75 percent of the square footage of commercial buildings in the project must be registered for the LEED green building rating system. State and local governments must contribute at least $5 million to a project, which can include tax abatements and in-kind contributions. See

http://www.cdfa.net/cdfa/cdfaweb.nsf/pages/greenbuildingfactsheet.html (accessed August 4, 2009).

78. U.S. Green Building Council; see http://www.usgbc.org/News/USGBCIn TheNewsDetails.aspx?id=2971 (accessed June 18, 2008).

79. Moriarty, 2008.

80. In March 2006, the New York Supreme Court ordered the city to maintain the tax abatement. In June 2008, the same court ruled that the state (New York Department of Environmental Conservation) could not deny Destiny the brownfield tax credits.

81. See http://www.grist.org/article/little-destiny

82. Little, 2005.

83. Personal interview, July 25, 2008. Indeed, Destiny's construction has gone through a number of starts and stops. First proposed in 1997, construction for Phase I didn't start until March 2007. Hotel construction started in October 2002, but stopped a few months later. In January 2006, Destiny laid off 190 out of 210 workers due to uncertainties in the retail sector and disputes with the city and state on tax abatements; see http://blog.syracuse.com/news/2006/01/destiny_usa_lays_off_190.html (accessed August 20, 2008). In February 2007, the Syracuse Industrial Development Agency sold $322.59 million in industrial bonds to complete the financing of the project. In March 2008, 45 workers were laid off, again due to financing delays.

84. Moriarty, 2008.

85. Palmateer, 2007.

86. "Triple bottom line" refers to cost accounting that incorporates economic, environmental, and social goals.

87. The plant will begin at a capacity of about 200 tons of soy or canola per day and produce up to 5 million gallons of biodiesel.

88. Personal interview, April 20, 2008.

89. The entire plan is available online at http://www.nyc.gov/html/planyc2030/html/plan/plan.shtml.

90. The Clinton Foundation's Clinton Climate Initiative (CCI) started the Energy Efficiency Building Retrofit Program in August 2006 to initiate energy efficiency retrofitting projects in cities throughout the world. Five banks—ABN AMRO, Citi, Deutsche Bank, JPMorgan Chase, and UBS—are contributing $1 billion each to the project. Owners will complete the retrofits at no initial cost and repay the loans with interest using savings in energy costs. Honeywell, Johnson Controls, Siemens, and Trane will conduct energy audits and perform building retrofits. The participating cities are Bangkok, Berlin, Chicago, Houston, Johannesburg, Karachi, London, Melbourne, Mexico City, New York, Rome, Sao Paulo, Seoul, Tokyo, and Toronto.

91. Personal interview, September 16, 2008.

92. See the Alliance to Save Energy Web site for a breakdown of the funding: http://ase.org/content/article/detail/5478 (accessed May 22, 2009).

93. For more information about Living Cities, see http://www.livingcities.org/about/ (accessed 12 July, 2009).

94. See http://greenbootcamp.livingcities.org/ for more detail (accessed 24 July, 2009).

95. RW Ventures and O-H Community Partners, 2008.

96. Shapiro, 2009.

97. Personal communication, April 13, 2009.

98. Fitzgerald and Leigh, 2003: 106.

99. These include energy-efficient building, construction, and retrofitting; renewable electric power; energy-efficient and advanced drive train vehicles; biofuels; deconstruction and materials use; energy efficiency assessment for the residential, commercial, or industrial sector; and manufacturing of sustainable products using sustainable processes. See http://www07.grants.gov/search/search.do?&mode=VIEW&f lag2006=false&oppId=46337 (accessed May 29, 2009).

100. The program closed when demand dried up due to President Reagan withdrawing federal incentives for efficiency in 1988. Then the college received a grant from the state's public power providers to reopen the program in 1992 to address worker shortages they were experiencing. The program was threatened with closure again in 1997, but program director Roger Ebbage convinced college administrators to keep the program as long as he could find funding for it.

101. See Fitzgerald, 2006 for a more extensive discussion of the limitations of career ladder programs for low-income workers.

102. Related by Dee Patel, Sustainability Consultant, Facilities, Planning & Development, LACCD (May 29, 2009).

103. See http://www.bpi.org/content/home/index.phps (accessed May 15, 2009).

CHAPTER 5

1. Platt et al., 2008.

2. Kaufman and Kaufman, 2004.

3. U.S. Environmental Protection Agency, 2007.

4. Gitlitz and Franklin, 2007: 3.

5. Environmental Protection Agency, http://www.epa.gov/industrialwaste/.

6. The three main federal laws regulating hazardous and industrial waste are the Resource Conservation and Recovery Act (1976), the Comprehensive Emergency Response, Compensation and Liability Act (1980, commonly known as CERCLA or the Superfund), and the Safe Drinking Water Act (1974).

7. Pernick and Krupp, 2007: 200.

8. See http://cawrecycles.org/issues/ghg.

9. See http://www.ecocycle.org/zero/world.cfm#four (accessed July 23, 2008) for more detail on such laws in California, Maine, and Maryland. States must be careful that such policies do not have unintended effects. Seven states have banned e-waste, which, along with higher fees for dumping it, may be contributing to

increased exporting of this waste to China (see http://chinadigitaltimes.net/china/
e-waste/ accessed September 1, 2009).

10. Beck, 2001.

11. Classification 562.

12. Pellow, 2002: 125.

13. Pellow, 2002; Weinberg, Pellow, and Schnaiberg, 2000.

14. Weinberg, Pellow, and Schnaiberg, 2000: 4.

15. Ibid. 8.

16. Gibbs, Deutz, and Proctor, 2002; Dunn and Steinemann, 1998.

17. See Goss, Kane, and Street, 2006. Industrial symbiosis has been practiced
for at least a century, particularly by European companies. And cities have recovered
resources, particularly sewage, to use as soil supplements for years. In *The Economy of
Cities*, Jane Jacobs speaks of cities as mines for resources. Others have chronicled quite
complex urban resource exchanges emanating from slaughterhouses and other industries. More recently, the Clinton administration's President's Council on Sustainable
Development created a task force on eco-industrial parks that provided assistance for
developing them in Baltimore, Chattanooga, and other cities. That none of them has
been successful is due to a combination of technical, informational, economic, regulatory, and motivational barriers (see Gibbs, Deutz, and Proctor, 2002).

18. See Gonzalez, 2008; Sullivan, 2008; Millar, 2007.

19. New York City's asthma hospitalization rate is twice as high as the nation's,
and East Harlem and the South Bronx have the highest rates in the city (Garg et al.,
2003). Two reports have been issued from the NYU asthma study, Restrepo and
Zimmerman, 2004, and Zimmerman et al., 2002.

20. Urban Ore, which salvages building supplies, furniture, lamps, etc., and
resells them in a retail store in Berkeley, is one of five reuse centers in the Bay Area.
The city provided financial assistance for the start-up in 1980, and the operation now
generates $1.6 million per year in sales. It employs 32 and has a $750,000 annual pay-
roll. The ReBuilding Center in Portland, Oregon, operates under a similar model.

21. See the Sustainable South Bronx website for publicity on Carter and the
organization: http://www.ssbx.org/press.html.

22. The organization was formed as the city was figuring out how it would
dispose of its waste once the infamous Fresh Kills landfill on Staten Island closed
in 2001. OWN supports sustainable solutions to waste disposal based on recycling
and reuse.

23. The Oak Point site was purchased from Conrail by Britestarr Homes in 1988.
The company never built its proposed modular-housing factory, and the site soon
became an illegal dump. The property was purchased by the president of Britestarr,
who intended to build a power plant, but this project never moved forward.

24. The plan is available at http://www.nyc.gov/html/dsny/html/swmp/swmp-
40ct.shtml.

25. This paragraph summarizes Sustainable South Bronx and Green Worker
Cooperatives, 2007.

26. The city is now looking for another site for a smaller, 1,500-bed jail. Since the jail was initially proposed, the projected number of jail beds needed has decreased.

27. See Sze, 2007, for a detailed history of the environmental justice movement and the campaign for a more equitable approach to trash processing and disposal in New York City. Chapter 4 focuses specifically on the Bronx.

28. Personal interview, August 11, 2008.

29. Personal interview, August 21, 2008.

30. Cited in Hirsch, 2007.

31. See Sze, 2007: 111.

32. One cannot easily compare recycling rates, as there is no consistent method used across cities and states. California calculates recycled material by weight, not volume. Los Angeles recycles green waste (organics), which tends to be heavier than blue-bin recycling content (e.g., plastics, glass, newspaper).

33. Goldman and Ogishi, 2001.

34. California Integrated Waste Management Board, 2003; Goldman and Ogishi, 2001.

35. Delaware recently hired the Institute for Local Self-Reliance, a nonprofit organization focused on sustainable economic development, to estimate the job creation potential of recycling and reuse. This analysis found that the state could create 1,574 jobs and realize $40 million in annual gross revenue from sale of materials if 50 percent of the waste stream were recycled and composted. If that increased to 75 percent, the numbers would increase to 2,360 jobs and $60 million in materials revenues. Households, local government, and businesses would avoid $25 million annually in disposal fees at the 50 percent recycling and composting level and $35.5 million at the 75 percent level. The state would have to invest $20 million over six years to provide the infrastructure for recycling and composting (Seldman and Anthony, 2007).

36. See http://www.ciwmb.ca.gov/RMDZ/LACity/Default.asp and http://www.lacity.org/san/solid_resources/pdfs/rmdz.pdf.

37. All quotes from personal interview, March 18, 2008.

38. See www.clkrep.lacity.org/councilfiles/06–1512_rpt_bos_6-5-08.pdf.

39. Sanitation District of Los Angeles: http://www.cd12.0rg/cd12r11.htm (accessed June 13, 2008). Note that this cost comparison does not take into account externalities such as pollution or CO_2 emitted due to having to transport waste to distant landfills, or methane from landfills.

40. The trip is financed by resources from Smith's office and from funds generated from a surcharge on tipping fees at the Sunshine Canyon landfill.

41. Personal communication, June 12, 2008.

42. There is some variation in the process and the output, depending on the specific technologies used by different equipment manufacturers. The biogas is 55 to 60 percent methane; the remainder is mostly CO_2. The amount of biogas produced varies with the type of input material. One ton of organic waste produces 110 cubic meters of biogas, the equivalent of 670 kWh of electricity—enough to power and heat ten houses during a 24-hour period (Kelleher, 2007).

43. To make compost, digestate is shipped to rural sites where it is mixed with leaf and yard waste in long rows called windrows. Naturally occurring bacteria and fungi break down the organic material to produce compost in about six months.

44. See http://www.adnett.org, the European Anaerobic Digestion Network.

45. Young, 2008.

46. Personal interview with Louis Circeo, Georgia Institute of Technology, July 23, 2008.

47. Vogel, 2008; personal interview, Louis Circeo, July 23, 2008.

48. See Platt, 2004, for an alternative view. Platt reports on zero-waste initiatives in several countries and argues against all forms of incineration.

49. See http://www.geni.org/globalenergy/library/technical-articles/generati on/wind/renewableenergyaccess.com/ladwp-moves-to-accelerate-renewable-energy-goal/index.shtml (accessed September 15, 2008).

50. Some of the information in this section was taken from interviews with Karen Wan, director of Sustainability and Competitiveness at the Chicago Manufacturing Center (September 29, 2007) and several interviews and e-mail exchanges with Sadhu Johnston (September–October, 2007).

51. Waste-to-profit networks represent a step toward a cradle-to-cradle production concept developed by Walter Stahl. Stahl analyzed energy use in making a product from the mining or production of the inputs through final manufacturing and argued that enormous efficiencies could be gained by reconditioning and reprocessing rather than starting with virgin materials (Lovins, 2008).

52. In addition to CMC and the City of Chicago, the partnership includes the Illinois Department of Natural Resources, the U.S. Business Council for Sustainable Development, and World Business Chicago.

53. Data are reported on the network's website, http://www.cmcusa.org/index2.cfm (accessed March 11, 2008).

54. The confidentiality agreement, data gathering, working groups, etc., are all part of the U.S. BCSD by-product synergy project process; they are delivered to organizations like CMC, which learn the ropes and become the local operators. The process is being used to develop projects in other parts of the country.

55. In addition to plastics and other recyclables, China receives 70 percent of the world's electronic waste for recycling (Renner, Sweeney, and Kubit, 2008).

56. To view products go to http://www.curbappealmaterials.com/.

57. There are several U.S. companies making countertops from recycled material. Canopy, in Portland, Oregon, uses 70 percent agricultural by-products and 30 percent acrylic resin on a wheat board or sunflower husk board. Fuez, also in Portland, uses recycled glass and fly ash concrete. Paperstone Certified, in Hoquiam, Washington, uses 100 percent postconsumer recycled paper bonded with a water-based, petroleum-free resin system. Squak Mountain Stone, in Woodinville, Washington, uses postconsumer recycled paper, postindustrial recycled glass, coal fly ash, and cement. Icestone, in Brooklyn, New York, uses all recycled glass and concrete (Wise et al., 2007: 12).

58. In addition to the U.S. Environmental Protection Agency, other funders include the City of Chicago, the Illinois Department of Commerce's Economic Opportunity, Recycling Expansion and Modernization Program, and the National Institute of Standards and Technology/Manufacturing Extension Partnership.

59. See World Business Council for Sustainable Development, 2008, for a history of the organization and a summary of its work.

60. As companies realize cost savings in one arena, they will be more open to taking energy-conserving measures. These investments are highly profitable. McKinsey (2007) estimates that manufacturers could make a 10 percent profit on investments in energy conservation and collectively reduce their energy demand by 16 percent by 2020.

61. The World Business Council for Sustainable Development started publishing energy efficiency by-product synergy case studies. See http://wbcsd.org/plugins/DocSearch/details.asp?type=DocDet&ObjectId=Mjk0MTk.

62. A state affiliate of the U.S. Business Council for Sustainable Development was created in April 2007 to lead it. Other organizations involved include the Center for Resilience, the Solid Waste Authority of Central Ohio (SWACO), the Ohio BioProducts Innovation Center (OBIC), the Ohio Environmental Protection Agency, the City of Columbus, and others.

63. Personal interview, March 31, 2008.

64. The funding is from the Business Resource Efficiency and Waste (BREW) Programme, which is operated by the Department for Environment, Food and Rural Affairs.

65. The government agency responsible for the landfill tax and for distributing funds is the BREW Programme.

66. Companies report data in each category based on indicators developed by NISP. A third party corroborates the reporting.

67. Personal interview, March 14, 2008.

68. Information supplied in a worker affidavit prepared in opposition to the company's hardship waiver application.

69. Connelly, Mary Jo. 2003. Testimony on the Boston Department of Public Works Application for a Hardship Waiver from the Jobs and Living Wage Ordinance for the Acceptance of Recycling Materials from Various Districts in Boston 2002–2005 contract.

70. International Brotherhood of Teamsters. 2009.

71. Mattera, 2009.

72. International Brotherhood of Teamsters, 2007.

CHAPTER 6

1. Krupp and Horn, 2008: 73.

2. Shapiro, Hassett, and Arnold, 2002: 24.

3. See http://www.icfi.com/newsroom/news.asp?ID=27

4. Economic Development Research Group, 2009.

5. Public transportation requires a certain level of density to be economically feasible. Bus systems with fairly frequent schedules require 12,096 people per square mile, light-rail systems need 15,552, and subways need 20,736 (Pushkarev and Zupan, 1977). Brookings Institution urbanist Anthony Downs (2004) estimates that only about one-third of the population lives in places with sufficient density to support public transportation.

6. See the Center for Neighborhood Technology H+T Affordability Index at http://htaindex.cnt.org/ (accessed May 29, 2009).

7. Cervero, 2003; Boarnet, 1998.

8. Handy, 2005.

9. See http://www.drcog.org/documents/2020_Metro_Vision_Plan-1.pdf (accessed June 12, 2009).

10. See http://www.metrodenver.org/transportation-infrastructure (accessed June 12, 2009).

11. See http://www.lightrailnow.org/news/n_newslog2007q3.htm#DEN_20070910 (accessed June 12, 2009).

12. Proctor, 2009.

13. Berke, 2008.

14. Denver Office of Community Planning and Development, 2006.

15. Proctor, 2003.

16. Florida, 2005.

17. Lipman, 2006.

18. See http://www.portoflosangeles.org/CAAP/CTP_O&B.pdf (accessed March 27, 2009).

19. Sahagun, 2007.

20. California Air Resources Board, 2006.

21. Bensman, 2009.

22. Belzer, 2000.

23. See http://oehha.ca.gov/public_info/facts/dieselfacts.html (accessed March 26, 2009).

24. See http://www.nrdc.org/ej/partnerships/air.asp (accessed March 26, 2009).

25. See http://www.arb.ca.gov/diesel/documents/rrpapp.htm (accessed March 26, 2009).

26. Los Angeles Alliance for a New Economy (LAANE) is part of a coalition that has negotiated community benefits agreements for six major economic development deals since 2001. The first was the Staples Center, a mixed-use sports and entertainment district that received $150 million in public subsidies and in return provided job training programs, public space, affordable housing units, a $650,000 interest-free loan to a nonprofit housing developer, and $1 million investment in existing local parks (see Gross, 2005 for details of this and other CBAs). Los Angeles has had a living

wage amendment that covers all developments using public subsidies since 1997, but community-benefits agreements are negotiated on a deal-by-deal basis.

27. See http://www.cleanandsafeports.org/index.php?id=8 for a complete list of member organizations (accessed May 21, 2009).

28. Matsuoka, 2008: 27.

29. Los Angeles and Long Beach, 2006.

30. Roberts, 2006.

31. See http://www.portworld.com/news/i69183/Cold_ironing_record_set_in_ Los_Angeles (accessed March 27, 2009).

32. The plan follows a successful system developed by Port Metro Vancouver, which was implemented after examining practices in ports around the world, using electronic information systems to manage deliveries and pickups and minimize truck wait times (see http://www.portmetrovancouver.com/users/landoperations/trucking.aspx and http://www.tc.gc.ca/pol/en/report/ContainersBCLowerMainlandPorts/1-e-05 .htm).

33. For a detailed compliance schedule, see http://www.portoflosangeles.org/ CAAP/CTP_CARB Presentation_Sept2007.pdf (accessed May 20, 2009).

34. Frequent and semifrequent truck visitors are those that enter the port at least three days a week.

35. Concessionaires are eligible for grants that cover up to 80 percent of the purchase price of a truck that meets emissions standards. Low-cost leases are also available. The port has other incentive programs in place as well.

36. For details of the transition, see http://www.portoflosangeles.org/CAAP/ CTP_Concession_Agreement.pdf (accessed May 20, 2009).

37. See http://www.calchamber.com/Headlines/Pages/CalChamberUrges GovernortoVetoJobKillerBill.aspx (accessed May 20, 2009).

38. See http://www.portoflosangeles.org/newsroom/2009_releases/news_ 012209_ctp_fee.pdf (accessed May 20, 2009) for a file of articles on the Clean the Portsprograms and legal battles. See also http://www.portoflosangeles.org/CAAP/ CTP_Notice_of_Court_Decision.pdf (accessed May 20, 2009).

39. See http://switchboard.nrdc.org/blogs/dpettit/a_preview_of_the_issues_ in_the.html (accessed May 22, 2009).

40. Estimates provided by Port of Los Angeles Executive Director Geraldine Knatz (May 22, 2009) and Clean Trucks program manager Chris Cannon (June 9, 2009).

41. Sahagun, 2007.

42. City of Portland, 2009.

43. Inslee and Hendricks, 2008: 118–119.

44. Portland's TriMet commuter light rail, MAX, connects residents in the cities of Gresham, Beaverton, and Hillsboro to Portland. Residents have voted three times to expand the system. A 5.5-mile spur to Portland International Airport was added in 2001, and a 5.8-mile spur opened the EXPO center in May 2004.

45. The 70-acre River District was an old rail area just north of downtown. The 128-acre South Waterfront contained numerous vacant industrial buildings in need of environmental remediation.

46. E.D. Hovee & Company, 2005.

47. Speech by Michael Powell available at http://reconnectingamerica.org/public/stories/417 (accessed August 3, 2009).

48. Belzer and Poticha, 2009.

49. See http://www.portlandstreetcar.org/history.php (accessed 17 May, 2009).

50. Personal interview with Chandra Brown, May 21, 2009.

51. Marshall, 2007.

52. See http://www.altaplanning.com/oregon+bicycling+economic+study+update.aspx (accessed May 18, 2009).

53. Jacklet, 2009.

54. See http://chrisking.com/company (accessed May 16, 2009).

55. Cited in Tucker, 2009.

56. Cited in Tucker, 2009.

57. Interview with Jennifer Nolfi, May 20, 2009.

58. A 2007 report estimates that outdoor recreation generates $730 billion annually and supports 6.5 million direct, indirect, and induced jobs (Southwick Associates, 2007).

59. Personal interview with Jerry Norquist, May 28, 2009.

60. In February 2005, Nichols was one of 11 mayors who challenged the nation's mayors to follow the mandates of the Kyoto Protocol (signed the day before) to reduce greenhouse gas emissions to 7 percent below 1990 levels by 2012. His challenge became the U.S. Mayor's Climate Protection Agreement.

61. See http://www.seattlechannel.org/issues/soundTransit.asp

62. See http://www.seattle.gov/Transportation/lightrail.htm

63. See http://seattletimes.nwsource.com/html/localnews/2008355167_websoundtransit05m.html

64. See http://www.psrc.org/publications/pubs/trends/t6jun09.pdf (accessed September 4, 2009).

65. Senator Patty Murray, a high-ranking member of the Senate Transportation Appropriations Subcommittee, helped secure federal funding to defray the $200,000 difference in price between a standard diesel bus and a hybrid. See http://www.metrokc.gov/kcdot/news/2004/nr040527_hybrids.htm (accessed May 4, 2008).

66. Personal interview, May 1, 2008.

67. The company also secured $101 million in debt financing; see Clean Tech Network: http://media.cleantech.com/2246/imperium-renewables-puts-ipo-on-hold and http://media.cleantech.com/770/imperium-renewables-lands-214-million (accessed May 5, 2008).

68. In Washington, 81 percent of biosolids are applied to land or distributed as soil amendments for building soils, revegetating barren areas, and fertilizing crops. It's a lot of biosolids—King County alone produces about 300,000 wet tons of biosolids a day.

University of Washington analysts conclude that the county achieves CO_2 credits for using biosolids as fertilizer, even when accounting for transporting it to rural sites. The county could increase the credit by reducing the transport distance (Brown and Leonard, 2004).

69. See Bloomberg.com, http://www.bloomberg.com/apps/news?pid=2060108 9&sid=a_FUqHBBcElU&refer=china, and http://findarticles.com/p/articles/mi_qn4174 /is_20031126/ai_n12920462 (accessed July 3, 2008).

70. See Krupp and Horn, 2008, for a discussion of research and advances in bio-fuel production.

71. González, 2008.

72. Cook, 2008.

73. Federal renewable fuels mandates require consuming approximately 500 million gallons of diesel from renewable sources in 2009; see http://www.epa.gov/EPA-AIR/2008/November/Day-21/a27613.htm.

74. Brasher, 2009.

75. This came from a $23 million appropriation over and above the original $100 million specifically for biofuels projects.

76. Personal interview, July 16, 2008.

77. See http://www.regionalstewardship.org/ARS_forums/washington/materials/ FasTracks.pdf (accessed June 21, 2009).

78. Speech by Michael Powell available at http://reconnectingamerica.org/ public/stories/417 (accessed 6 August, 2009).

79. Cervero, 1998.

80. Filion and McSpurren, 2007.

81. See Wood and Brooks, 2009.

82. See Belzer and Poticha, 2009.

83. See http://www.reconnectingamerica.org/public/reports/375 (accessed May 20, 2009).

84. This includes amount for various highway programs authorized by the Transportation Equity Act for the 21st Century (TEA-21, covering 1998 to 2003) and the Safe, Accountable, Flexible and Efficient Transportation Equity Act of 2003 (SAFETEA, covering 2004 to 2009). See http://www.fhwa.dot.gov/tea21/; http:// www.fhwa.dot.gov/reauthorization/safetea.htm

85. See http://www.recovery.gov/?q=node/202; http://www.recovery.gov/?q=content /rebuilding-infrastructure

86. See http://www.chinadaily.com.cn/china/2008–11/12/content_7195456.htm

87. U.S. Department of Transportation, 2009.

88. Feldman, 2009.

89. Feldman, 2009.

90. The Buy America provisions have a complicated history. The original Buy America Act was passed in 1933. The first Buy America provision to apply directly to transit was the Urban Mass Transportation Act of 1964. The provisions were revised in the Surface Transportation Assistance Acts of 1978 and 1982 (see Federal Transit Administration, 2001).

91. Feldman, 2009.

92. Wust, 2009.

93. In January 2009, Siemens Transportation Systems located the headquarters for its mobility division in Sacramento. This division includes units that develop operating systems for rail and road traffic; technology systems for airport logistics; postal automation and rail electrification; and railcars for mass transit, regional and long-distance transportation. See http://sacramento.bizjournals.com/sacramento/stories/2009/01/19/story7.html (accessed May 22, 2009).

94. See http://findarticles.com/p/articles/mi_qn4176/is_20070406/ai_n19000461/ (accessed May 9, 2009).

95. Boucher, 2004.

96. Paaswell at http://www.fiveborough.org/5boroughreport/railcars_paaswell .html (accessed May 20, 2009).

97. Boucher, 2004: 3.

98. This estimate is for direct jobs only. Some of these jobs already exist in railcar assembly.

99. See http://www.dot.ca.gov/hq/MassTrans/MAIN-Bus-Rapid-Transit.htm (accessed June 19, 2009) for a list of California cities and counties that are developing BRT systems.

100. See http://www.newflyer.com/index/news-app/story.59/title.new-flyer-receives-845-bus-orders-valued-at-us-484-million/menu.no/sec./home (accessed December 12, 2008).

101. Personal communication, David Hochman, June 19, 2009.

102. Kuttner, 1997, ch. 6.

103. Fitzgerald, 2006.

CHAPTER 7

1. The rankings are produced from an index developed by Climate Action Network Europe.

2. Amundsen, Bergman, and von der Fehr, 2006: 165–168.

3. For information on the European Green Capital award, see http://ec.europa. eu/environment/europeangreencapital/green_cities_submenu/awardwinner_2010 .html (accessed June 25, 2009). Stockholm is one of 70 ecomunicipalities in Sweden, defined by their commitment to the sustainability goals of the Sustainable Sweden Association, formed in 1983. Members agree to use a participatory planning process to meet the following goals: reduce or eliminate substances removed from earth's crust (e.g., oil) or produced by humans (synthetic chemicals); reduce or eliminate ecosystem degradation; and meet human development needs in as equitable a manner as possible (Spencer, 2005). A few smaller U.S. cities, such as Madison, Wisconsin, and Portsmouth, New Hampshire, have adopted an American Planning Association version of the four objectives.

4. Gould, 1997: xxi.

5. Gould, 1997: xxii.

6. Eliasson, 2006.

7. See http://www.terrapass.com/blog/posts/congestion-tax and http://www.streetsblog.org/2007/08/01/congestion-charging-returns-to-stockholm/

8. See http://www.stockholmbusinessregion.se/templates/indexpage_39354.aspx ?epslanguage=EN (accessed June 20, 2009).

9. Stockholm Business Regional Development, 2006.

10. Reed and Sains, 2009.

11. Växjö, a city of 85,500, has cut its use of fossil fuels in half without sacrificing economic development. Like Sweden, Växjö announced it would become independent of fossil fuels and now gets 51 percent of its energy from renewable sources. Fossil Fuel Free Växjö's goal was mainly achieved by building a central combined heat and power plant powered by wood waste from the forestry industry. Other efficiencies were obtained in transportation, including a common municipal green car fleet, bio-gas buses, promoting bicycle use, and satellite tracking of cabs so the closest cabs can be dispatched for pickups; see http://postcarboncities.net/node/261 (accessed October 16, 2008). Växjö has reduced its per capita greenhouse gas emissions 24 percent to 3.5 tons, compared to 5 tons for Sweden (and 23.5 tons in the United States).

12. Cited in Williams, 2007.

13. See http://www.mjardevi.se/opencms/msp/en/index.html (accessed June 24, 2009).

14. Business Week online, http://bx.businessweek.com/green-energy/view?url= http%3A%2F%2Ftwurl.nl%2F76nqe5 (accessed 26 July, 2009).

15. Kuttner, 1997.

References

Aeppel, Timothy. 2008. "Stung by Soaring Transport Costs, Factories Bring Jobs Home Again." *Wall Street Journal*, June 13.

Agyeman, Julian. 2005. *Sustainable Communities and the Challenge of Environmental Justice*. New York: New York University Press.

Alta Planning and Design. 2006. *Bicycle-Related Industry Growth in Portland*. Portland, Ore.: Portland Office of Transportation.

Alternative Resources, Inc. 2007. *Los Angeles County Conversion Technology Evaluation Report. Phase II—Assessment: Converting Waste into Renewable Resources*. Concord, Mass.: American Council on Renewable Energy.

American Council of Renewable Energy. 2007. *Outlook on Renewable Energy*. Washington, D.C.: Author.

American Institute of Architects. 2008. *Local Leaders in Sustainability—Green Incentives*. Washington, D.C.: American Institute of Architects.

American Planning Association. 1998. *The Principles of Smart Development*. Report 479. Chicago: American Planning Association.

American Planning Association. 2000. *Policy Guide on Planning for Sustainability*. Available at http://www.planning.org/policy/guides/adopted/sustainability.htm (accessed April 9, 2009).

Amundsen, Eirik S., Lars Bergman, and Nils-Henrik M. von der Fehr. 2006. "The Nordic Electricity Market: Robust by Design?" Pages 145–170 in *Electricity Market Reform: An International Perspective*, edited by Fereidoon P. Sioshansi and Wolfgang Pfaffenberger. San Diego: Elsevier.

Apollo Alliance. 2004. *New Energy for America*. San Francisco: author.

Apollo Alliance. 2008. *The New Apollo Program: Clean Energy, Good Jobs*. San Francisco: author.

Apollo Alliance. 2009. *Imagining Newark's Green Future: A Year Building the Green Economy*. San Francisco: Apollo Alliance. Available at http://apolloalliance.org/downloads/newarksgreenfuture.pdf (accessed July 23, 2009).

Asmus, Peter. 2008. *Harvesting California's Renewable Energy Resources: A Green Jobs Business Plan*. Sacramento, Calif.: Center for Energy Efficiency and Renewable Technologies.

Bailey, John. 2007. *Lessons from the Pioneers: Tackling Global Warming at the Local Level*. Washington, D.C.: Institute for Local Self-Reliance.

Bailie, Alison, Stephen Bernow, William Dougherty, Michael Lazarus, Sivan Kartha, and Marshall Goldberg. 2001. *Clean Energy: Jobs for America's Future*. Washington, D.C.: World Wildlife Fund.

Barringer, Felicity. 2008. "In Many Communities, It's Not Easy Going Green." *New York Times*, February 7.

Barringer, Felicity. 2008. "A City Committed to Recycling Is Ready for More." *New York Times*, May 8.

Barringer, Felicity. 2009. "Environmentalists in a Clash of Goals." *New York Times*, March 24.

Barron, Rachel. 2008. "Power-Purchase Agreements to Spike." Greentech Media, February 14. Available at http://www.greentechmedia.com/articles/power-purchase-agreements-to-spike-591.html (accessed February 11, 2009).

Basel Convention on the Control of Transboundary Movements of Hazardous Wastes and Their Disposal. 2008. http://www.basel.int (accessed October 17, 2008).

Battelle Technology Partnership Practice. 2007. *Central Upstate New York's Green Industry Sector: Opportunities and Prospects*. Columbus, Ohio: Battelle Memorial Institute.

Beatley, Timothy. 2000. *Green Urbanism: Learning from European Cities*. Washington, D.C.: Island Press.

Beck, R.W. 2001. *U.S. Recycling Economic Information Study*. St. Paul, Minn.: National Recycling Coalition.

Beck, R.W. 2004. *Anaerobic Digestion Feasibility Study for the Bluestem Solid Waste Agency and Iowa Department of Natural Resources*. St. Paul, Minn.: Bluestem Solid Waste Agency.

Belzer, Michael H. 2000. *Sweatshops on Wheels: Winners and Losers in Trucking Deregulation*. New York: Oxford University Press.

Belzer, Dana, and Shelley Poticha. 2009. "Understanding Transit-Oriented Development: Lessons Learned 1999–2009." Pages 4–11 in *Fostering Equitable and Sustainable Transit-Orientated Development*. New York: Ford Foundation.

Bensman, David. 2009. *Port Trucking Down the Low Road: A Sad Story of Deregulation*. New York: Demos.

Berke, Philip R. 2008. "The Evolution of Green Community Planning, Scholarship, and Practice: An Introduction to the Special Issue." *Journal of the American Planning Association*. 74(4): 393–407.

Bezdek, Roger. 2007. *Renewable Energy and Energy Efficiency: Economic Drivers for the 21st Century*. Boulder, Colo.: American Solar Energy Society.

Bharvirkar, Ranjit, Charles Goldman, Donald Gilligan, Terry E. Singer, David Birr, Patricia Donahue, and Scott Serot. 2008. *Performance Contracting and Energy Efficiency in the State Government Market*. Berkeley, Calif.: Lawrence Berkeley National Laboratory.

Blackwell, Angela Glover. 2006. "Regional Equity and Smart Growth: Opportunities for Advancing Social and Economic Justice in America." Pages 407–428 in *Urban Sprawl: A Comprehensive Reference Guide*, edited by David C. Soule. Westport, Conn.: Greenwood Press.

Blair, Nate, Walter Short, Paul Denholm, and Donna Heimiller. 2006. *Long-Term National Impacts of State-Level Policies: Preprint*. NREL Report No. CP-620–40105.

Blue-Green Alliance. 2009. *How to Revitalize America's Middle Class with the Clean Energy Economy*. Minneapolis, Minn.: Blue-Green Alliance. Available at http://www.blue-greenalliance.org/admin/publications/files/0012.4.pdf (accessed July 24, 2009).

Boarnet, Martin. 1998. "Spillovers and the Locational Effects of Public Infrastructure." *Journal of Regional Science* 38: 381–400.

Böhme, Dieter. 2008. *Development of Renewable Energies in Germany in 2008*. Berlin: German Federal Ministry for the Environment, Nature Conservation and Nuclear Safety.

Bolinger, Mark. 2007. *Annual Report on U.S. Wind Power Installation, Cost, and Performance Trends: 2006*. Berkeley, Calif.: Lawrence Berkeley National Laboratory.

Boucher, Tom. 2004. "Stability of Public Financing and Re-industrialization in Rail Car Manufacture." Working paper, Department of Industrial & Systems Engineering, Rutgers University.

Boyd, John D. 2009. "Hard Times for Railcar Makers." *Journal of Commerce Online*. Available at http://www.joc.com/node/409352.

Bradsher, Keith. 2009. "China Races Ahead of U.S. in Drive to Go Solar." *New York Times*, August 25, pp. 1, 3.

Brasher, Philip. 2009. "European Union Duty Cuts Biodiesel Demand." *Des Moines Register*, May 5.

Breckenridge, Tom. 2009. "Port Seeks $26.5 Million for Makeover of Docks, Warehouses." *Cleveland Plain Dealer*, February 20. Available at http://blog.cleveland.com/business/2009/02/port_seeks_265_million_for_mak.html (accessed April 22, 2009).

Brettman, Allan. 2009. "Port of Vancouver Announces Wind-Turbine Cargo Deals." *The Oregonian*, February 5.

Bronstein, Zelda. 2009. "Industry and the Smart City." *Dissent* (Summer): 27–34.

Brown, Marilyn A., Frank Southworth, and Andrea Sarzynski. 2008. *Shrinking the Carbon Footprint of Metropolitan America*. Washington, D.C.: The Brookings Institution Metropolitan Policy Program.

Brown, Marilyn, Frank Southworth, and Therese Stovall. 2005. *Towards a Climate-Friendly Built Environment*. Philadelphia: Pew Center on Global Climate Change.

Brown, Sally, and Peggy Leonard. 2004. "Biosolids and Global Warming: Evaluating the Management Impacts." *BioCycle* 45(8): 54–56, 58–61.

Brown, Sally, and Peggy Leonard. 2004. "Building Carbon Credits with Biosolids Recycling." *BioCycle* 45(9): 25–29.

Browning, Adam. 2008. "Feed-In Tariff versus Marginal Incentives." Renewable Energy World.com. Available at http://www.renewableenergyworld.com/rea//news/article/2008/02/feed-in-tariff-versus-marginal-incentive-51362.

Bruno, M.S., J.T. Young, O. Moghaddam, H. Wong, and J.A. Apps. 2007. "Thermal Treatment, Carbon Sequestration, and Methane Generation through Deep-Well Injection of Biosolids." Pages 587–604 in *Underground Injection Science and Technology*, edited by C.F. Tang and J. Apps. Amsterdam: Elsevier. Available at http://www.terralog.com/biosolids_management.asp.

Buckman, Rebecca. 2008. "Betting on Green." *Wall Street Journal*. February 11.

Bullard, Robert D. 2005. *The Quest for Environmental Justice*. San Francisco: Sierra Club Books.

Burgermeister, Jane. 2008. "Renewable Energy Jobs Soar in Germany." Renewable Energy World.com, April 8. Available at http://www.renewableenergyworld.com/rea/news/story?id=52089 (accessed September 24, 2008).

Burgermeister, Jane. 2009. "Lessons from Europe." *The American Prospect*, March 23.

Burns, Patrick, and Daniel Flaming. 2006. *Jobs in the L.A. Green Tech Sector*. Los Angeles, Calif.: Economic Roundtable.

Burtis, Patrick R. 2004. *Creating the California Cleantech Cluster: How Innovation and Investment Can Promote Job Growth and a Healthy Environment*. Washington, D.C.: National Resources Defense Council and E2 Environmental Entrepreneurs.

Burtis, Patrick R., Bob Epstein, and Nicholas Parker. 2006. *Creating Cleantech Clusters: 2006 Update. How Innovation and Investment Can Promote Job Growth and a Healthy Environment*. E2 and Cleantech Venture Network.

Caldwell, Evan. 2007. "Port Windfall: Wind Farm Imports Buoy Economy." *Longview* (Wash.) *Daily News*.

California Air Resources Board. 2006. *Emissions Reduction Plan for Ports and Goods Movement in California*. Available at http://www.arb.ca.gov/planning/gmerp/march21plan/march22_plan.pdf (accessed July 24, 2009).

California Integrated Waste Management Board. 2003. "Recycling Zones Promote Jobs, Economic Development: City of L.A.'s Recycling Market Development Zone Is Renewed." Press release, November 3.

Campbell, Scott. 1996. "Green Cities, Growing Cities, Just Cities?: Urban Planning and the Contradictions of Sustainable Development." *Journal of the American Planning Association* 62 (3): 296–312.

Carey, John. 2008. "Is Ethanol Getting a Bum Rap?" *Business Week*, May 12: 60–63.

Carlton, Jim. 2007. "Toledo Finds the Energy to Reinvent Itself." *Wall Street Journal*, December 18.

Carson, Iain, and Vijay V. Vaitheeswaran. 2007. *Zoom: The Global Race to Fuel the Car of the Future*. New York: Twelve.

Casteool, Daniel. 2003. *The Returning City: Historic Preservation and Transit in the Age of Civic Renewal*. Washington, D.C: National Trust for Historic Preservation.

Center for Neighborhood Technology. 2009. Available at http://www.epa.gov/green-building/ (accessed September 2, 2009).

Center of Excellence. 2008. *Environmental Scan: Solar Industry, San Francisco Bay and Greater Silicon Valley Regions*. San Francisco: Chancellor's Office, California Community Colleges.

Cervero, Robert. 1998. *The Transit Metropolis: A Global Inquiry*. Washington, D.C.: Island Press.

Cervero, Robert. 2003. "Road Expansion, Urban Growth, and Induced Travel: A Path Analysis." *Journal of the American Planning Association* 69: 145–163.

Cervero, Robert. 2003. *Transit-Oriented Development in the United States: Experiences, Challenges, and Prospects*. Washington, D.C.: Transit Research Board of the National Academies.

Chavez, Jon. 2008. "First Solar to Enter Residential Markets: To Take $25M Stake in California Firm." *Toledo Blade*, October 30.

Christopherson, Susan, and Jennifer Clark. 2007. "Power in Firm Networks: What It Means for Regional Innovation Systems." *Regional Studies* 41(9): 1223–1236.

Chun, Yoon-Moon, Peter Claisse, and Tarun R. Naik. 2007. Sustainable construction materials and technologies: International Conference on Sustainable Construction Materials and Technologies. Coventry, UK.

City of Portland Mayor's Office. 2009. *Economic Development Strategy: A Five-Year Plan for Promoting Job Creation and Economic Growth*. Available at http://www.pdxeconomicdevelopment.com/docs/Portland-Ec-Dev-Strategy.pdf (accessed July 24, 2009).

City of Seattle. 2006. *Seattle, a Climate of Change: Meeting the Kyoto Challenge*. Seattle, Wash.: Mayor Nichols' Green Ribbon Commission on Climate Protection. Available at http://www.4cleanair.org/Documents/SeaCAP_plan.pdf (accessed July 24, 2009).

City of Toronto Waste Diversion Task Force, Canada. 2001. *Waste Diversion Task Force 2010 Report*. Available at http://www.toronto.ca/taskforce2010/2010_report.htm (accessed July 24, 2009).

Clark-Madison, Mike. 2003. "AE Drops a Soar Bomb." *Austin Chronicle* (December 5).

Clean Energy Development Plan for the Heartland. 2003. *Repowering the Midwest*. Chicago, Ill.: Environment Law and Policy Center.

Conway, Maureen, Amy Blair, Steven L. Dawson, and Linda Dworak-Muñoz. 2007. *Sectoral Strategies for Low-Income Workers: Lessons from the Field*. Washington, D.C.: Aspen Institute.

Cook, John. 2008. "Imperium Loses Biodiesel Contract." *Seattle Post Intelligencer* (August 14). Available at http://www.seattlepi.com/business/375065_imperium15.html.

Corpus Christi Metropolitan Planning Organization. 2009. "Green Energy—Papalote Creek Wind Farm." *Metro-Mobility Talks* 14(4). Available online at http://www.corpuschristi-mpo.org/Newsletter_V14_I4_Green.html (accessed July 24, 2009).

Cowell, Stephen. 2008. "Energy Efficiency Is the New Oil." *Huffington Post*, December 16. Available at http://www.huffingtonpost.com/stephen-cowell/energy-efficiency-is-the_b_151553.html (accessed December 16, 2008).

Cuyahoga Regional Energy Development Task Force. 2007. *Building a New Energy Future*. Report to the Board of Commissioners of Cuyahoga County, Ohio. Available at http://www.cuyahogacounty.us/pdf/RegEnergyTF.pdf (accessed July 24, 2009).

Dafoe, Jack. 2007. *Growing Green Collar Jobs: Energy Efficiency*. New York: Urban Agenda. Delphi Group. 2007. *People, Planet, & Profit: Catalyzing Economic Growth and Environmental Quality in the City of Toronto*. Available at http://www.toronto.ca/business_publications/pdf/green_economic_development_22may2007.pdf (accessed July 24, 2009).

Denver Office of Community Planning and Development. 2006. *Strategic Plan for Transit-Oriented Development*. Available at http://www.rtd-fastracks.com/media/uploads/main/StrategicPlan-final_100708.pdf (accessed July 24, 2009).

Denver Regional Transportation District. 2008. *Transit Oriented Development 2008 Status Report*. Available at http://www.rtd-fastracks.com/media/uploads/main/TOD_Status_Report_2008.pdf (accessed July 24, 2009).

Devuvst. 2001. *How Green Is the City?* New York: Columbia University Press.

Deyette, Jeff, and Steve Clemmer. 2005. *Increasing the Texas Renewable Energy Standard: Economic and Employment Benefits*. February. Union of Concerned Scientists.

Dicus, Howard. 2004. "Next Generation Gasification Technology Proposed for Oahu Refuse Crisis." *Pacific Business News*, October 7.

Dimino, Resa, and Barbara Warren. 2004. *Reaching for Zero: The Citizens Plan for Zero Waste in New York City*. New York: New York City Zero Waste Campaign and Consumer Policy Institute / Consumers Union.

Doe, Paula. 2008. "Explosive Growth Reshuffles Top 10 Solar Ranking." RenewableEnergyWorld.com. Available at http://www.renewableenergyworld.com/rea/news/article/2008/09/explosive-growth-reshuffles-top-10-solar-ranking-53559 (accessed July 15, 2009).

Dorn, Jonathan G. 2007. "Solar Cell Production Jumps 50 Percent in 2007." Earth Policy Institute. Available at http://www.earthpolicy.org/Indicators/Solar/2007.htm (accessed November 8, 2008).

Downs, Anthony. 2004. *Still Stuck in Traffic: Coping with Peak-Hour Traffic Congestion*. Washington D.C.: Brookings Institution.

Dreier, Peter. 2009. "Good Jobs, Healthy Cities." *The American Prospect* 20(10): A10–A13.

Duamy, Andres, and Elizabeth Plater-Zyberk. 2000. *Suburban Nation: The Rise of Sprawl and the Decline of the American Dream*. New York: North Point Press.

Dunn, B.C., and A. Steinemann. 1998. "Industrial Ecology for Sustainable Communities." *Journal of Environmental Planning and Management*. 4(6): 661–672.

Dupressoir, Sophie, Joaquín Nieto, Ana Belen Sanchez, Patrick Nussbaumer, Jorge Riechmann, Pierre Bobe, Daniel Dubois et al. 2007. *Climate Change and*

Employment—Impact on Employment in the European Union-25 of Climate Change and CO₂ Emission Reduction Measures by 2030. Brussels, European Trade Union Confederation.

Dürrschmidt, Wolfhart, and Michael van Mark. 2006. *Renewable Energy Employment Effects: Impact of the Expansion of Renewable Energy on the German Labour Market.* Berlin: Federal Ministry for the Environment, Nature, Conservation, and Nuclear Safety.

Dykes, Katherine, Fletcher Miller, Bob Weinberg, Aaron Godwin, and Emily Sautter. 2008. *A Wind Resource Assessment for Near-Shore Lake Erie: Cleveland Water Crib Monitoring Site Two Year Report.* Cleveland: Green Energy Ohio.

Economic Development Research Group. 2009. *Job Impacts of Spending on Public Transportation: An Update.* Available at http://www.apta.com/research/info/online/jobs_impact.cfm (accessed July 24, 2009).

E.D. Hovee & Company. 2005. *Portland Streetcar Development Impacts.* Portland, Ore.: Portland Streetcar Inc.

Eichholtz, Piet, Nils Kok, and John M. Quigley. 2008. *Doing Well by Doing Good? Green Office Buildings.* Berkeley: Institute of Business, University of California, Berkeley.

Eliasson, Jonas. 2006. "Cost-Benefit Analysis of the Stockholm Congestion Charging System." Available at http://siteresources.worldbank.org/INTTRANSPORT/Resources/StockholmcongestionCBAEliassonn.pdf

Energy Information Administration. 1999. Commercial Buildings Energy Consumption Survey—Commercial Buildings Characteristics. Available at http://www.eia.doe.gov/emeu/cbecs/char99/intro.html (accessed February 6, 2009).

Energy Information Service. 2003. Table 3. Number of Buildings and Floorspace by Size of Building. Available at http://www.eia.doe.gov/emeu/cbecs/cbecs2003/introduction.html (accessed May 30, 2008).

Energy Information Service. 2005. Table HC3.3 Household Characteristics by Owner-Occupied Housing Unit, http://www.eia.doe.gov/emeu/recs/recs2005/hc2005_tables/hc3demographics/pdf/tablehc3.3.pdf; Table B11. Selected Principal Building Activity: Part 1, Number of Buildings for Non-Mall Buildings, 2003.http://www.eia.doe.gov/emeu/cbecs/cbecs2003/detailed_tables_2003/2003set4/2003pdf/set4.pdf (accessed May 30, 2008).

EPA (United States Environmental Protection Agency). 1998. *International Trade in Hazardous Waste: An Overview (EPA-305-K-98–001).* Available at http://www.epa.gov/compliance/resources/policies/civil/rcra/intnltrahazwas-rpt.pdf

EPA (United States Environmental Protection Agency). 2004. Buildings and the Environment: A Statistical Summary. http://www.epa.gov/greenbuilding/

European Renewable Energy Council. 2004. *Renewable Energy in Europe: Building Markets and Capacity.* Brussels: European Commission.

Evamy, Michael. 2007. *In the Black: The Growth of the Low Carbon Economy.* London: Climate Group. Available at http://www.theclimategroup.org/assets/resources/TCG_ITB_SR_FINAL_COPY.pdf (accessed August 7, 2009).

Farrell, Diana, Jaana Remes, Florian Bressand, Mark Laabs, and Anjan Sundaram. 2008. *The Case for Investing in Energy Productivity.* San Francisco: McKinsey & Company.

Federal Transit Administration, Transit Cooperative Research Program. 2001. "Guide to Federal Buy America Requirements." *Legal Research Digest* 17: 1–27.

Feist, Christian, Dirk Schlesinger, and Wes Frye. 2008. *Smart Grid: The Role of Electricity Infrastructure in Reducing Greenhouse Gas Emissions*. Cisco Internet Business Solutions Group.

Feldman, Jonathan. 2009. "From Mass Transit to New Manufacturing." *The American Prospect* (March 23).

Fell, Hans-Josef. 2009. *Feed-in Tariff for Renewable Energies. An Effective Stimulus Package Without New Public Borrowing*. Available at http://solar.gwu.edu/index_files/Resources_files/Fell_Feed-in-Tariffs.pdf.

Fiksel, Joseph. 2006. "Sustainability and Resilience: Toward a Systems Approach." *Sustainability: Science, Practice, and Policy* 2(2): 14–21.

Filardo, Mary. 2008. *Good Buildings, Better Schools: An Economic Stimulus Opportunity with Long-Term Benefits*. Briefing Paper # 216. Washington, D.C.: Economic Policy Institute.

Filion, P., and Kathleen McSpurren. 2007. "Smart Growth and Development Reality: The Difficult Coordination of Land Use and Transportation Objectives." *Urban Studies* 44(3): 501–523.

Fitzgerald, Joan. 2006. *Moving Up in the New Economy*. Ithaca, N.Y.: Cornell University Press.

Fitzgerald, Joan. 2007. "Help Wanted—Green." *The American Prospect*. 18(1): A16–A19.

Fitzgerald, Joan, and Nancey Green Leigh. 2003. *Economic Revitalization: Cases and Strategies for City and Suburb*. Thousand Oaks, Calif.: Sage.

Flavin, Christopher. 2008. "Building a Low-Carbon Economy." Pages 75–90 in *2008 State of the World: Innovations for a Sustainable Economy*, edited by Worldwatch Institute, Gary Gardner, and Thomas Prugh. New York: W.W. Norton.

Fletcher, Michael A. 2008. "In Toledo, Promises of Change Ring Hollow." *Washington Post*, February 24.

Flora, Rebecca L. 2006. *Green Building Products: Defining and Verifying the Opportunity for Western Pennsylvania*. Pittsburgh: Green Building Alliance.

Flora, Rebecca L. 2006. *Green Building Products: Positioning Southwestern Pennsylvania as the U.S. Manufacturing Center*. Pittsburgh: Green Building Alliance.

Florida, Richard. 2005. *Cities and the Creative Class*. New York: Routledge.

Francis Mary Kate. 2008. "Wind's Splash at U.S. Ports." American Wind Energy Association, March. Available at: http://www.awea.org/windletter/wl_08mar.html (accessed August 7, 2009).

Frantzis, Lisa, Jay Paidipati, Matt Stanberry, and Daniel Tomlinson. 2008. *Economic Impacts of Extending Federal Solar Tax Credits*. Burlington, Mass.: Navigant Consulting.

Friedman, Adam. 2008. "City Launches Green Manufacturing Initiative." *Real Estate Weekly*, June 6.

Friedman, Thomas. 2008. *Hot, Flat, and Crowded*. New York: Farrar, Straus and Giroux.

Furnas, Ben. 2009. *We Must Seize the Energy Opportunity or Slip Further Behind.* Washington, D.C.: Center for American Progress.

Galbraith, Kate, and Matthew L. Wald. 2008. "Energy Goals a Moving Target for States." World of Renewables.com, July 24. Available at http://www.worldofrenewables. com/index.php?do=viewarticle&artid=2770&title=energy-goals-a-moving-target-for-states (accessed December 31, 2008).

Galbraith, Kate. 2009. Dark Days for Green Energy. *New York Times.* (February 4, pp B1, 7).

GAO (United States Government Accountability Office). 2008. *Electronic Waste: EPA Needs to Better Control Harmful U.S. Exports through Stronger Enforcement and More Comprehensive Regulation* (GAO-08–1044). Available at http://www.gao.gov/products/GAO-08–1044.

Garg, Renu, Adam Karpati, Jessica Leighton, Mary Perrin, and Mona Shah. 2003. *Asthma Facts.* 2nd ed. New York: New York City Department of Health and Mental Hygiene.

Gavron, Nicky. 2007. "The Role of Cities in Tackling Climate Change." Sustainable Development International, November 26. Available at http://www.climateaction-programme.org/features/article/the_role_of_cities_in_tackling_climate_change/ (accessed December 10, 2007).

Gelbspan, Ross. 1997. *The Heat Is On: The Climate Crisis, the Cover-Up and the Prescription.* New York: Perseus.

Gelbspan, Ross. 2004. *Boiling Point: How Politicians, Big Oil and Coal, Journalists, and Activists Have Fueled a Climate Crisis—And What We Can Do to Avert Disaster.* New York: Basic.

Gibbs, David, Pauline Deutz, and Amy Proctor. 2002. *Sustainability and the Local Economy: The Role of Eco-Industrial Parks.* Paper presented at the Ecosites and Eco-Centres in Europe, Brussels, June 19, 2002.

Gifford, Henry. 2008. *A Better Way to Rate Green Buildings.* Available at http://www. aiact.org/userfiles/file/COTE/GreenGoals_Resources/LEED_Critique_ Gifford.pdf (accessed July 24, 2009).

Gillham, Oliver. 2002. *The Limitless City: A Primer on the Urban Sprawl Debate.* Washington, D.C.: Island Press.

Giloth, Robert, ed. 2004. *Workforce Intermediaries for the Twenty-first Century.* Philadelphia: Temple University Press.

Giloth, Robert, and John Betancur. 1988. "Where Downtown Meets Neighborhood: Industrial Displacement in Chicago, 1978–1987." *Journal of the American Planning Association* 53: 279–290.

Gitlitz, Jennifer, and Pat Franklin. 2007. "Water, Water Everywhere: The Growth of Non-Carbonated Beverages in the U.S." Washington, D.C.: Container Recycling Institute. Available at http://www.container-recycling.org/assets/pdfs/reports/2007-waterwater.pdf (accessed July 24, 2009).

Glaeser, Edward L., and Matthew Kahn. 2008. *The Greenness of Cities.* Cambridge, Mass.: Harvard University, Rappaport Institute for Greater Boston.

Glasmeier, Amy, Ron Feingold, Amanda Guers, Gillian Hay, Teresa Lawler, Alissa Meyer, Ratchan Sangpenchan, et al. 2007. *Energizing Appalachia: Global Challenges and the Prospect of a Renewable Future*. Washington, D.C.: Appalachian Regional Commission. Available at http://www.arc.gov/index.do?nodeId=3292 (accessed July 24, 2009).

Goldman, George, and Aya Ogishi. 2001. *The Economic Impact of Waste Disposal and Diversion in California*. Report to the California Integrated Waste Management Board. Berkeley: Department of Agricultural and Resource Economics, University of California, Berkeley.

Goldstein, David. 2007. *Saving Energy Growing Jobs: How Environmental Protection Promotes Economic Growth, Profitability, Innovation, and Competition*. Berkeley, Calif.: Bay Tree Publishing.

Goldstein, Nora. 2005. "Source Separated Organics as Feedstock for Digesters." *Bio-Cycle* 46(8): 42–46. Available at http://www.jgpress.com/archives/_free/000508.html (accessed July 24, 2009).

González, Ángel. 2008. "Biofuel Backlash: High Prices, Pollution Worries Hit Consumers." *Seattle Times*, June 8.

Gonzalez, David. 2008. "Greening the Bronx, One Castoff at a Time." *New York Times*, April 21.

Goodman, Peter S. 2008. "A Splash of Green for the Rust Belt." *New York Times*, November 2.

Gordon, Kate, and Jeremy Hays. 2008. *Green-Collar Jobs in America's Cities: Building Pathways out of Poverty and Careers in the Clean Energy Economy*. Washington, D.C.: The Apollo Alliance, March 13. Available at http://www.americanprogress.org/issues/2008/03/pdf/green_collar_jobs.pdf (accessed July 24, 2009).

Gordon, Kate, Jeremy Hays, Leon Sompolinsky, Elizabeth Tan, and Jackie Tsou. 2007. *Community Jobs in the Green Economy*. Madison, Wisc.: Apollo Alliance and Urban Agenda.

Gordon, Kate, Ragini Kapadia, Satya Rhodes-Conway, Jeff Rickert, Dan Seligman, and Brian Siu. 2007. *State Leadership for a New Energy Future: A Four-Point Initiative for Clean Energy and Good Jobs*. Madison, Wisc.: Apollo Alliance.

Gordon, Kate, Matt Mayrl, Satya Rhodes-Conway, and Brian Siu. 2006. *New Energy for Cities*. Madison, Wisc.: Apollo Alliance.

Goss, Sam, Gareth Kane, and Graham Street. 2006. *The Eco-Park: Green Nirvana or White Elephant?* Middlesbrough, U.K.: University of Teesside Clean Environment Management Centre. Available at http://www.tees.ac.uk/docs/DocRepo/Clemance/Ecopark.pdf (accessed July 24, 2009).

Gould, Kenneth, David N. Pellon, and Allan Schnaiberg. 2009. *The Treadmill of Production: Injustice and Unsustainablility in the Global Economy*. Boulder, Colo.: Paradigm Publishers.

Grama, Sorin, and Travis Bradford. 2008. *Thin-Film PV 2.0: Market Outlook through 2012*. Cambridge, Mass.: Prometheus Institute.

Green Building Alliance. 2008. *Shades of Green*. Annual report. Available at http://www
.gbapgh.org/Files/GBA%20Shades%200f%20Green%202008.pdf (accessed July
24, 2009).

Gross, Julian. 2005. *Community Benefits Agreements: Making Development Projects
Accountable*. Washington, D.C.: Good Jobs First.

Grossman, Elizabeth. 2006. *High Tech Trash: Digital Devices, Hidden Toxics, and Human
Health*. Washington, D.C.: Island Press.

Gunder, Michael. 2006. "Sustainability: Planning's Saving Grace or Road to Perdition?"
Journal of Planning Education and Research 26: 208–221.

Gurnon, Emily. 2003. "The Problem with Plastics: Recycling It Overseas Poses Risks
to Workers. Doing It Here Doesn't Pay." *North Coast Journal Weekly*, June 5.
Available at http://www.mindfully.org/Plastic/Recycling/Problem-With-Plastics
5jun03.htm (accessed October 1, 2008).

Handy, Susan. 2005. "Smart Growth and the Transportation-Land Use Connection:
What Does the Research Tell Us?" *International Regional Science Review*. 28(2):
146–167.

Harvey, Fiona, Chris Bryant, and Kathrin Hille. 2009. "Feeling the Heat." *Financial
Times*, June 2. Available at http://www.ft.com/cms/s/0/dd496434–4fa2–11de-a692–
00144feabdc0.html (accessed July 24, 2009).

Hecht, Ben. 2009. *Green Cities: How Urban Sustainability Efforts Can and Must Drive
America's Climate Change Policies*. Washington, D.C.: Living Cities.

Helper, Susan. 2008. *Renewing U.S. Manufacturing: Promoting a High-Road Strategy*.
Briefing Paper #212. Washington, D.C.: Economic Policy Institute.

Henton, Doug, John Melville, Tracey Grose, and Gabrielle Maor. 2008. *Clean
Technology and the Green Economy: Growing Products, Services, Businesses and Jobs in
California's Value Network*. Sacramento, Calif.: California Economic Strategy
Panel.

Hewings, Jeffrey, and Moshe Yanai. 2001. *Job Jolt: The Economic Impacts of Repowering
the Midwest: The Clean Energy Development Plan for the Heartland*. Washington,
D.C.: Environmental Law and Policy Center.

Hildt, Natalie. 2001. *Appliance and Equipment Efficiency Standards: New Opportunities for
States*. Boston: Appliance Standards Awareness Project.

Hill, Jeffrey. "Taken for a Ride: The Insanity of Escalators." *Next American City*.
Summer: 19–20. Available at http://americancity.org/magazine/article/taken-for-
a-ride-the-inanity-of-escalators/ (accessed July 24, 2009).

Hirsch, Joe. 2007. "Allies Split Over Rail Yard Plan." *Hunts Point Express*, November
30. Reprinted in http://nycitynewsservice.com/2007/11/30/bronx-allies-split-
over-rail-yard-plan/ (accessed July 25, 2008).

Hogan, John. 2005. "2001 Seattle Energy Code: Striving for 20% Total Building Energy
Savings compared to Standard 90.1–1999." *ASHRAE Transactions* 111: 444–456.

Holdren, John P, William K. Reilly, John W. Rowe, Philip R. Sharp, and Jason Grumet.
2004. *Ending the Energy Stalemate: A Bipartisan Strategy to Meet America's Energy*

Challenges. Washington, D.C.: National Commission on Energy Policy, December 2004.

Holtzclaw, J., J.R. Clear, H. Dittmar, D. Goldstein, and P. Haas. 2002. "Location Efficiency: Neighborhood and Socioeconomic Characteristics Determine Auto Ownership and Use—Studies in Chicago, Los Angeles and San Francisco." *Transportation Planning and Technology* 25(1): 1–27.

Inslee, Jay, and Bracken Hendricks. 2008. *Apollo's Fire: Igniting America's Clean Energy Economy*. Washington, D.C: Island Press.

Institute for America's Future, Center on Wisconsin Strategy, and Perryman Group. 2004. *New Energy for America: The Apollo Jobs Report: Good Jobs and Energy Independence*. Madison, Wisc.: Center on Wisconsin Strategy.

Intergovernmental Panel on Climate Change. 2007. *Climate Change 2007: Synthesis Report*. Available at http://www.ipcc.ch/pdf/assessment-report/ar4/syr/ar4_syr_spm.pdf.

International Brotherhood of Teamsters. 2007. *Trash and the Public Interest*. Washington, D.C.: Author.

International Brotherhood of Teamsters. 2009. Greening San Francisco. *Teamster* (May/June pp. 22–25).

International Energy Agency. 2008. *Energy Technology Perspectives 2008: Scenarios and Strategies to 2050*. Paris: Organization for Economic Cooperation and Development.

Jacklet, Ben. 2009. Geared Up. *Oregon Business* (January). Available at http://www. oregonbusiness.com/articles/15-january-2009/38-oregons-bicycle-industrial-complex (accessed July 20, 2009).

Johnston, Robert A. 2006. *Review of U.S. and European Regional Modeling Studies of Policies. Intended to Reduce Motorized Travel, Fuel Use, and Emissions*. Victoria, B.C.: Victoria Transport Policy Institute, August. Available at http://www.vtpi.org/ johnston.pdf (accessed July 24, 2009).

Joint Global Change Research Institute. 2006. *Renewable Energy Policy in Germany: An Overview and Assessment*. College Park, Md.: Joint Global Change Research Institute.

Jones, Carolyn. 2009. "Bright Future as Berkeley Starts Solar Program." *San Francisco Chronicle*, February 28.

Jones, Van. 2008. *The Green Collar Economy*. New York: HarperOne.

Kammen, Daniel M., Kamal Kapadia, and Matthias Fripp. 2004. Updated 2006. *Putting Renewables to Work: How Many Jobs Can the Clean Energy Industry Generate?* Berkeley: University of California, Berkeley, Goldman School of Public Policy Energy and Resources Group.

Kammen, Daniel M., and Gregory F. Nemet. 2005. "Reversing the Incredible Shrinking Energy R&D Budget." *Issues in Science and Technology* 22: 84–88. Available at http:// rael.berkeley.edu/files/2005/Kammen-Nemet-ShrinkingRD-2005.pdf (accessed August 7, 2009).

Karlenzig, Warren, 2006. "US city rankings," SustainLane.com. Available at http://www.sustainlane.com/us-city-rankings/ (accessed July 25, 2009).

Kaufman, Themelis, and Scott M. Kaufman. 2004. Waste in a Land of Plenty—Solid Waste Generation and Management in the US. *Waste Management World*, (September-October). Available at http://www.seas.columbia.edu/earth/wtert/sofos/Themelis_kaufman_WMW.pdf

Kelleher, Maria. 2007. "Anaerobic Digestion Outlook for MSW Streams." *BioCycle* 48(8): 51–55. Available at http://www.jgpress.com/archives/_free/001406.html (accessed December 16, 2007).

Klein, Ezra. 2007. "Inner-City Futurism." *The American Prospect* 17(7): 38–41.

Klein, Arne, Anne Held, Mario Ragwitz, Gustav Resch, and Thomas Faber. 2007. *Evaluation of Different Feed-In Tariff Design Options: Best Practice Paper for the International Feed-In Cooperation*. Karlsruhe, Germany: Fraunhofer Institut für Systemtechnik und Innovationsforschung. Available at http://www.feed-in-cooperation.org/images/files/best_practice_paper_final.pdf (accessed July 25, 2009).

Krueger, Rob, and David Gibbs, eds. 2007. *The Sustainable Development Paradox*. New York: The Guilford Press.

Krumholz, Norman. 1991. "Equity and Local Economic Development." *Economic Development Quarterly* 5(4): 291–300.

Krumholz, Norman, and John Forester. 1991. *Making Equity Planning Work*. Philadelphia: Temple University Press.

Krupp, Fred, and Miriam Horn. 2008. *Earth: The Sequel*. New York: W.W. Norton.

Kutcher, Charles F. 2007. *Tackling Climate Change in the U.S.: Potential Carbon Emissions Reductions from Energy Efficiency and Renewable Energy by 2030*. Boulder, Colo.: American Solar Energy Society.

Kuttner, Robert. 1997. *Everything for Sale*. New York: Alfred A. Knopf.

Lacoste, Elisabeth, and Philippe Chalmin. 2007. *From Waste to Resource: 2006 World Waste Report*. Paris: Economica.

Lake, Robert W. 2000. "Contradictions at the Local State: Local Implications of the U.S. Sustainability Agenda in the USA." Pages 71–91 in *Consuming Cities: The Urban Environment in the Global Economy after the Rio Declaration*, edited by Nicholas Low and Brendan Gleeson. London: Routledge.

LaPedus, Mark. 2006. "China Preps Huge Ramp in Solar Production." *EETimes*, March 22. Available at http://www.eetimes.com/news/semi/showArticle.jhtml?articleID=183701996 (accessed November 8, 2008).

Lee, Joanna, and Jennifer Ito. 2008. *A Greener Future for Los Angeles*. Los Angeles, Calif.: Strategic Concepts in Organizing and Policy Education (SCOPE).

Lerch, Daniel. 2008. *Post Carbon Cities: Planning for Energy and Climate Uncertainty*. Sebastopol, Calif.: Post Carbon Press.

LeRoy, Greg. 2005. *The Great American Jobs Scam*. San Francisco: Berrett-Koehler.

Ling, Catherine. 2009. "Obama Administrations Releases Initial 'Smart Grid' Standards." *New York Times* (September 24).

Lipman, Barbara J. 2006. *A Heavy Load: The Combined Housing and Transportation Burdens of Working Families*. Washington, D.C.: Center for Housing Policy.

Little, Amanda Griscom. 2005. "The Mall That Would Save America." *New York Times Magazine*, July 3. Available at http://syracusethenandnow.org/Dstiny/MallSaveAmerica.htm (accessed July 25, 2009).

Lovins, Hunter L. 2008. "Rethinking Production." Pages 32–44 in *2008 State of the World: Innovations for a Sustainable Economy*, edited by Worldwatch Institute, Gary Gardner, and Thomas Prugh. New York: W.W. Norton.

Lstiburek, Joseph. 2008. "Mis—LEED—ing." Building Science Corporation. Available at http://www.buildingscience.com/documents/insights/mis20141eed-2014ing/ (accessed July 25, 2009).

Lu, Xi, Michael B. McElroy, and Juha Kiviluoma. 2009. "Global Potential for Wind-Generated Electricity." *Proceedings of the National Academy of Sciences*, April 29: 1–6.

Luo, Michael, and Lydie Polgreen. 2003. "Layoffs by Carrier Corp. Strike Syracuse in Heart." *New York Times*, October 7.

Mack, Chuck, and Tom Politeo. 2007. "Together at Last: Teamsters and Sierra Club Join Forces for Good Jobs and Clean Air." *Social Policy* 38: 20–26.

Magnusson, Jemilah. 2005. "The Top 10 Green Cities in the U.S.: 2005." *National Geographic Green Guide*. Available at http://www.thegreenguide.com/doc/107/cities (accessed 8/10/07).

Makower, Joel, Ron Pernick, and Clint Wilder. 2008. *Clean Energy Trends 2008*. Portland, Ore.: Clean Edge.

Makower, Joel, Ron Pernick, and Clint Wilder. 2009. *Clean Energy Trends 2009*. Portland, Ore.: Clean Edge.

Malin, Nadav. 2008. "Lies, Damn Lies, and…(Another Look at LEED Energy Efficiency)." BuildingGreen.com, September 2. Available at http://www.buildinggreen.com/live/index.cfm/2008/9/2/Lies-Damn-Lies-and-Are-LEED-Buildings-iLessi-Efficient-Than-Regular-Buildings (accessed July 25, 2009).

Mangan, Andrew, and Elsa Olivetti. 2008. By-product Synergy Networks, Driving Innovation through Waste Reduction and Carbon Mitigation. Unpublished manuscript. Available at http://www.usbcsd.org/resources/documents/Clean%20Tech%20BPS%20Networks.pdf (accessed July 25, 2009).

Marshall, Alex. 2007. "The Streetcar Surge." *Governing*, December 1. Available at http://www.governing.com/column/streetcar-surge (accessed May 29, 2009).

Martinot, Eric. 2007. *Renewables 2007: Global Status Report*. Paris: Renewable Energy Policy Network for the Twenty-First Century (REN21).

Matsuoka, Martha. 2008. Clean and Safe Ports: Building a Movement, Region by Region. Available at http://urbanhabitat.org/node/2753 (accessed September 1, 2009).

Mattera, Philip. 2009. "A Green Industrial Economy." *The American Prospect*, March 23. Available at http://www.prospect.org/cs/articles?article=a_green_industrial_economy (accessed July 25, 2009).

Maycock, Paul. 2007. "World Average Photovoltaic Production and Module Cost per Watt, 1975–2006." Compiled by Earth Policy Institute. Available at http://www.earthpolicy.org/Indicators/Solar/2007_data.htm (accessed November 8, 2008).

Mazria, Edward, and Kristina Kershner. 2008. *The 2030 Blueprint: Solving Climate Change Saves Billions.* Available at http://www.architecture2030.0rg/pdfs/2030Blueprint.pdf (accessed July 25, 2009).

McGinn, Daniel. 2007. "Workers Find Jobs in Emerging Green Economy." *Newsweek,* October 8.

McGraw-Hill Construction. 2006. *Green Building SmartMarket Report.* New York: McGraw-Hill Construction.

McElroy, Michael. 2008. Global Potential for Wind-Generated Electricity. PubMed Central (PMC3—NLM DTD) (United States), http://www.pubmedcentral.nih.gov/articlerender.fcgi?artid=2700152 (accessed September 2, 2009).

McKinsey Global Institute. 2007. *Curbing Global Energy Demand Growth: The Energy Productivity Opportunity.* New York: McKinsey Global Institute.

McKinsey Global Institute. 2008. Newsletter. Available at http://www.mckinsey.com/mgi/BlackberryNewsletter/newsletter_dec2008/index.asp (accessed August 3, 2009).

McKnight, Jenna. 2007. "Destiny USA Breaks Ground in Syracuse." *Business Week Online,* November 5.

McMahon, Síle. 2008. "Crystalline Solar Cell Market Grew 39 Percent in 2007, Says Gartner." PV-tech.org, April 7. Available at http://www.pv-tech.org/news/_a/crystalline_solar_cell_market_grew_39_percent_in_2007_says_gartner/(accessed August 2, 2009).

McRandle, P.W., and Sara Smiley Smith. 2006. "The Top 10 Green Cities in the U.S.: 2006." *National Geographic Green Guide.* Available at http://www.thegreenguide.com/doc/113/top10cities.

Menz, Fredric C., and Stephan Vachon. 2006. "The Effectiveness of Different Policy Regimes for Promoting Wind Power: Experiences from the States." *Energy Policy* 34: 1786–1796.

Mier, Robert. 1993. *Social Justice and Local Development Policy.* Newbury Park, Calif.: Sage.

Millar, Heather. 2007. "Profile: Your Trash, His Inventory." *Sierra Magazine,* November/December. Available at http://www.sierraclub.org/sierra/200711/profile.asp.

Milligan, Susan. 2004. "Energy Bill a Special-Interests Triumph." *Boston Globe,* October 4.

Moriarty, Rick. 2008. "Judge Reverses Decision Denying Destiny USA Millions in 'Brownfield' Tax Credits." *Syracuse Post-Standard,* June 13. Available at http://www.syracuse.com/news/index.ssf/2008/06/judge_reverses_state_decision.html (accessed July 25, 2009).

Moritz, Jennifer, Christopher McMahan, and Keith R. Phillips. 2006. "Austin's High-Tech Industry: Played Out or Just Beginning?" *Vista—South Texas Economic Trends and Issues,* Issue 1. Available at http://dallasfed.org/research/vista/vista0601.pdf (accessed July 25, 2009).

Morris, Craig. 2006. *Energy Switch.* Gabriola Island, B.C.: New Society Publishers.

Mottola, Dan. 2005. "Why Has Austin's Solar Program Stalled?" *Austin Chronicle*, September 30.

Nelson, Arthur C. 2004. *Toward a New Metropolis: The Opportunity to Rebuild America.* Washington, D.C.: Brookings Institute.

Neuman, William, and Sewall Chan. 2008. "Judge Kills Mayor's Try at Greening Taxi Fleets." *New York Times*, November 1.

New Energy Finance. 2009. "Wind Developers Eye Long-term Gain after Short-term Pain." *Week in Review* 4(86): 1.

Newman, Peter, and Jeffrey Kenworthy. 1999. Sustainability and Cities: Overcoming Automobile Dependence. Island Press, Washington, DC.

Newman, Peter, and Jeffrey Kenworthy. 2006. "Urban Design to Reduce Automobile Dependence." *Opolis: An International Journal of Suburban and Metropolitan Studies* 2(1): 35–52. Available at http://repositories.cdlib.org/cssd/opolis/v012/iss1/art3 (accessed June 1, 2008).

New York League of Conservation Voters Education Fund. 2007. *Building a Greener Future: A Progress Report on New York City's Sustainability Initiatives*. New York: NYLCVEF.

New York State Energy Research and Development Administration. 2007. *New York Energy Smart Program Evaluation and Status Report, 2006*. Albany: NYSERDA.

Oakes, Larry. 2008. "Wind Power Is Pushing Duluth Port to a New Age." *Minneapolis-St. Paul Star Tribune*, November 23.

O'Brien, Keith. 2008. "In Praise of Plastic." *Boston Globe*, September 28.

OECD (Organization for Economic Co-operation and Development). 2002. *Decision of the Council Concerning the Transfrontier Movements of Wastes Destined for Recovery Operations.* www.olis.oecd.org/olis/2001doc.nsf/LinkTo/NT00005016/$FILE/JT00160032.PDF

Olofsson, Maud. 2008. "One Country's Success Story: Building a Green Economy." *eGov Monitor*, March 31. Available at http://www.egovmonitor.com/node/17936 (accessed March 25, 2009).

O'Neill, Meaghan. 2006. "Pittsburgh: From Steel to Sustainability." *Interior Design*, November 16.

O'Toole, Christine H. 2009. The Greening of Pittsburgh. *New York Times*, April 1.

Pakulski, Gary T. 2003. "First Solar Renews Its Push for Viability." *Toledo Blade*, February 16.

Palmateer, Paige. 2007. "NuClimate Offers Energy-efficient HVAC Units." *CNY Business Journal*, May 18.

Palmer, Thomas C. 2007. "Cambridge Sets $70m Energy Initiative." *Boston Globe*, March 29.

Panoska, Christina, and William A. Spratley. 2004. *Green Energy Ohio: Growing Clean Energy Opportunities from the Grassroots Up*. Columbus, Ohio: Green Energy Ohio. Available at http://www.greenenergyohio.org/page.cfm?pageId=463 (accessed July 26, 2009).

Patel-Predd, Prachi. 2007. "Carbon-Dioxide Plastic Gets Funding." *Technology Review*, November 14. Available at http://www.technologyreview.com/Biztech/19697/ (accessed July 26, 2009).

Pellow, David Naguib. 2002. *Garbage Wars: The Struggle for Environmental Justice in Chicago*. Cambridge, Mass.: MIT Press.

Pellow, David Naguib. 2007. *Resisting Global Toxics: Transnational Movements for Environmental Justice*. Cambridge, Mass.: MIT Press.

Pernick, Ron, and Clint Wilder. 2007. *The Clean Tech Revolution*. New York: HarperCollins.

Peters, Alan, and Peter Fisher. 2004. "The Failures of Economic Development Incentives." *Journal of the American Planning Association* 70(1): 27–37.

Pinderhughes, Raquel. 2006. "Green Collar Jobs: Work Force Opportunities in the Growing Green Economy." *Race, Poverty & the Environment* 13(1).

Pinderhughes, Raquel. 2007. *Green Collar Jobs: An Analysis of the Capacity of Green Businesses to Provide High-Quality Jobs for Men and Women with Barriers to Employment*. Berkeley, Calif.: Office of Energy and Sustainable Development.

Pittsburgh. 2007. *Code of Ordinances. Title Nine, Zoning, subsection 915.04, Sustainable Development Bonuses for Green Buildings*.

Platt, Brenda. 2004. *Resources Up in Flames: The Economic Pitfalls of Incineration versus a Zero Waste Approach in the Global South*. Washington, D.C.: Institute for Local Self-Reliance.

Platt, Brenda, David Ciplet, Kate M. Bailey, and Eric Lombardi. 2008. *Stop Trashing the Climate*. Washington, D.C.: Institute for Local Self-Reliance.

Pollin, Robert, Heidi Garrett-Peltier, James Heintz, and Helen Scharbar. 2008. *Green Recovery: A Program to Create Good Jobs and Start Building a Low-Carbon Economy*. Washington, D.C.: Center for American Progress.

Pollin, Robert, James Heintz, and Heidi Garrett-Peltier. 2009. *The Economic Benefits of Investing in Clean Energy*. Amherst: University of Massachusetts, Political Economy Research Institute.

Pollin, Robert, and Jeannette Wicks-Lim. 2008. *Job Opportunities for the Green Economy: A State-by-State Picture of Occupations that Gain from Green Investments*. Amherst: University of Massachusetts, Political Economy Research Institute.

Pollin, Robert, Jeannette Wicks-Lim, and Heidi Garrett-Peltier. 2009. *Green Prosperity: How Clean-Energy Policies Can Fight Poverty and Raise Living Standards in the United States*. Amherst: University of Massachusetts, Political Economy Research Institute.

Port of Longview, 2007. "Port of Longview Handles Siemens Wind Turbines." Press release. Available at http://www.portoflongview.com/page.asp?view=4322 (accessed August 7, 2009).

Port of Los Angeles and Long Beach. 2006. "San Pedro Bay Ports Clean Air Action Plan." Los Angeles, Calif: Authors.

Porter, Michael. 1997. "New Strategies for Inner-City Economic Development." *Economic Development Quarterly* 11(1): 11–27.

Porter, Michael. 1998. "Clusters and the New Economics of Competition." *Harvard Business Review*, November-December: 77–90.

Portney, Kent E. 2003. *Taking Sustainable Cities Seriously*. Cambridge, Mass.: MIT Press.

Proctor, Cathy. 2003. "Hickenlooper, Owens Plan California Eco-Devo Trip." *Denver Business Journal*, June 26.

Proctor, Cathy. 2009. "New FasTracks Campaign Faces Recession Realities." *Denver Business Journal*, March 20.

Puckett, Jim, and Ted Smith, eds. 2002. *Exporting Harm: The High-Tech Trashing of Asia*. Seattle: Basel Action Network. Available at http://www.ban.org/E-waste/technotrashfinalcomp.pdf (accessed July 26, 2009).

Pushkarev, Boris S., and Jeffrey M. Zupan. 1977. *Public Transportation and Land Use Policy*. Bloomington: Indiana University Press.

Rabe, Barry G. 2002. *Greenhouse and Statehouse: The Evolving State Government Role in Climate Change*. Philadelphia: Pew Center of Global Climate Change.

Rabe, Barry G. 2003. *Statehouse and Greenhouse: The Stealth Politics of America Climate Change Policy*. Philadelphia: Pew Center of Global Climate Change.

Rabe, Barry G. 2006. 1996. "Challenges to Climate Policy Development in Canada's Multi-Level Governance System." Pages 71–85 in *Comparative Smart Practices for Innovation in Public Management*, edited by Colin Campbell. Ottawa: Canada School for Public Service, 2006.

Rabe, Barry G. 2006. *Race to the Top: The Expanding Role of U.S. State Renewable Portfolio Standards*. Arlington, Va.: Pew Center on Global Climate Change, Available at http://www.pewclimate.org/docUploads/RPSReportFinal.pdf (accessed July 26, 2009).

Rabe, Barry G. 2006. "Power to the States: The Promise and Pitfalls of Decentralization." Pages 34–56 in *Environmental Policy: New Directions for the Twenty-First Century*, edited by Norman J. Vig and Michael Kraft. Washington, D.C.: CQ Press, 2006. 34–56.

Rabe, Barry G. 2006. "Second Generation Climate Policies in the American States: Proliferation, Diffusion, and Regionalism." *Issues in Governance Studies* 6 (August): 1–9. Available at http://www.brookings.edu/papers/2006/08energy_rabe.aspx

Reed, Stanley, and Ariane Sains. 2009. "Sweden Puts Its Bets on Green Tech." *Business Week*, January 15. Available at http://www.businessweek.com/globalbiz/content/jan2009/gb20090115_287438.htm?campaign_id=rss_daily (accessed June 10, 2009).

Renner, Michael. 2000. *Working for the Environment: A Growing Source of Jobs*. Washington, D.C.: Worldwatch Institute.

Renner, Michael, Sean Sweeney, and Jill Kubit. 2008. *Green Jobs: Towards Sustainable Work in a Low-Carbon World*. Washington, D.C.: Worldwatch Institute.

Restrepo, Carlos E., and Rae Zimmerman, eds. 2004. *South Bronx Environmental Health and Policy Study: Transportation and Traffic Modeling, Air Quality, Waste Transfer Stations, and Environmental Justice Analyses in the South Bronx. Final Report for Phase II & III*. New York: Robert F. Wagner Graduate School of Public Service.

Revkin, Andrew. 2009. "California Utility Looks to Mojave Desert Project for Solar Power." *New York Times*, February 11.

Rickerson, Wilson. 2002. "German Electricity Feed Law Policy Overview." WindWorks.org. Available at http://www.wind-works.org/articles/fl_Rickerson.html (accessed July 26, 2009).

Rickerson, Wilson, Florian Bennhold, and James Bradbury. 2008. *Feed-in Tariffs and Renewable Energy in the USA—A Policy Update*. Washington, D.C.: Heinrich Böll Foundation.

Rickerson, Wilson, and Robert C. Grace. 2007. *The Debate over Fixed Price Incentives for Renewable Electricity in Europe and the United States: Fallout and Future Directions*. Washington, D.C.: The Heinrich Böll Foundation.

Roberts, Allen P. 2006. "Port of Long Beach, Matson on Board for 'Cold Ironing.' " *Los Angeles Business Journal*, May 8.

Rogers, Joel. 2007. *Improving Building Energy Efficiency: Why Building Retrofits Don't Happen at Scale, and How to Fix That*. Madison, Wisc.: Center on Wisconsin Strategy.

Rogol, Michael. 2005. Sun Screen II. Investment Opportunities in Solar Power. Available at http://photon-magazine.com/news/PI%202005–08%20ww%20med%20feat%20SunScreen%20Study.pdf (accessed June 20, 2009).

Rogol, Michael, Mark Farber, Hilary Flynn, Martin Meyers, Scott Paap, Christopher Porter, Joshua Rogol, and Joonki Song. 2008. *Solar Annual 2008*. Boston, Mass.: Photon Consulting.

Roland-Holst, David. 2008. *Energy Efficiency, Innovation, and Job Creation in California*. Berkeley, Calif.: Center for Energy, Resources, and Economic Sustainability.

Romm, Joseph. 2007 *Hell and High Water. Global Warming—The Solution and the Politics and What We Should Do*. New York: HarperCollins.

Rowan, Colin. 2008. *Igniting Texas' New Energy Economy*. Austin: The Catalyst Project.

Royte, Elizabeth. 2005. *Garbage Land: On the Secret Trail of Trash*. New York and Boston: Little, Brown.

Runci, Paul. 2005. *Renewable Energy Policy in Germany: An Overview and Assessment*. Baltimore, Md.: Joint Global Change Research Institute.

Rusk, David. 2006. "Social Framework: Sprawl, Race, and Concentrated Poverty—Changing the 'Rules of the Game.' " Pages 90–102 in *Urban Sprawl: A Comprehensive Reference Guide*, edited by David C. Soule. Westport, Conn.: Greenwood Press.

RW Ventures and O-H Community Partners. 2008. *Market Development for Building Energy Efficiency Retrofits*. Chicago: Authors.

Sahagun, Louis. 2007. "Ports Turn Over a New, Green Leaf." *Los Angeles Times*, December 25.

Salon, Deborah, Daniel Sperling, Alan Meier, Sinnott Murphy, Roger Gorham, and James Barrett. 2008. *City Carbon Budgets: Aligning Incentives for Climate-Friendly Communities*. Davis: Institute of Transportation Studies, University of California, Davis.

Sawin, Janet L. 2004. *National Policy Instruments: Policy Lessons for the Advancement & Diffusion of Renewable Energy Technologies around the World*. Washington, D.C.: Worldwatch Institute. Available at http://www.issuelab.org/research/national_policy_instruments_policy_lessons_for_the_advancement_and_diffusion_of_renewable_energy_technologies_around_the_world (accessed August 7, 2009).

Schaefer, Louisa. 2007. "Despite Climate Concerns, Germany Plans Coal Power Plants." Deutsche Welle, March 21. Available at http://www.dw-world.de/dw/article/0,2144,2396828,00.html (accessed September 23, 2008).

Schneider, Werner. 2006. "German Alliance for Work and Environment." Presentation to the Trade Union Assembly on Labor and Environment, Nairobi, Kenya, January 15–17.

Scott, Robert E. 2008. *The Importance of Manufacturing: Key to Recovery in the States and the Nation*. Washington, D.C.: Economic Policy Institute.

Seldman, Neil, and Richard Anthony. 2007. *Resource Management in the State of Delaware*. Washington, D.C.: Institute for Local Self-Reliance.

Senville, Wayne. 2007. "What's Syracuse's Destiny?" *Planning Commissioners Journal*, November 9. Available at http://pcj.typepad.com/planning_commissioners_jo/2007/11/whats-syracuses.html (accessed June 18, 2008).

Shapiro, Robert J., Kevin A. Hassett, and Frank S. Arnold. 2002. *Conserving Energy and Preserving the Environment: The Role of Public Transportation*. Washington, D.C.: American Public Transportation Association. Available at http://www.apta.com/gap/policyresearch/Documents/shapiro.pdf

Shapiro, Shari. 2009. "Barriers to Entry—Analyzing Barriers to Greening Building Codes." Green Building Law Blog, March 22. Available at http://www.green-buildinglawblog.com/2009/03/articles/codes-1/barriers-to-entryanalyzing-barriers-to-greening-building-codes/ (accessed July 26, 2009).

Sheppard, Kate. 2008. "Big Trucking Deal." *In These Times*, April 7.

Shiels Obletz Johnsen, Inc. 2006. *Portland Streetcar Development Summary*. Portland, Ore.: Shiels Obletz Johnsen. Available at http://www.portlandstreetcar.org/pdf/development_200804_project_list.pdf (accessed July 26, 2009).

Siegel, Beth, and Peter Kwass. 1995. *Jobs and the Urban Poor: Publicly Initiated Sectoral Strategies*. Somerville, Mass.: Mount Auburn Associates.

Sijm, J.P.M. 2002. "The Performance of Feed-in Tariffs to Promote Renewable Electricity in European Countries." Petten: Energy Research Centre of the Netherlands. Available at http://www.ecn.nl/docs/library/report/2002/c02083.pdf (accessed July 26, 2009).

Singh, Virinder, and Jeffrey Fehrs. 2001. *The Work That Goes Into Renewable Energy*. Washington, D.C.: Renewable Energy Policy Project.

Sissine, Fred. 2006. *Renewable Energy: Tax Credit, Budget and Electricity Production Issues*. Washington, D.C.: Congressional Research Service.

Smart Growth America. n.d. "What Is Smart Growth?" Available at http://www.smartgrowthamerica.org/whatissg.html (accessed January 4, 2007).

Solarenergie-Forderverein, 1994. A New Path to Self-Sustaining Markets for PV. World Conference on Photovoltaic Energy Conversion. Pp. 2357–2360.

Soule, David C. 2006. "Defining and Managing Sprawl." Pages 3–11 in *Urban Sprawl: A Comprehensive Reference Guide*, edited by David C. Soule. Westport, Conn.: Greenwood Press.

Southwick Associates. 2007. *State-Level Economic Contributions of Active Outdoor Recreation*. Fernandina Beach, Fla.: Outdoor Industry Foundation.

Spencer, Miranda. 2005. "Building Sustainable Cities: Scandinavia's 'Eco-Municipalities' Show the Way." *E Magazine*, September/October.

Sperling, Daniel, and James Cannon. 2009. *Reducing Climate Impacts in the Transportation Sector*. Dordrecht, The Netherlands: Springer Transportation.

Stanley, Dean. 2005. "ECD-Ovonics Tests Solid Storage in Prius Hybrid." Hydrogen Forecast, http://www.hydrogenforecast.com/ArticleDetails.php?articleID=241

Stephenson, John B. 2008. *Electronic Waste: EPA Needs to Better Control Harmful U.S. Exports through Stronger Enforcement and More Comprehensive Regulation*. United States Governmental Accountability Office. Available at http://www.gao.gov/new.items/d081044.pdf (accessed September 24, 2008).

Stern, Nicholas. 2006. *The Economics of Climate Change: The Stern Review*. Cambridge, U.K.: Cambridge University Press.

Sterzinger, George. 2008. *Energizing Prosperity: Renewable Energy and Re-Industrialization*. Washington, D.C.: The Economic Policy Institute.

Sterzinger, George. 2009. "Beyond Sunny Hopes and Windy Rhetoric." *The American Prospect*, March 23.

Sterzinger, George, and Jerry Stevens. 2006. *Renewable Energy Potential: A Case Study of Pennsylvania*. Washington, D.C.: Renewable Energy Policy Project.

Sterzinger, George, and Matt Svrcek. 2004. *Wind Turbine Development: Location of Wind Manufacturing*. Washington, D.C.: Renewable Energy Policy Project.

Sterzinger, George, and Matt Svrcek. 2005. *Component Manufacturing: Ohio's Future in the Renewable Energy Industry*. Washington, D.C.: Renewable Energy Policy Project.

Stone, Andy. 2009. "Smart Grid, Stupid Policy?" Forbes.com, January 29.

Stryi-Hipp, Gerhard. 2004. "How Municipalities Can Profit from Solar Energy—Experiences in Germany." International Economic Forum of the Americas, December 9.

Stryi-Hipp, Gerhard. 2008. Renewable Energy India 2008 Expo, International Exhibition & Conference, August 22, 2008, New Delhi.

Stryi-Hipp, Gerhard. 2009. Experience with the German Performance-Based Incentive Program. Volume II: Joint Summary Report.

Sullivan, Robert. 2008. "The Green Urbanist." *Men's Vogue*, May. Available at http://www.mensvogue.com/business/articles/2008/05/freilla.

Sustainable Pittsburgh. 2004. *Southwestern Pennsylvania Regional Sustainability Indicators Report*. Pittsburgh: Sustainable Pittsburgh. Available at http://www.sustainablepittsburgh.org/pdf/2004Indicators.pdf (accessed July 26, 2009).

Sustainable South Bronx and Green Worker Cooperatives. 2007. *The Oak Point Eco-Industrial Park: A Sustainable Development Proposal for the South Bronx*. New York: Sustainable South Bronx.

Svoboda, Elizabeth. 2008. "America's 50 Greenest Cities." PopSci.com, February 8. Available at http://www.popsci.com/environment/article/2008–02/americas-50-greenest-cities?page=1 (accessed July 26, 2009).

Syracuse Center of Excellence in Environmental and Energy Systems. 2006. *Excellence Rising: Creating Innovations to Improve Built and Urban Environments*. Progress Report 2006. Syracuse, N.Y.: Syracuse Center of Excellence. Available at http://www.syracusecoe.org/pdfs/coe%20progress%20report%202006%20final.pdf (accessed July 26, 2009).

Syracuse Center of Excellence in Environmental and Energy Systems. 2007. *Collaborating for a Sustainable Future*. Progress Report 2007. Syracuse, N.Y.: Syracuse Center of Excellence. Available at http://www.syracusecoe.org/pdfs/File/SCoEAPR-LR.pdf (accessed July 26, 2009).

Sze, Julie. 2007. *Noxious New York: The Racial Politics of Urban Health and Environmental Justice*. Cambridge, Mass.: MIT Press.

Talbot, David. 2009. "Lifeline for Renewable Power." *Technology Review*, January/February: 1–5.

Talley, Ian. 2009. "Obama Renewable-Energy Plans Must Hurdle Local Opposition." *Wall Street Journal*, March 20.

Theodore, Nik, and Virginia Carlson. 1998. "Targeting Job Opportunities: Developing Measures of Local Employment." *Economic Development Quarterly* 12(2): 137–149.

Tobias, Leanne. 2009. "Green Business Investment: Energetic and Evolving." Greenbiz.com, March 9. Available at http://www.greenbiz.com/blog/2009/03/09/green-building-investment (accessed April 12, 2009).

Tucker, Libby. 2009. "In-Depth: Could Portland Be America's Bike Manufacturing Hub?" BikePortland.org, May 1. Available at http://bikeportland.org/2009/05/01/in-depth-could-portland-become-a-bike-industry-hub/ (accessed May 18, 2009).

Turner, Cathy, and Mark Frankel. 2008. *Energy Performance of LEED for New Construction Buildings*. Washington, D.C.: U.S. Green Building Council.

Urban Land Institute. n.d. "What Is Smart Growth?" Available at http://www.uli.org/LearnAboutULI/WhereWeAre/Asia/What%20is%20Smart%20Growth.aspx (accessed December 12, 2006).

U.S. Department of Commerce. 2008. *The Future of the Hollings Manufacturing Extension Partnership*. Washington, D.C.: National Institute of Standards and Technology.

U.S. Department of Energy. 2008. *20% Wind by 2030: Increasing Wind Energy's Contribution to U.S. Electricity Supply*. Washington, D.C.: author.

U.S. Department of Transportation. 2009. *Vision for High-Speed Rail in America*. Washington, D.C.: Department of Transportation.

U.S. Environmental Protection Agency. 2001. *What Is Smart Growth?* Factsheet. Available at http://www.epa.gov/dced/pdf/whtissg4v2.pdf (accessed July 26, 2009).

U.S. Environmental Protection Agency. 2004. *Buildings and the Environment: A Statistical Summary*. Washington, D.C.: author. http://www.epa.gov/greenbuilding/pubs/gbstats.pdf (accessed February 16, 2009).

U.S. Environmental Protection Agency, 2004. *Buildings and the Environment: A Statistical Summary*. Available at *http://www.epa.gov/greenbuilding/pubs/gbstats.pdf* (accessed February 16, 2009).

U.S. Environmental Protection Agency. 2007. *Municipal Solid Waste Generation, Recycling and Disposal in the United States: Facts and Figures for 2006*. Washington, D.C.: Environmental Protection Agency.

U.S. Environmental Protection Agency. 2008. *Inventory of U.S. Greenhouse Gas Emissions and Sinks, 1990–2006*. Washington, D.C.: Environmental Protection Agency.

U.S. Green Building Council. 2002. *Building Momentum: National Trends and Prospects for High-Performance Green Buildings*. Washington, D.C.: Green Building Council.

Vardon, Joe. 2007. "Lucas County OKs $2M Loan to Toledo Solar-panel Firm." *Toledo Blade*, December 18.

Vogel, Jennifer. 2008. "Rural Renewal." *Mother Jones*, May/June: 54–55.

Vogel, Mike. 2008. "Incinerating Garbage, the High-Tech Way." *Florida Trend*, July 1.

Warner, Kee. 2002. "Linking Sustainability Initiatives with Environmental Justice." *Local Environment*. 7(1): 35–47.

Warren, Barbara. 2000. *Taking Out the Trash: A New Direction for New York City's Waste*. New York: Organization of Waterfront Neighborhoods and Consumer Policy Institute/Consumers Union. Available at http://www.consumersunion.org/pdf/trash%20report.pdf (accessed July 26, 2009).

Weinberg, Adam S., David N. Pellow, and Allan Schnaiberg. 2000. *Urban Recycling and the Search for Sustainable Community Development*. Princeton, N.J.: Princeton University Press.

White, Rodney. 2001. "Sustainable Development in Urban Areas: An Overview." In *How Green Is the City?*, edited by Dimitri Devuyst. New York: Columbia University Press.

White, Sarah. 2001. Voluntary Instruments: Predicting Green Power. Presentation at Project Workshop Green-X, September 23.

White, Sarah, and Jason Walsh. 2008. *Jobs and Workforce Development in the Clean Energy Economy*. Madison, Wisc.: Center on Wisconsin Strategy, the Workforce Alliance, and the Apollo Alliance.

Wilhelm, Steve, 2008. "Washington Ports Feed Growing Wind Industry with Turbines." *Puget Sound Business Journal (Seattle)*, March 7. Available at http://seattle.bizjournals.com/seattle/stories/2008/03/10/story8.html (accessed August 7, 2009).

Williams, Louise. 2007. "Sweden: Going Green." *Sydney Morning Herald* (Australia), June 23.

Williams, Stockton. 2008. *Bringing Home the Benefits of Energy Efficiency to Low-Income Households: The Case for a National Commitment*. Columbia, Md.: Enterprise Community Partners.

Wilson, Alex. 2007. "Driving to Green Buildings: The Transportation Energy Intensity of Buildings." *Environmental Building News*, September 1. Available at http://www.buildinggreen.com/auth/article.cfm?fileName=160901a.xml

Wise, Robert N., Ellie Fiore, Clark Brockman, and Eden Brukman. 2007. *Economic Development Opportunities for Portland's Green Building Industry*. Report prepared for the Portland Development Commission. Portland, Ore.: Portland Development Commission.

Wiser, Ryan, and Mark Bolinger. 2007. *Annual Report on U.S. Wind Power Installation, Cost and Performance Trends: 2006*. U.S Department of Energy.

Wiser, Ryan, and Ole Langniss. 2001. "The Renewable Portfolio Standard in Texas: An Early Assessment." Berkeley, Calif.: Ernesto Lawrence Berkeley National Laboratory. Available at http://www.osti.gov/bridge/servlets/purl/790029–9pmNCT/native/790029.pdf (accessed July 26, 2009).

Wiser, Ryan, Kevin Porter, and Robert Grace. 2004. *Evaluating Experience with Renewables Portfolio Standards in the United States*. Berkeley, Calif.: Lawrence Berkeley National Laboratory (LBNL). March. Available at http://eetd.lbl.gov/EA/EMS/reports/54439.pdf (accessed July 26, 2009).

Wood, David, and Allison Brooks. 2009. Fostering Equitable and Sustainable Transit-Oriented Development. Overview of Briefing Papers, Boston University.

World Business Council for Sustainable Development. 2008. *Collaborative Action for Energy Regional Network Case Study*. Washington, D.C.: WBCSD. Available at http://www.usbcsd.org/resources/documents/USBCSD%20BPS%20Case%20Study%20Final.pdf (accessed July 26, 2009).

World Business Council for Sustainable Development. 2009. China Responds Better to Policy Shifts than to Caps, Climate Group Says. http://www.wbcsd.org/plugins/DocSearch/details.asp?type=DocDet&ObjectId=MzUzOTU (accessed August 28, 2009).

Wust, Christian. 2009. Woo Car-Loving US with Eco-Friendly Trans. http://www.spiegel.de/international/business/0,1518,536892,00.html (accessed 12 May, 2009).

Ye, Lin, Sumedha Mandpe, and Peter B. Meyer. 2005. "What Is Smart Growth, Really?" *Journal of Planning Literature* 19(3): 301–315.

Young, Gary C. 2006. "Zapping MSW with Plasma Arc." *Pollution Engineering*, December.

Young, Gary C. 2008. "From Waste Solids to Fuel." *Pollution Engineering*, February 15. Available at http://www.pollutionengineering.com/Articles/Cover_Story/BNP_GUID_9-5-2006_A_10000000000000263119 (accessed July 26, 2009).

Zakaria, Fareed. 2008. *The Post-American World*. New York: W.W. Norton.

Zerolnick, Jon. 2007. *The Road to Shared Prosperity: The Regional Economic Benefits of the San Pedro Ports' Clean Trucks Program.* Los Angeles: Los Angeles Alliance for a New Economy.

Zimmerman, Rae, Carlos Restrepo, Cary Hirschstein, José Holguín-Veras, Jennifer Lara, and David Klebenov. 2002. *South Bronx Environmental Health and Policy Study: Public Health and Environmental Policy Analysis: Final Report for Phase I.* New York: Robert F. Wagner Graduate School of Public Service. Available at http://www.icisnyu.org/assets/documents/SouthBronxPhaseIReport.pdf (accessed July 26, 2009).

Zweibel, Ken, James Mason, and Vasilis Fthenakis. 2008. "A Solar Grand Plan." *Scientific American*, January. Available at http://www.scientificamerican.com/article.cfm?id=a-solar-grand-plan (accessed July 26, 2009).

Index

Agyeman, Julian, 19
American Clean Energy and Security
    Act of 2009, 22, 88, 183
American Planning Association, 19
American Public Transportation
    Association, 146, 171
American Recovery and Reinvestment
    Act (ARRA), 10, 25, 70, 83, 111,
    170
American Society of Heating,
    Refrigerating and Air-Conditioning
    Engineers (ASHRAE), 87
American Trucking Association, 155
American Wind Energy Association, 37
Anaerobic digestion, 129, 132–134
Apollo Alliance, 10, 23–28
Architecture 2030, 85–87
Austin, 11, 16, 20, 27, 32, 47–55, 69, 84
Austin Energy, 47–49, 53, 77, 84
Austin Polytechnic Academy, 74

Berkeley, Calif., 32, 40–43, 124, 173
Berkeley FIRST, 16, 32, 41, 94
Bike-related business, 210–212
Biodiesel, 16, 37, 40, 105, 143, 146,
    164–167
Boston, 11, 19, 84, 110, 142–143
Brown, Senator Sherrod 59, 73
Building efficiency, 78, 81
    in Cambridge, 89–90
    and employment, 79–80, 81–82

and link to manufacturing, 95
and link to manufacturing in New
    York City, 105–108
and link to manufacturing in
    Pittsburgh region, 95–98
and link to manufacturing in Syracuse,
    98–105
in Los Angeles, 90–92
and Los Angeles Community College
    Green Build Program, 92–93
in Milwaukee, 93–95
Bus rapid transit, 148–149, 173

California
    and California Green Stimulus
        Coalition, 25–26
    and California Integrated Waste
        Management Act, 129
    and employment in solar energy, 42
    and energy efficiency, 80, 88, 114
    Green Wave Initiative, 182
    Million Solar Roofs, 46, 182
    and renewable energy policy, 46,
        50, 68
Cambridge, 89, 93, 101, 142
Cambridge Energy Alliance, 89–90,
    111
Carbon emissions, 1, 12, 78, 81, 138,
    146, 182
Carbon tax, 178
Carter, Majora, 124–125

Case Western Reserve University, 61
Center of Excellence in Environmental
    and Energy Systems (Syracuse
    CoE), 99
Center on Wisconsin Strategy (COWS),
    93
Chicago
    Austin Polytechnic Academy, 74–75
    and energy efficiency, 109
    Waste to Profit Network, 135–138,
    141
China
    and greenhouse gas emissions, 21
    and solar production, 5, 35, 36, 69–70,
    182
    and waste recycling, 118–119, 137
Clean Renewable Energy Bonds
    (CREBs), 174
Cleveland, 14, 16
    and recycling, 118–119
    and renewable energy production, 5,
    36, 69
    and wind energy development, 59–63
Cleveland Foundation, 59–61
Climate change, 8, 9, 20–22, 174, 176,
    177, 183
Coalition for Clean and Safe Ports,
    151, 153
Colorado, 53, 54, 75
Conversion technologies, 131–134

Denver, 145, 147–151, 172
DeVries, Cisco, 41
Dreier, Peter, 19
Dukakis, Michael, 177

Efficiency standards, 45, 78, 80, 82
Elam, Rob, 167
Ella Baker Center, 23–25
Energy efficiency, 78, 80–81, 89. See also
    building efficiency
Energy Service Companies (ESCOs), 89
Energy Star Rating System, 88–89, 166
Environmental justice, 18–19, 22–25,
    115, 123, 146, 153

Federal Production Tax Credit, 34,
    37, 65
Feed-in tariff, 3–7, 35, 45, 54, 67–68
First Solar, 36, 56–57, 75
Flora, Rebecca, 96

Freiburg, Germany, 1–4, 7, 177
Freilla, Omar, 122–127

Gamesa, 38, 69, 75
Gemini Solar Development Company,
    49, 53
Germany
    Aachen and energy policy, 4, 18
    Freiburg and energy policy, 1–4
    renewable energy policy, 4–8, 14, 67,
    70, 82, 177, 183
Global warming, 20–22, 25, 45–46,
    122, 182
Good Jobs First, 73–76
Great Lakes Wind Network, 63
Green building, 8, 87, 92–93, 96,
    98–101, 106–108, 181. See also
    building efficiency
    market for, 80
    policy to promote, 83–89
Green Building Alliance, 95–96, 110
Green for All, 23, 25
Greenhouse gas emissions, 9, 11, 15, 20,
    22–25, 40, 47, 78–79, 145, 147, 180
Green Jobs Act, 25, 111
Green LA, 90, 111
Green Worker Cooperative, 122–125

Hammarby Sjöstad, 178–179
HelioVolt, 51–54

Imperium Renewables, 163–164
Industrial policy, 27, 72–73, 183–184
    in transit, 171–175
International Brotherhood of Electrical
    Workers (IBEW), 44, 74, 114

Jones, Van, 23–25

Kim, Ian, 23
King County Metro Transit, 163–164,
    167

Lane Community College, 112
Leadership in Energy and
    Environmental Design (LEED),
    83–87, 92, 98, 102, 105, 109
Leapfrogging strategies, 15–17, 95, 98,
    121, 146, 165, 183
Light rail, 14, 146, 148–150, 162,
    170–172

Linking strategies, 2, 8, 15–17, 145, 151
Los Angeles, 14, 80, 88, 111, 145–146
    and Coalition for Clean and Safe
        Ports, 151–156
    and GREEN LA, 90–92
    and RENEW LA, 128–135, 182,
Los Angeles Alliance for a New
    Economy, 153
Los Angeles Community College Build
    Green Program, 92
Los Angeles Trade Technical College, 91

Mangan, Andrew, 138–139
Mazria, Ed, 87
Methane emissions, 117–118
Metropolitan Development Association
    (MDA) of Syracuse and Central
    New York, 99
Milwaukee, 14, 81, 90, 93–95
Milwaukee Energy Efficiency (Me2),
    93–94

Nanosolar, 49, 68–69, 76
National Industrial Symbiosis
    Programme, 136, 139, 141
National Renewable Energy Laboratory,
    51, 71
Natural Resources Defense Council, 71,
    151–152
New York City, 81, 95, 101, 110
    Green Manufacturing Initiative,
        105–108
    Local Law 86, 84, 105–106
    and recycling initiatives in the Bronx,
        122–128
New York Industrial Retention Network
    (NYIRN), 106–108

Oakland, 24–26, 173
Ohio, 60, 61, 73
    and by-product synergy networks, 139
    Department of Development, 56
    Third Frontier Program, 57
Oregon Iron Works, 158, 169, 174

Paaswell, Robert, 172–173
Pellow, David, 120–121
Peterson, Kent, 88, 109
Pittsburgh, 14, 81, 95–98
PlaNYC, 106
Plasma arc, 132–134

Portland, 14, 81, 94, 124, 156–161, 168,
    170, 175
    bicycling, 156, 159, 162
    public transportation in, 10–11, 14,
        20, 27, 105, 145–147, 149, 156–157,
        163, 167, 170–173, 178
Portney, Kent, 19
Propel Fuel, 167
Public transportation, 10–11, 14, 20, 27,
    105, 145–147, 149, 156–157, 163,
    167, 170–173, 178

Recology, 143–144
Reconnecting America, 170
Recycling, 14, 29, 105, 118–121, 123,
    127–130, 135, 142–143, 156, 176, 184
Regional Growth Partnership, 55, 57
RENEW LA, 128–131, 142
Renewable energy, 33–34, 176
    cities promoting, 31–32, 33–34
    and education and training, 73–75
    in Freiburg, Germany, 2–5, 6
    industry in the United States, 40
    policy in California to promote, 45–46
    policy to promote in the United
        States, 66–67
    research and production of, 34–35,
        37–38
    in Sweden, 178–181–183
    top manufacturers, 36
    and transmission capacity, 70–72
Renewable Energy Policy Project, 29, 72
Renewable Energy Systems Americas, 54
Renewable Portfolio Standards, 29, 37,
    45, 50, 68, 134, 164
Richard, Ron, 59–60
Richmond Build, 42–44, 73–74
Richmond, California, 32, 42

Sectoral strategies (economic
    development), 12–13
Sims, Ron, 163
Smart grid, 49, 51, 71
Smart growth, 2, 11, 148, 178
Smith, Greig, 129, 131–134
Social justice, 4, 9, 13, 19, 23, 27, 90–91,
    121, 129, 132, 168, 176
Solar array, 1, 53–54
Solar energy, 2–3, 32–33, 49, 76, 182
    policy and production in Toledo,
        55–59

Solar energy (*Continued*)
  policy to promote in Austin, 47–56
  policy to promote in Berkeley, 40–45
  policy to promote in Germany, 2–5, 6
  solar manufacturers, 37, 38
  value chain in solar production, 39
Solargystics, 58
Solar Richmond, 42
Sprawl, 103, 146, 148–149, 178
Steubi, Richard, 60
Stockholm, 178–181
  urban planning, 178
Strategic Concepts in Organizing and
    Policy Education (SCOPE), 91
Streetcars, 14, 146, 156–157, 159, 174
  cities developing, 14, 146, 157–159,
    170–174
  production, 146, 158
Sustainability, 12
  defined, 18–20
Sustainable South Bronx, 124–127
Sweden, 177–183
  carbon tax, 178
  land-use planning, 170
Swinney, Dan, 74
Syracuse, 8, 81, 95, 98–105
Strickland, Governor Ted, 58, 61–62

Thin-film solar, 34
Third Frontier Program, 57–58
Toledo, 14, 32, 75
  and solar energy development,
    56–59
Transformational strategies, 15–17, 121
Transit-oriented development, 2, 10,
    147–151, 157–158, 168–170

U.S. Business Council for Sustainable
    Development, 136, 138–140
U.S. Conference of Mayors, 20, 87
U.S. Department of Energy, 34, 51, 56,
    66, 69, 71, 83
U.S. Green Building Council, 83, 86–87,
    96, 103–104

United States
  employment in renewable energy,
    39–40
  and investment in energy efficiency,
    81, 83
  and investment in renewable energy,
    35–38, 69–72
  and need for industrial policy,
    171–175, 183–184
  and recycling, 118
  and spending on public transportation,
    145, 170–171
  and waste, 116–117
University of Toledo, 56–58
Urban planning, 2, 109, 148, 178

Vestas, 38, 66
Villaraigosa, Mayor Antonio, 91, 153, 169

Waste to Profit Network (Chicago), 122,
    135–139
Weathers, Steve, 55, 57
Westside Industrial Retention and
    Expansion Network (WIRE-Net),
    63
Wind energy, 29, 33–35, 61, 69, 72, 76.
    See also renewable energy
  opposition to, 76
  policy and production in Germany, 5–6
  policy to promote in Cleveland, 59–62
  and production tax credit, 38
  and supply chains, 63–64
  world wind turbine manufacturers, 37
Wind turbines, 15, 60, 62, 65
  shipping through U.S. ports, 65–67
Workforce development, 12, 15, 73,
    91, 111
Wright Center for Photovoltaic
    Innovation, 56–58
Wynn, Will, 48

Xunlight, 57–58

Zoning, 109–111, 157, 170